Global Terrorism
A Beginner's Guide

D1396179

ONEWORLD BEGINNER'S GUIDES combine an original, inventive, and engaging approach with expert analysis on subjects ranging from art and history to religion and politics, and everything in between. Innovative and affordable, books in the series are perfect for anyone curious about the way the world works and the big ideas of our time.

Global Terrorism
A Beginner's Guide

Leonard Weinberg

ONEWORLD

OXFORD

A Oneworld Book

First published by Oneworld Publications, 2005
First published in the new *Beginners Guide* series, 2008

Copyright © Leonard Weinberg, 2005

ISBN 978–1–85168–608–7

Typeset by Jayvee, Trivandrum, India
Cover design by Two Associates
Printed and bound in the United States
of America by Thomson-Shore Inc.

Oneworld Publications
185 Banbury Road
Oxford OX2 7AR
England
www.oneworld-publications.com

*The author would like to thank
Kristen Kabrin for help in the preparation
of the manuscript.*

Contents

Foreword

It is hard to think of a more appropriate scholar than Leonard Weinberg to author *Global Terrorism: A Beginner's Guide*. Leonard is Foundation Professor of Political Science at the University of Nevada, Reno and has a formidable track record as a specialist in the study of terrorism, political violence and extremism.

He has a masterly knowledge of the experience of political violence and extremism by major countries and this is reflected in his influential works, *The Transformation of Italian Communism* (1995) and *The Emergence of a Euro-American Radical Right* (1998, with Jeffrey Kaplan). Leonard's understanding of the complexities of extremism and violence in the European democracies was deepened by his tenure of a Fulbright senior research fellowship in Italy and a visiting professorship at the University of Florence. However, he is a scholar with a wide range of interests and his work on the Radical Right with Jeffrey Kaplan, and his book *Revival of Right-Wing Extremism in the Nineties* (1997), which he co-edited with Peter Merkl, provided some ground-breaking cross-national comparisons of extremist movements, including analysis of developments in the United States. Leonard has also been applying his specialist knowledge to the daunting problems of Christian–Jewish reconciliation for which work he received the Thornton Peace Prize in 1999. As co-editor of the academic journal *Terrorism and Political Violence*, I particularly value Leonard's work as our book review editor, for which his qualities of academic rigour, fairness and breadth of knowledge have proved invaluable.

I warmly commend this book to readers who desire a concise, clear and balanced guide to the phenomenon of terrorism in today's world. The opening chapter on the concept of terrorism is both shrewd and immensely practical. He accepts that it is a contested concept. In that respect it is no different from other terms in our vocabulary of politics, such as 'democracy', 'imperialism' and 'liberalism'. Yet just as we cannot manage without concepts of 'democracy' and 'imperialism' we cannot dispense with 'terrorism'. As Professor Weinberg makes clear, it is not a philosophy or a movement, it is an *activity*, which has been employed in a myriad of different political causes and campaigns. It follows that even those who sympathise with the beliefs and political aims of those who commit acts of terrorism are often profoundly opposed to the use of terrorism as a weapon to achieve such aims. In a democracy, where, by definition, dissenters can use the freedoms of an open society to campaign for their views peacefully, resort to the bomb and the bullet instead of the ballot box is morally indefensible. It is a fascinating paradox, therefore, that terrorist groups appear more frequently in democracies than they do in non-democratic societies. The good news is that well-established operative democracies generally show more resilience in withstanding and defeating the attempts of terrorists to undermine them. The majority of citizens of democratic countries generally prefer to hold on to their freedoms, despite the imperfections of democracy, and rally to support their government's attempts to suppress terrorism.

However, in reviewing the current terrorist scene, Leonard Weinberg makes clear that the al Qaeda network is far more dangerous to international peace and security than any previous international terrorist organisation. It is explicitly committed to the mass killing of civilians. In 1998 it announced the formation of the 'World Islamic Front for Jihad' against 'Jews and Crusaders', saying it was the duty of all Muslims to kill US citizens – civilian or military, and their allies, everywhere. The 9/11 attacks, and the series of deadly acts of terrorism since 9/11 show beyond doubt that al Qaeda has both the intent and the capability to kill large numbers of civilians in attacks around the globe. This is one of the key features of al Qaeda terrorism, which differentiates it from the more traditional groups. As Brian Jenkins famously observed, terrorist groups in 1970s wanted 'a lot of people watching, not a lot of people dead'. It is all too clear that al Qaeda wants a lot of people watching *and* a lot of people dead. Another key difference is that al Qaeda's political aims are non-negotiable. The terrorists want nothing less than the restructuring of the entire international order, including the removal of all the current Muslim governments they accuse of betraying the 'true Islam' as defined by bin Laden. These aims are clearly non-negotiable. By contrast, more traditional separatist groups, for example, in Northern Ireland and Sri Lanka, have more limited and pragmatic aims and it is possible to conceive of peace processes in such conflicts succeeding, despite all the difficulties.

Yet perhaps the most important lesson to be drawn from Leonard Weinberg's wise and provocative guide is that one of the greatest dangers of contemporary terrorism for democracy is not so much from the capability of the terrorist to inflict great physical harm but from the consequences of blundering overreaction. By introducing draconian measures and suspending basic human rights and freedoms in the name of national security, a government could end up collapsing democracy far more swiftly and efficiently than any terrorist group could manage on its own. As this excellent book consistently reminds us, a balanced response to terrorism, which preserves human rights and democracy, is absolutely vital.

Paul Wilkinson
Chairman, Centre for the Study of Terrorism
and Political Violence
University of St Andrews

1

Introduction

Defining terrorism

What is terrorism? How do or should we define it? Despite the vast publicity the subject has received in recent years sensible answers to these important questions are hard to come by. Writing about terrorism in the middle of the 1970s, the political historian Walter Laqueur threw up his hands; he thought that providing a comprehensive definition was virtually impossible because of the great variety of circumstances in which this type of violence had appeared and the numerous and often competing political causes whose advocates had used it.[1] Decades later and after the publication of literally thousands of articles and books on the subject, Martha Crenshaw, another leading observer, wrote that the absence of a consensual definition continued to plague those interested in studying terrorism.[2]

For some the very idea of "terrorism" is a snare and delusion, a way of diverting the public's attention from the failings of Western governments, the American and British ones especially. Consider this remark: "It is clear that so-called terrorism is the logical and just resistance of the people against state terrorism, capitalism, racism, sexism and imperialism."[3] Or, in other words, "terrorism" is a semantic technique employed by government spokespersons to change the subject, a slick way of transforming the victims of injustice into its perpetrators. These comments convey some sense of the difficulties involved in defining the subject.

One of these difficulties is that "terrorism" is hardly a value-neutral term. No matter how detached the observer, it is hard to ignore the fact that the application of the term, calling some activity or group or organization engaged in it "terrorist" conveys a moral judgment. Few groups, organizations, or states these days are willing to accept the label. They typically respond to an attempt at such labeling by denial and by making what amounts to a counter-accusation. The government or organization that made the initial claim is the "real" terrorist by virtue of its commission of a long litany of criminal or immoral acts. Frequently what follows is a war of the words, fought in the mass media, as each side denies that its behavior constitutes terrorism as it struggles to reach the moral high ground.

Not uncommonly the mass media compound the confusion by applying the term "terrorist" on a highly selective basis. Newspaper and television accounts will often oscillate back and forth, sometimes referring to a particular group as consisting of extremists, militants, guerrillas, or "terrorists" depending upon exceptionally hazy criteria.

Another problem derives from the statement that "one man's terrorist is another man's freedom fighter." The point is that choosing the label "terrorist" or "freedom fighter" depends on the point of view, the political sympathies of the observer. If you like the goals of the individual she or he is a freedom fighter; if you don't she or he is a terrorist. Those of us living in the wealthy Western democracies call "terrorists" the same people many inhabitants of the impoverished parts of the world would think of as "freedom fighters" – viewing them in virtually the same way, for example, that young Americans and Britons learn to think of Robin Hood and his Merry Men.

But by saying "one man's terrorist is another man's freedom fighter" the observer is simply confusing the goal with the activity. Almost everyone concedes that terrorism is a tactic, one involving the threat or use of violence. If this is true, there is in principle no reason why this tactic cannot be used by groups seeking to achieve any number of goals and objectives, including a fight for freedom or national liberation.

Despite the various problems associated with the effort (see above), the world is hardly lacking comprehensive definitions of terrorism. The word itself entered the vocabulary of Western civilization during the French Revolution and derived, in particular, from the period (1793–94) of Jacobin rule under Robespierre known as the "Reign of Terror." The new revolutionary regime in France granted wide powers to the Committee of General Security and the Revolutionary Tribunal to ferret out and try suspected opponents of the People, counter-revolutionaries in other words. Some forty thousand people lost their lives in the process, many executed by the guillotine. We should remember then that "terrorism" at the end of the eighteenth century meant a campaign of violence undertaken by a government apparatus and was intended to consolidate the government's hold on the country.

Today when we think about "terrorism" we are more likely to associate it with the activities of private groups and organizations, what students of international relations frequently describe as "non-state" actors: al Qaeda, Jemaah Islamiyah (Indonesia), Sendero Luminoso (Peru), People's Revolutionary Armed Forces (Colombia), and a long list of others. When we describe them as engaged in terrorism, what exactly do we mean?

Academics have hardly been reluctant to propose definitions. Here are two: terrorism is

> the deliberate creation and exploitation of fear through violence or the threat of violence in the pursuit of political change.[4]

> An anxiety-inspiring method of repeated violent action, employed by (semi) clandestine individual, group, or state actors, for idiosyncratic, criminal or political reasons ... whereby the direct targets of the violence are not the main targets. The immediate human victims of violence are generally chosen randomly (targets of opportunity) or selectively (representative

or symbolic targets) from a target population, and serve as message generators.[5]

The laws of various democratic states also provide definitions, devised for purposes of prosecution or extradition of those accused of perpetrating or planning to perpetrate certain acts. Here are three:

1. German Federal Republic: "Terrorism is the enduringly conducted struggle for political goals, which are intended to be achieved by means of assaults on the life and property of other persons, especially by means of severe crimes as detailed in art. 129a of the penal code."
2. United Kingdom: "For purposes of the legislation, terrorism is the use of violence for political ends, and includes any use of violence for the purpose of putting the public or any section of the public in fear."
3. United States: "Premeditated, politically motivated violence perpetrated against noncombatant targets by subnational groups or clandestine agents, usually intended to influence an audience."[6]

What, if anything, do these definitions have in common? With the exception of the German one (drafted by the Federal Office for the Protection of the Constitution), they make reference to a psychological element. The academic and legal definitions identify terrorism as a type of violence (or threat of violence) intended to achieve a psychological effect. Or, in other words, the immediate target or victim of a terrorist attack is only part of an operation whose main aim is to change the thinking and often the behavior of some audience. Late nineteenth-century anarchists set off bombs in public places and assassinated prominent figures in politics and business in order to make "propaganda by deed."

If we see terrorism, at least in part, as a theatrical endeavor performed to influence some audience or multiple audiences, the next question we need to pose is: What purposes do its practitioners hope to achieve by their acts of violence? The list is not exhaustive, but here are some of the more obvious benefits they hope to achieve.

Purposes

First, as V. I. Lenin put it, "The purpose of terrorism is to terrify." The perpetrators of terrorist acts often hope to create a generalized sense of anxiety and fear among the public. That is why, as Jessica Stern reminds us, chemical and biological weapons in the hands of terrorists seem so threatening. Nothing seems more dreadful than the possibility of being overcome by an unseen vapor or microbe floating in the air which has been dispersed by some hostile clandestine organization.[7] If people become terrified they may become immobilized, incapable of mounting a coherent response to the dangers they confront. They may very well blame their government for its inability to eliminate the danger to public safety. For a comparatively few individuals equipped with relatively primitive weapons, terrorism has the benefit of multiplying their power well beyond what it would appear to be on paper.

We ought not to forget that sowing widespread fear may have quite tangible benefits. The tourist economy in Israel and on the Indonesian island of Bali suffered serious losses because of fears resulting from terrorism. The same may be said of the airline industry throughout the United States in the year following the 9/11 attacks on the World Trade Center and the Pentagon.

Another purpose motivating those who carry out terrorist attacks is attention, publicity for whatever cause they claim to embody. Previously obscure causes or previously unknown groups achieve instant celebrity through the mass media when a terrorist attack is shown to a live television audience. Symbolic targets such as the World Trade Center or the Pentagon are exceptionally attractive in this regard. Countries where the mass media are tightly controlled by the government, the People's Republic of China or the former Soviet Union for example, seem to experience little terrorism. Perpetrators or potential perpetrators of terrorist attacks there are aware their deeds will attract little if any attention, except perhaps from the secret police.

A third purpose, and the purposes need not be mutually exclusive, is to provoke an over-reaction by the authorities. Not uncommonly, terrorist groups are small aggregations located at the margins of society with little popular support among the very people whose cause they claim to lead. If the forces of order react to a series of terrorist attacks by lashing out indiscriminately against people belonging to the segment of the population, e.g. students, workers, ethnic minorities, on whose behalf the terrorists claim to act, they may really do the terrorists' job for them. The violent reaction often persuades the relevant population that the government is brutal and oppressive and needs to be challenged in the way the terrorist group thinks necessary. Among other things, indiscriminate reactions by the authorities may help glamorize the terrorist group and help it win new recruits.

Clearly related to the above, spectacular acts of violence may raise the morale not only of the terrorist group's own members but also and more importantly of the segment of the population whose cause the terrorists hope to champion. Acts of terrorism often disclose the vulnerability of governments previously believed to be so strong as to be unchallengeable. Terrorist violence then can serve as a way of restoring hope to those who have lost it. It may also provide sympathetic observers with a psychologically satisfying sense of vengeance when wealthy or powerful individuals are assassinated or when members of a long-dominant class or ethnic group are harmed. The events of September 11, 2001 horrified millions of Americans but gratified millions of others in the Middle East and elsewhere, since an arrogant United States was perceived as getting what it had long deserved.

Frequently, terrorist groups commit especially dramatic or lethal attacks in order to polarize the situation and make a compromise settlement between two (or more) contending sides harder to achieve. Atrocities may be used to prevent moderate forces from reaching an agreement. Or, if an agreement appears to be in the immediate offing, terrorists may act as "spoilers" by sabotaging peace negotiations and re-inflame a troubled situation. The recent history of the Israeli–Palestinian conflict following the 1993 Oslo Agreement offers a particularly good example, with Hamas and Islamic Jihad playing the spoiler roles.

To this point we have focused on the emotional or psychological benefits to be gained from terrorism, but there are often quite tangible benefits as well. Compared with more conventional means of armed conflict terrorism is relatively cheap, but cheap but does not mean completely cost free. In staging bank robberies, kidnapping wealthy individuals, and other such escapades terrorist bands acquire the ability to maintain their operations and acquire new and better weapons. In some instances such terrorist groups as the late Abu Nidal's organization become guns for hire, staging terrorist attacks on targets selected by some paymaster, usually a state sponsor, rather than on the basis of their own religious or ideological convictions. The danger here is that the organization will become so corrupted that its political goals get displaced in the process and it is transformed into a straightforward criminal enterprise.

We have hardly exhausted the list, but still another important purpose for carrying out terrorist attacks is the maintenance of discipline within the terrorist organization itself. The willingness of an organization to kill a defector or someone suspected of wishing to defect sends a powerful message to its other members about the fate that awaits them if they attempt to leave and disclose what they know to the authorities. The family members of defectors become attractive targets of assassination in these situations as well.[8]

Goals

The groups and individuals who carry out terrorist attacks usually have some broader goals in mind above and beyond the immediate purposes of these violent operations. We need to repeat that terrorism is a tactic not a goal in and of itself. What do those who use this tactic hope to achieve?

Revolution

Before the collapse of the Soviet empire in 1989 and the subsequent disintegration of the Soviet Union itself in 1991, the world abounded with groups willing to use terrorism to bring about revolutionary social, economic, and political change. Marx, Trotsky, Mao were typically their patron saints and Latin America was most often their venue. Argentina, Brazil, Uruguay, Colombia, and Peru had substantial "urban guerrilla" groups that sought to bring an end to the economic exploitation of workers and peasants and replace the prevailing political order with one more compatible with their socialist principles. Japan and the highly industrialized Western democracies also had a substantial number of like-minded organizations. The Italian Red Brigades, West Germany's Red Army Fraction, and the Japanese United Red Army may serve as examples. Some of the revolutionary groups have persisted: Peru's Shining Path remains active in the first decade of the twenty-first century.

Nationalism/Separatism

The objectives of terrorist groups in this case are national independence, the creation of independent states carved from territories that were previously under the control or part of some other country. For instance, the Liberation Tigers of Tamil Eelam has carried out literally thousands of terrorist acts over more than two decades with the goal of establishing an independent homeland for Sri Lanka's Tamil minority. Analogously, during the 1980s groups claiming to represent the Sikh population of India's Punjab state committed an extensive series of terrorist attacks, e.g. machine-gunning to death dozens of bus passengers, in order to create a separate state of Khalistan for the Sikh population. In the Western world the two most prominent cases of terrorist campaigns waged on behalf of the nationalist/separatist causes are those of Basque Homeland and Liberty (ETA), which hopes to establish an independent state for the Basques in what is now northern Spain, and the Irish Republican Army, whose long-standing aim has been to detach Northern Ireland from the United Kingdom and make it part of the Irish Republic. The groups espousing nationalist/separatist causes usually display greater staying power than their social revolutionary counterparts.

Reaction

It is common, particularly among academics, writers, artists, and journalists, to regard those who use terrorist violence as in some sense the proponents of "progressive" causes. This is hardly the case. Terrorist violence has been used extensively by groups wishing to maintain or restore systems of racial supremacy, such as the Ku Klux Klan in the United States, or to promote the establishment or re-establishment of a right-wing dictatorship in the name of neo-Nazi or neo-Fascist ideas. Furthermore, in the recent past Latin American countries, e.g. El Salvador and

Colombia, have been sites of "death squads," bands of killers (frequently off-duty soldiers or police officers in civilian dress) who wage assassination campaigns against land reformers, union organizers, members of the Catholic clergy and others identified with promoting the interests of the poor. In Northern Ireland, Loyalist paramilitary organizations have repeatedly carried out terrorist attacks with the goal of maintaining the region's link to the United Kingdom. And we should not forget that the most lethal single act of domestic terrorism in the United States, the April 1995 bombing of the Murrah Federal Building in Oklahoma City was carried out by Timothy McVeigh, an individual on the fringes of far right militia groups with racist and anti-Semitic agendas.

Religion

Since the Iranian Revolution of 1979 and the Soviet Union's military intervention in Afghanistan in the same year, groups claiming inspiration from religious ideas have come to play leading roles in terrorist dramas around the world. Not religions in general but groups asserting their fidelity to Islam have become widely associated with particularly horrendous terrorist attacks, such as the September 11, 2001 attack by al Qaeda on the World Trade Center towers in New York City. Given the severity and volume of attacks carried out around the world by admirers or followers of Osama bin Laden the pre-occupation with Muslim fundamentalists or Islamist groups is perfectly understandable. We should not forget, however, that adherents of other religious traditions have been responsible for a signifi-cant number of terrorist attacks in recent years. In Israel follow-ers of the late Rabbi Meier Kahane were responsible for the execution of terrorist attacks or acts of "vigilante justice" against Palestinians on the West Bank. An Israeli zealot, the law student Yigal Amir, invoked religious principles for his assassination of

Prime Minister Yitzhak Rabin because of the latter's commitment of trading "land for peace" with the Palestinian Authority. In the United States followers of the Christian Identity movement, such as the Aryan Nations figures Robert Mathews and Buford Furrow, Jr., have carried out terrorist attacks against Jewish targets in order to carry out what they believe is the will of God by restoring the country to its rightful Aryan Christian people. In Japan members of the eclectic "new religion" Aum Shinrikyo (Supreme Truth), headed by the half-blind "prophet" Shoko Asahara, set off a canister of Sarin gas on a crowded Tokyo subway, killing twelve passengers and injuring many more.

Precisely why religiously motivated terrorism appears to be so lethal is a subject we propose to discuss in detail later in this book. For now it will suffice to say that those who believe themselves to be acting on behalf of God and against the enemies of God feel less restrained in killing large numbers of people than terrorists driven by secular concerns.

Single issues

Whether religious or secular in outlook most terrorist organizations claim to act on behalf of some broad political goal or set of goals. Campaigns of terrorist violence, though, have been carried out to achieve far more restricted aims. The legally protected ability of women to obtain abortions performed by licensed physicians in the United States has caused a backlash: a "right-to-life" movement has emerged which is committed to ending this practice. On the movement's fringes single individuals (usually operating with networks of supporters) and small groups have assassinated doctors and nurses and bombed abortion clinics in order to make those seeking and performing abortions so fearful they will desist from the practice. Also in the United States, the cause of environmental protection has led members of such groups as the Environmental Liberation Front (ELF) to fire-bomb expansion-minded ski resorts, construction sites and automobile dealerships in order to deter further air pollution and the degradation of wildlife habitat.

State terror

One question that almost invariably arises in discussions about terrorism concerns the role of the state. Don't states commit acts of terrorism? Those posing this question usually mean to strike a kind of ethical balance on behalf of moral relativism. If terrorism is a morally repugnant activity it is important to show that states do it too, especially those targeted for attack by non-state organizations, i.e. terrorist groups. In the context of these discussions the assertion that governments do it too is intended to serve as a moral equalizer, an argument to the effect that, since a state may initiate terrorist attacks against innocent civilians, those challenging the state are justified in responding in kind. In effect, the violence of the challengers becomes redefined as acts of legitimate self-defense. What should we make of this argument?

Its advocates certainly have a point. Various states do wage terrorist campaigns against their own citizens or subjects, with far higher casualties than those resulting from the efforts of all but the most bloodthirsty of the non-state organizations. During the first half of the twentieth century Stalinist Russia was the site of the "Great Terror," a brutal campaign that consigned millions of Soviet citizens to the Gulag or the grave. During the second half of the century approximately the same occurred in the People's Republic of China under the leadership of Mao Tse-tung. We could multiply the examples. The states implicated would range from Central America to sub-Saharan Africa to the Middle East to Southeast Asia. However, virtually none of the states systematically employing terrorism against its own citizens was challenged by terrorism from below, at least not for very long. On the rare occasions when some were, they typically reacted with great brutality and swiftly brought the threat, along with those making it, to a rapid end. Thomas Friedman's vivid description of how the Baathist regime of Hafez al-Asad killed thousands of suspected Muslim Brothers in the city of Hama in 1983 is suggestive of the more general practice.[9]

State terror or the use of terrorist tactics by states against their own citizens would be the subject of another volume. This volume focuses on non-state or private organizations waging terrorist campaigns. We need to point out, however, that a government may provide assistance to and may even covertly sponsor groups conducting terrorist operations against countries on which it wishes to inflict harm but without taking direct responsibility. During the Cold War the Soviet Union and some of its allies, e.g. East Germany, were accused by some of furnishing sanctuary and other types of assistance to such groups as the German Red Army Fraction and Turkey's Red Road with the aim of destabilizing the NATO alliance. Until recently Libya, under the leadership of Colonel Muammar al Qaddafi, evidently offered succor to groups ranging from the Irish Republican Army to the Moro National Liberation Front in the Philippines. The advantage of covert sponsorship is that it furnishes a state with a cover, a means of avoiding direct responsibility for violent acts against a particular state. Violent attacks carried out directly by one state against another's citizens or territory are, of course, acts of war. Modern warfare is an expensive and risky undertaking. It is cheaper and usually less dangerous to carry out attacks through "cut-outs" or intermediaries. International condemnation may be deflected and direct retaliation by the target state usually avoided. The governments of Great Britain and the United States presently have statutes in place that require the Foreign Office and the State Department to compile lists of terrorism-supporting states on an annual basis. Under the provisions of British and American law states so designated, e.g. Iran, are then subject to a variety of economic and political sanctions – as are those firms and individuals seeking to do business with them.

Terrorism and warfare

In addition to the phenomenon of state sponsorship of terrorist organizations we need to take into account in this volume another consideration. There are a number of countries and parts of countries where state authority has broken down and no effective government authority exists. These locales provide near ideal sanctuaries for terrorist groups because there is no armed force available to oppose their operations. Somalia on the Horn of Africa and the tribal areas of northeast Pakistan are venues where al Qaeda operates with impunity for this reason. The no-go sections of some of the vast urban conurbations in the Third World offer an analogous type of sanctuary.[10] The governments of these countries do not sponsor terrorist groups. They simply lack the power to do much about their presence. In any case, in this volume we certainly need to investigate the role of the state as both sponsor and inadvertent host of terrorist organizations.

What is the relationship between terrorism and warfare? During the conduct of modern warfare states certainly do engage in military operations for the purpose of terrorizing the enemy's civilian population, to break the latter's will to resist or to cause it to pressure the government into surrender. The Allied bombing of Dresden in 1945 had such an objective in mind as did earlier Luftwaffe attacks on Britain and other opponents of the Nazi dictatorship. What else, for instance, was the "Shock and Awe" campaign waged by the American and British air forces against Saddam Hussein's Iraq in March 2003 all about? In a century (the twentieth) the late French analyst

Raymond Aron described as one of "total war," the aim of demoralizing the enemy's civilian population became an important component of the general war strategy.

Most commonly, however, the political terrorism with which we are concerned has been linked to guerrilla warfare and placed under the more general heading of "unconventional" or "low intensity" conflict. Furthermore, perpetrators of terrorist attacks are not uncommonly described in the mass media as "guerrillas" or "urban guerrillas." What then is the relationship between terrorism and guerrilla war?

Guerrilla warfare is an age-old tactic practiced by weak or irregular forces confronted by superior conventional military establishments. (The name "guerrilla" comes from the Spanish resistance to French occupation in the first years of the nineteenth century.) The doctrine was summarized by Mao Tse-tung, who put the idea into winning practice in rural China during the 1930s and later:

> Divide our forces to arouse the masses, concentrate our forces to deal with the enemy. The enemy advances, we retreat; the enemy camps, we harass; the enemy tires, we attack; the enemy retreats, we pursue. To extend stable base areas, employ the policy of advancing in waves; when pursued by a powerful enemy, employ the policy of circling around. Arouse the largest number of masses in the shortest possible time and the best possible methods. These tactics are just like casting a net; at any moment we should be able to cast it or draw it in. We cast it wide to win over the masses and draw it in to deal with the enemy.[11]

In other words, what Mao is proposing is a strategy of waging unconventional war in rural areas while simultaneously winning the support of the area's peasantry. The enemy to which Mao refers is the government's police or military forces or outposts of government authority, not civilians or non-combatants. If the logic of a guerrilla insurgency works, the result will be the progressive "liberation" of more and more territory and the formation of a new "counter-government" over which insurgents will begin to rule. Finally, if the guerrillas' plans unfold successfully, the insurgents will reform into a large, conventional armed force, such as the Chinese People's Liberation Army (PLA). This new revolutionary army will then defeat in open battle the armed forces of the government. This form of insurgency ends when the revolutionaries march into Beijing, Saigon, Havana, etc. and set up their own government – often as the incumbents they displaced flee into exile. What, if anything, do these rural-based guerrilla tactics employing largely peasant armies have to do with political terrorism, a tactic many regard as a way of challenging governments in urban settings by attacking civilians and highly symbolic targets?

Some writers have maintained that terrorist violence is often used during the early "agitation-propaganda" phase of a guerrilla war.[12] Terrorism, e.g. killing local officials or setting off bombs in front of public buildings, becomes propaganda by deed, a means of calling the public's attention to the presence of those who would threaten the seemingly powerful. After terrorism for agitation-propaganda purposes has had the desired effect on the relevant audiences, the insurgents should be prepared to move to a new and higher level of violent engagement with the forces of the old order. Groups that are unable to move beyond this preliminary stage of activity, such as the communist insurgents in British-controlled Malaya during the early 1950s, simply reflect their own weakness. They are unable to transform the struggle into one likely to jeopardize the government's hold on power. Hence the observation that terrorism is a weapon of the weak. That, at least, is the theory, but what is the reality?

In fact some guerrilla campaigns have been waged with virtually no terrorism at their beginning. Fidel Castro's success in Cuba at the end of the 1950s is a case in point. (Castro once claimed that cities were the graveyards of revolution.) Other cases abound in which terrorism and rural guerrilla warfare are conducted simultaneously by the same group of insurgents. For instance, the Revolutionary Armed Forces of Colombia (FARC) and the Shining Path in Peru have employed a mix of these tactics, attacking government forces in the hinterland while carrying out attention-getting terrorist spectaculars in Bogotá and Lima.[13] The United States is presently (2004) engaged in a low level conflict in post-Saddam Iraq. The attacks carried out, apparently by those still loyal to the old regime, against American and British forces resemble the kind of hit-and-run attacks advocated by Mao and other exponents of guerrilla warfare, the so-called "war of the flea" against a far more powerful enemy. But the bombings carried out against the Jordanian embassy and United Nations headquarters in Baghdad and a high-ranking Shiite cleric in Najaf are pretty clearly terror-ist acts. In short, on occasion terrorism may be one of several tools at the disposal of insurgent groups. They may also conduct guerrilla operations at the same time.

Still another take on the relationship between terrorist violence and conventional warfare should be mentioned. Before the events of September 11, 2001 the following observation seemed eminently sensible:

> Counterterrorism, even though it shares some attributes with warfare, is not accurately represented by the metaphor of a war. It has neither a fixed set of enemies nor the prospect of coming to closure, be it through a "win" or some other kind of denouement. There will be victories and defeats but not big, tide-turning victories ... Perhaps a better analogy is the effort by public health authorities to control communicable diseases.[14]

Or, to put it somewhat differently, those who regard the United States and its allies as engaged in a "war" against terror-ism are using an inappropriate, and potentially dangerous, metaphor, one that leads to unrealistic expectations about what can be achieved and who the enemy is. If it is a war, it is a war in the shadows fought by covert forces and psychological operations. This view is certainly a sophisticated interpretation of the terrorist challenge before 9/11. But we should bear in mind the fact that the United States suffered more casualties on that date than it did on December 7, 1941, the day of the Japanese attack on Pearl Harbor, an event that was quintessentially an act of war.

Some analysts have come to believe that the nature of warfare itself has changed or is undergoing profound changes. It may be misleading or even preposterous to apply the term "war" to a conflict between the forces of order in a particular country and a small terrorist organization that may consist of a few dozen or a few hundred members and whose weapons' store contains some pistols and a few sticks of dynamite: the armed revolutionary groups active in Italy and West Germany during the 1970s, for example. But what should we make of al Qaeda and its various subsidiaries?

In this case we are dealing with an organization of an entirely different order of magnitude than the erstwhile Italian and German revolutionary bands of the 1970s. Al Qaeda is to the latter as a vast multinational corporation is to a neighborhood grocery store. By one recent account there is an al Qaeda presence in more than seventy countries, with cells to be found not only in the Middle East but also in most of the Western democracies, East Africa, Indonesia, the Philippines, and many of the other countries of South and Southeast Asia.[15] It is, furthermore, an organization that conducts military training exercises much in the manner of a more conventional armed force and which by most accounts has for some years been in hot pursuit of highly lethal, mass casualty weapons. It has thousands of members and supports them through an intricate series of financial transactions also carried out on a worldwide basis. It learns from its failures as well as its defeats. It is resilient. And its unrelenting conflict with the United States in fact may be the first war of the twenty-first century. There seems to be no good reason why twenty-first-century warfare has to resemble World War II any more than that conflict resembled the War of the Spanish Succession. Unconditional surrender may be an unrealistic expectation or an impossible achievement but the same was true of many wars fought on the European continent and elsewhere before the twentieth century.

Outline of the book

By this point we have been able to define terrorism and distinguish this tactic from other types of politically motivated violence. We have also described the principal purposes and long-term objectives of those who wage terrorist campaigns. Now we need to call attention to what lies ahead, what the rest of this book is about. Where do we go from here?

Terrorism did not begin in 2001 or in the 1990s for that matter. There is a long history behind the kind of violence that the mass media show us seemingly on a daily basis. In chapter 2 we will trace this history back to its origins in the world's revealed religions and forward to its manifestations in the nineteenth and twentieth centuries.

In chapter 3 we examine the current situation: the challenges posed by al Qaeda and other groups engaged in what some leaders regard as the first war of the twenty-first century. In offering this account of recent developments, we consider terrorists' quest for and use of chemical, biological, radiological, and, at least potentially, nuclear weapons and the dangers of their use to inflict mass casualties on the civilian populations of the Western democracies. Here we also need to consider the phenomenon of suicide bombing as carried out by such groups as Hezbollah, Hamas, the Liberation Tigers of Tamil Eelam, and other groups active in Kashmir and Chechnya.

Next, we respond to two questions: Who are they? And why do they do it? We shall look at evidence concerning the social backgrounds of terrorists. Some maintain that terrorists come from such diverse social circumstances that no generalizations are possible. For example, some modern terrorists have come from wealthy and even aristocratic backgrounds whereas others have emerged from exceptionally humble ones. Despite this, some general patterns do seem observable. In responding to the question, we need to pay attention not only to what psychologists tell us but also to what the terrorists themselves have to say about their motives in, for instance, killing large numbers of perfect strangers or what their families tell us about those who commit suicide with this objective in mind.

In chapter 5 we consider reactions to terrorist violence by the authorities, particularly in the wake of the September 11 attacks. We discuss how laws have been changed and law enforcement agencies restructured to better suppress those waging terrorist campaigns in various regions of the world. We also need to consider how the mass media, television especially, treat terrorist events. Do the mass media simply report the story or are they part of the story? Finally, in many cases the ultimate target of the violence is the general public, whose representatives or whose randomly selected members are frequently its immediate targets. There is now a body of evidence drawn from public opinion surveys about how Americans, Britons, Germans, Israelis, and other populations have reacted to protracted terrorist campaigns or spectacular individual acts of terrorism. Do these publics, for example, become terrified?

In the last chapter we suggest how terrorist campaigns reach their conclusions and terrorist groups end. Some have come to believe that terrorism is a never-ending scourge. But we intend to show that this is not the case. Almost all the terrorist groups that were active in Latin America and Western Europe during the 1970s and 1980s have passed from the scene. In the conclusion, we identify how terrorist campaigns reach their ends as well.

Further reading

Bruce Hoffman, *Inside Terrorism* (London: Victor Gollancz, 1998).

Mark Juergensmeyer, *Terror in the Mind of God* (Berkeley and London: University of California Press, 2001).

Gilles Kepel, *Jihad: The Trail of Political Islam* (Cambridge, MA: Harvard University Press, 2002).

Walter Laqueur (ed.), *Voices of Terror* (New York: Reed Press, 2004).

Walter Laqueur, *No End to War: Terrorism in the Twenty-First Century* (New York and London: Continuum, 2003).

Walter Laqueur, *The Age of Terrorism* (Boston: Little, Brown, 1987).

Alex Schmid, Albert Jongmann et al., *Political Terrorism: A New guide to Actors, Authors, Concepts, Data Bases, Theories and Literature* (New Brunswick, NJ: Transaction Books, 1988).

2
A brief history of terrorism

Beginnings

The facts that major terrorist attacks typically receive saturation coverage by the mass media, television especially, and the terrorists themselves often rely on encrypted email messages and satellite phones to communicate with one another give the impression that terrorism is a distinctively modern development. Some believe it to be a new kind of warfare that enables weak groups with meager resources to challenge far more powerful foes and come away with at least some of what they wish to get. Terrorism, though, is not a new phenomenon. It did not begin during the 1960s, much less at the beginning of the new millennium. Rather, terrorist violence has a long history but a history we intend to describe briefly in this chapter.

The word "terrorism" enters the vocabulary, first in French (*regime de la terreur*) and then in English, during the last decade of the eighteenth century at the time of the French Revolution. In particular, it came to be applied to the period of Jacobin rule (1793–94), under Robespierre, which became known as the "Reign of Terror." This episode was one in which the new revolutionary regime sought out and executed via the guillotine thousands of individuals suspected of opposing the dramatic transformation of French society then underway. But the fact that the label "terrorism" was first applied to an activity at the end of the eighteenth century does not mean that the activity itself only began at that point. Terrorism, as a kind of violent tactic, enters recorded history almost two thousand years before the outbreak of France's revolutionary upheaval.

There were no doubt terrorist campaigns in various parts of the ancient world and during the European Middle Ages which have escaped the attention of historians. Those episodes which have created the most interest were religious in character, campaigns whose perpetrators had a mix of religious and political motives. They hoped the violence would purge the world of its corruption and thereby accelerate the advent of a messianic era and the end of human history, at least as they understood it. But to accomplish this divine task, the terrorists needed to radically change the prevailing political order.

The first group we encounter who fit this pattern were the Zealots-Sicarri who sought to provoke a Jewish uprising against Roman rule in Judea during the middle of the first century A.D.[1] Members saw themselves as living in the End Times, a messianic period before the coming of the Messiah. In order to accelerate the latter's appearance Jews had to bring the period of Roman rule in the Holy Land to an end. This could be accomplished through an armed revolt. It seemed there would be little chance that the Judeans could defeat the foremost military power of that era. The Zealots-Sicarri appraised the situation differently because they believed God would intervene in human history on behalf of those who worshipped him as the one and only God. Armed with this belief the Zealots-Sicarri went about provoking war. They slaughtered members of a Roman garrison who surrendered to them. They used daggers to stab to death Jewish leaders who appeared too willing to compromise with Roman rule. They also murdered individual Roman soldiers and Greek residents of Judea in the hope of inviting an indiscriminate repression by the Romans. These murders characteristically occurred in and around Jerusalem and in public places during feast days or on days when large numbers of people were gathered in markets. A Zealot would appear suddenly, stab his victim in full view of a large audience, and then disappear back into the crowd from which he had come. The act of killing in full view of a large gathering was intended to attract the most public attention possible in an era lacking today's means of mass communication. The Zealots-Sicarri achieved their goal, a Jewish uprising against the Romans (A.D. 66–73). The results were catastrophic, at least for the Jews. Jerusalem fell and the Second Temple was burned to the ground (aside from the outer Western Wall or "Wailing Wall"). Thousands of Jews were forced into exile, the beginning of the Diaspora; some of the defeated Jews were taken as slaves to Rome. A small band of Zealots retreated to the mountain fortress of Masada near the Dead Sea, where they eventually committed suicide rather than surrender to a besieging Roman legion.

Religious motivations

The religious sect that became known in the West as the "Assassins" (based on a corruption of the Arabic word for hashish eaters) was active in the Middle East from the eleventh to the thirteenth century, when they were eliminated by the Mongols. Also known as the Ismailis-Nizari, the Assassins were a group of Shiite Muslims who believed in the necessity of purifying Islam, since it had come to be practiced and led by Sunnis.[2] The Assassins originated in Persia, where the Fedayeen received training, but spread to Syria and other parts of the region. The Fedayeen or "self-sacrificers," were taught to believe their deeds would earn them rewards in paradise. Accordingly, they would work their way into the inner circles of important Muslim political and religious figures and when the time was right would then take out a dagger and stab the victim to death. The Fedayeen were expected to remain at the side of their victims to await the judgment of the authorities, which always meant execution. Thus in carrying out the attacks the Fedayeen were permitting themselves to be killed, not unlike today's suicide bombers in the Middle East and elsewhere. The Assassins hoped that by murdering corrupt or unjust prefects, governors, and caliphs (they attempted but failed to kill Saladin) they would not only cleanse the world but also accelerate the arrival of the Mahdi or the Holy One and the advent of a messianic era.

In India and the Far East secret societies, religious and secular, existed for centuries. In India members of the Thugs, a Hindu sect, strangled unsuspecting travelers with a silk tie in order to satisfy the death god they hoped to propitiate. In the nineteenth century Chinese secret societies professed xenophobic sentiments that helped spark the Boxer Rebellion.

Christendom was not exempt. In Europe at the time of the Crusades, the Black Death during the thirteenth century, and then again during the Reformation small sects appeared, typically led by self-styled "prophets" or self-proclaimed "messiahs" who proclaimed the imminence of the Millennium.[3] To accelerate this age the world needed to be purged of sin and those deemed responsible for its commission. In the German town of Muenster during the sixteenth century Anabaptists came to identify both Catholics and Lutherans with the villainy and executed many before they were subdued by the armed forces of the surrounding rulers. Earlier, along the Rhine and in what is today Belgium, one or another "prophet" or "messiah" would lead his followers from one town to another, e.g. the Children's Crusade and the Flagellants, attacking the wealthy, bishops and other leaders of the Catholic Church, and Jews. (The latter were often given a choice of either conversion or death.) These activities were typically conducted in public so as to demonstrate the seriousness with which the followers regarded their mission.

What do these various religiously motivated groups have in common? And what, if anything, do they share with terrorist groups active in our own time?

We are dealing, for the most part, with small groups drawn

from one of the world's major revealed religions, whose leaders tell their followers and all others who listen to their statements that they are carrying out God's intent as discerned from readings of a holy book – Hebrew Scripture, New Testament, Qur'an. There also is a sense of living in a special time, when divine intervention in worldly affairs is imminent. But in addition to these purely religious concerns the Zealots, Assassins, Christian Millennial bands (or "Crusaders") had a political agenda, one that involved the conquest or recapture of holy territory, a "holy land," from those ungodly elements who controlled it. And to achieve this objective virtually any means are appropriate, no matter how merciless. The parallels with religiously inspired terrorist groups active in our own time are not difficult to draw. Osama bin Laden's *fatwa* of February 1998, urging all Muslims to wage jihad against the Americans, reads as if it might have been written a thousand years earlier (deliberately so no doubt):

> Praise be to God, who revealed the Book, controls the clouds, defeats factionalism, and says in His Book "But when the forbidden months are past, then fight and slay the pagans wherever ye find them, seize them, beleaguer them, and lie in wait for them in every stratagem (of war)."[4]

Bin Laden, then, is invoking the Qur'an as a justification for slaying the infidels (i.e. American "crusaders" and Jews) without mercy wherever they can be found until they relinquish control over the land regarded as holy by Muslims everywhere. Nothing in these 1998 remarks would have seemed out of place had they been uttered in the centuries when the *caliph* ruled the faithful from Baghdad.

Revolutionary motivations

In Europe at least until the French Revolution campaigns of terrorist violence or indiscriminate killing and blood-letting were typically justified in terms of religious ideas. The French Revolution had a profound effect not only on the practice of political murder but also on its rationale. Let us deal with the latter first. The extraordinary events in France following the storming of the Bastille in 1789 had the long-term effect of secularizing the source of political authority. "The People" as an abstract entity became the ultimate source of authority. Governments that did not act in the name of the People or whose conduct was not in accord with the People's will were thereafter to be regarded as illegitimate. Correlatively, groups, movements, political parties, and even individuals who asserted they were acting on behalf of the People felt themselves to be justified in doing almost anything to fulfill the latter's wishes – as defined by those who claimed to discern what the People really wanted. Over the course of the nineteenth century, as nationalism and industrialism spread through the continent, political writers disaggregated the idea of "the People" into subsidiary categories. For advocates of national unification in Germany and Italy and of national independence for the peoples under the dominion of the Austro-Hungarian, Russian, and Ottoman empires, the People became equated with the Nation, on whose behalf virtually all forms of political action became justifiable. In a similar vein, with the spread of industrial capitalism in Europe and beyond the idea of the People as a particular social class took hold. For Marx and his followers, it was the industrial working class, the urban proletariat, who became the People, that is, the ultimate source of political legitimacy and justification for political action. In both cases, it was typically small groups of the enlightened who believed they had the capacity to discern what the People really needed or wanted irrespective of what individuals belonging to this category in fact did or said.

In addition to the shift in the source of authority from heaven to earth, the French Revolution bequeathed a more concrete legacy. In subsequent decades of the nineteenth century secret societies appeared in Europe, such as the Carbonari groups which spread all over Italy, whose members were committed to keeping the revolutionary ideas of the French Revolution alive. How was a new revolution, in the manner of the French, to be achieved? What would bring the People onto the streets and make them storm the barricades? Opinions varied but some of the new revolutionaries believed that oppressive governments could be brought down by "imitating Brutus," in other words by the assassination of national rulers. In his 1849 essay "Murder" the German revolutionary Karl Heinzen argued that "murder is the principal agent of historical progress ... No clear thinking, rational person can accept the hair-splitting distinctions by which certain methods of obliterating the enemy are justified and others condemned; such distinctions rest on theological and legal fictions."[5]

Within a decade of Heinzen's observation individual revolutionaries began to translate his words into practice. In an era of monarchy, assassinating kings and other royal personages made the most sense. Felice Orsini, an Italian nationalist, attempted to assassinate Napoleon III in 1858 because of the latter's opposition to Italian unification. A few years later a young German law student made an attempt on the life of the Prussian ruler Wilhelm I because of his failure to unify Germany. This was the first of multiple attempts on the Prussian ruler's life.

During the 1860s and 1870s young European revolutionaries, often anarchists, made multiple attempts to kill important political figures, including (in 1866) Otto von Bismarck, the Prussian prime minister and architect of German unification. These were spectacular though relatively isolated incidents, attacks carried out by single individuals with little by way of organized support. The beginning of what the American terrorism expert David Rapoport refers to as the "first wave" of modern terrorism really began in the 1880s and continued into the first decades of the twentieth century.[6] Not only isolated individuals but various groups became involved in what became known as the "era of the attempts."

The first wave

It is possible to identify three separable strands of terrorist violence in this first wave: Russian revolutionaries, anarchists, and nationalists. To some extent the ideas and the groups that propounded them fed on each other. But the goals they pursued were sufficiently different to justify treating them separately.

The Russian People's Will (Narodnaia Volia) emerged in 1879 from a broader political movement committed to bringing down the czarist autocracy and replacing it with a liberal constitutional regime that would then become a way station on the path to popular socialism. The tactic by which they could achieve this goal was through a campaign of assassination directed against the czar himself, the most harmful figures in the regime, and police spies and in response to particularly brutal acts by the government. The People's Will's most spectacular act was its assassination of Czar Alexander II in 1881. Despite the massive repression that followed this killing, which included the complete elimination of its executive committee, the People's Will was able to carry out other acts of terrorism into the 1890s.

At the beginning of the twentieth century, during what proved to be the reign of Russia's last czar, Nicholas II, the Socialist Revolutionaries (SRs) launched a terrorist campaign aimed at the regime. This party's Combat Organization engaged in a far more extensive series of assassinations than the People's Will. The Russian interior was one of its major victims. The SRs' hope was that the killings would ignite a popular revolutionary uprising against the Romanov dynasty and bring about the advent of a socialist system.[7] The Bolsheviks headed by

Lenin objected to the SRs' terrorism. The cause of socialist revolution would not be advanced, they reasoned, through acts of individual assassination. In fact, the potentially revolutionary masses might be deluded into believing that the terrorism *was* the revolution rather than the spark that was intended to ignite it. Social revolution required careful organization and raising the class consciousness of the Russian working class. There were no shortcuts. Despite this objection to terrorism as a matter of revolutionary principle, the Bolsheviks, when they found it expedient, were willing to engage in a certain amount of terrorism themselves on occasions when they thought it would enhance their prospects. "Proletarian expropriations," bank robberies in other words, became a significant means of fundraising for Lenin's followers.

The view that small numbers of the most enlightened and far-sighted could spark a social revolution was adopted by the nineteenth-century European and American anarchists who became exponents of "propaganda by deed." Although many of its leading theorists were Russians, e.g. Michael Bakunin, Pyotor Kropotkin, and Serge Nechaev, revolutionary anarchism played its most visible role in Southern Europe. The anarchists believed they had discovered a new and more scientific way of making a revolution.[8] The state as an instrument of human oppression could be eliminated and workers and peasants freed from the bondage of their masters through the use of advanced technology, dynamite especially. In place of a mass revolution in which thousands of innocent bystanders would be killed or injured the modern revolution could be carried out with only minimal loss of life. Kings and queens, emperors, legislators, captains of industry, police chiefs, generals, and admirals – if they could be removed from the scene in spectacular ways the masses would find their way to revolution and the dissolution of the state.

Accordingly, during the 1880s and into the early twentieth century anarchists assassinated *inter alia* the president of France, the empress of Austria-Hungary, the Spanish foreign minister, and the king of Italy. A French anarchist threw a bomb into the Chamber of Deputies in Paris. In the United States anarchists assassinated President William McKinley in 1901 and former Idaho governor Frank Steunenberg in 1905. Anarchists set off bombs in front of the *Los Angeles Times* building (1910) and at a patriotic parade in San Francisco (1910). These events led to widespread fear in the US and throughout Europe that a vast conspiracy was at work, aimed at undermining public order and leading to a state of, well, anarchy. Criminal codes were often amended to make the practice of anarchism a punishable offense.

The era in which modern terrorism first appeared was an age of empire, a period in which the British, French, and other European powers controlled vast transoceanic empires in Africa, Asia, and the Pacific. We should not forget, however, that Europe itself was the site of large continental empires, the Austro-Hungarian, Russian, German, and on the periphery the Ottoman. These empires, which were to be swept away by World War I, contained various national groups, especially in Eastern and Southeastern Europe, whose members frequently achieved a level of consciousness sufficient to give rise to national independence movements. Among these movements there were those who were willing to make "propaganda by deed" in order to achieve their goals.

The Irish were the first to do so when (in 1882) members of the Invincibles (an offshoot of the Fenian Irish independence movement) committed the Phoenix Park murders, killing the British government's representative in Dublin along with his secretary on behalf of the cause.[9] During the 1890s the Armenian Revolutionary Federation (ARF), inspired in part by their Russian counterparts, launched a terrorist campaign to free Armenia from Ottoman Turkish control. At the same time the Inner Macedonian Revolutionary Organization (IMRO) carried out terrorist attacks against the Turkish authorities in order to achieve an independent Macedonia in the Balkans. In neither case did the group involved achieve their goals.

In the first decade of the twentieth century a number of shadowy groups emerged in the Balkans whose goal was the establishment of a federation of the southern Slavic peoples – Serbs, Croats, Slovenes – at the expense of the Austro-Hungarian Empire. Against this background we should not forget that it was a Serb nationalist and a member of Young Bosnia, Gavrilo Princip, who assassinated the Habsburg Archduke Franz Ferdinand on June 28, 1914 and thereby set in motion the sequence of events that led to the outbreak of World War I less than three months later.

The period between the end of World War I and the outbreak of World War II in 1939 was a time in which fascism became a powerful force in European politics, managing to secure power in Italy and Germany. Fascist ideas became widely attractive throughout the continent and beyond. What was the relationship between fascism and terrorist violence? That Fascist Italy and Nazi Germany engaged in state terrorism seems beyond dispute. But what about the sort of terrorism from below with which we have been concerned?

The answer is that in a number of East European states several ultra-nationalist movements appeared in the successor states (successors to the Russian and Habsburg empires) that mimicked the fascist style and expressed admiration for the Mussolini and Hitler dictatorships. Among the most prominent of these mimetic movements were the Romanian Iron Guard, the Hungarian Arrow Cross, and the Croat Ustascha. These organizations, with funding from Fascist Italy or the Nazis, carried out terrorist attacks, assassinations, and nocturnal bombings against their domestic and almost invariably left-wing domestic political opponents. Jews were frequent targets of anti-Semitic pogroms as well. The Ustascha, though, had wider-ranging ambitions. In its effort to create an independent Croatia, a state free of Belgrade and Serbian domination, a small band of Ustascha terrorists (who had received training for their mission in Mussolini's Italy) assassinated the Yugoslav King Alexander along with the French foreign minister in Marseilles in 1934. This act of international terrorism prompted the French government to seek redress through the League of Nations. On the basis of the French complaint the League considered the matter and drafted two treaties (in 1937), one on the suppression of international terrorism and the other calling for the establishment of an international criminal court to try those accused of committing or sponsoring international terrorist attacks. Before the outbreak of World War II put an end to the proceedings, only three states had ratified the first treaty and none the second.[10]

The second wave

The second wave of terrorism followed the end of that war and is associated with the cause of national independence among colonies seeking to free themselves from the control of the transoceanic empires of the European powers, Britain and France especially. The postwar era also encompassed the revolutionary upheaval in China which culminated in 1949 with the victory of the communists under the leadership of Mao Tse-tung and the retreat of his Nationalist adversaries to the island of Taiwan, where they remain to this day.

In some cases the colonial powers granted independence to the "new nations" of the Third World without putting up much of a fight. In some cases a few mass protests in the colony's capital city with threats of more to come were enough to persuade the Europeans to depart. Thus Britain's Gold Coast colony was transformed into the independent West African state of Ghana in 1957. India and Pakistan became independent countries a decade earlier following a long campaign of non-violent civil disobedience waged by the Congress party under Gandhi and Nehru.

In other instances, however, the colonial power chose to forcefully resist the demands of national independence movements. For example, the Dutch sought to retain control over their resource-rich possession in Southeast Asia which became the independent country of Indonesia in 1949. The French attempted to reassert their control over Indo-China despite the armed insurrection of the Viet Minh under Ho Chi Minh. And the British did likewise in Malaya, another resource-rich territory in Southeast Asia. In these and other locations the dominant form of armed struggle was not terrorism but rural guerrilla warfare, of the kind practiced with such success by Mao's followers in China.[11] To the extent that terrorism played a role it was a subsidiary one. In French Indo-China (which became the countries of Laos, Cambodia, and North and South Vietnam following the 1954 Geneva peace conference) the Viet Minh assassinated mayors and other local officials and notables identified as collaborators with the French administration. Terrorism was also of some significance in places where the forces of national independence were internally divided along ethnic lines or where communist insurgents sought to achieve dominance in the movement against other elements claiming to represent the colonized.

There were a few places, however, where political terrorism played a central role in the effort to make the colonial power depart. In the Protectorate of Aden, now the capital of Yemen, insurgents (1964) used urban terrorism extensively against the British because their leader reached the conclusion that no one paid attention when the fighting was restricted to the hinterland. In 1952 there began the Mau Mau uprising against British rule in Kenya. Led by members of the Kikuyu people, the Mau Mau carried out attacks against British settlers inside their homeland

and also, and far more extensively, against fellow tribesmen they suspected of aiding the colonists or of adhering to such British regulations as those which prohibited female circumcision.

The island of Cyprus in the eastern Mediterranean was another locale where terrorism was a significant factor in persuading the British to go home. In 1955 the National Organization of Cypriot Fighters (EOKA) under the leadership of Greek Colonel George Grivas launched a terrorist campaign in Cyprus's major cities against the British occupiers with the aim of capturing the attention and winning the sympathy of an international audience. Hit-and-run attacks against police and military personnel were mounted by a few hundred EOKA fighters. The British response was substantial but largely fruitless. Grivas's ultimate goal was the achievement of *Enosis*, a union between Cyprus and Greece. This goal could not be attained even with United Nations mediation because the island had a substantial Turkish population; nevertheless in 1958 the British government did sign an agreement granting Cyprus an independent status (in exchange for the retention of two air bases) with a Greek-Cypriot-dominated government.[12]

The two most attention-winning cases where terrorism was employed to achieve national independence in this era were Palestine and Algeria. In Palestine the British government's decision to maintain its 1939 white paper policy of severely restricting Jewish immigration, even after the events of the Holocaust became widely known, set off the Revolt. Two terrorist organizations, Irgun and LEHI (a Hebrew acronym for "Fighters for the Freedom of Israel") or "Stern Gang," reacted to London's decision by launching a series of terrorist attacks against British targets throughout the Holy Land in the period 1946–47. The most notorious of these attacks was the bombing of the King David Hotel in Jerusalem, which killed over ninety people. The goal was to make the cost to the British of maintaining their control over Palestine so high that the British government would withdraw, leaving the Zionist movement free to establish a Jewish state. The latter goal was achieved in 1948 with the formation of the state of Israel but the role of terrorist violence as practiced by Irgun and LEHI was limited. The terrorism may have made the British position less tenable but it was international pressures from the United States and the United Nations that were probably decisive in bringing an end to the Mandate.

Terrorism was of still greater significance in the case of Algeria. In 1953, when the National Liberation Front (FLN) launched an insurgency aimed at forcing an end to French rule, the government in Paris regarded the territory as part of France. Algerians, at least the European minority, elected deputies to serve in the Palais Boubon. Algeria was divided into departments presided over by prefects, the same arrangement as prevailed in metropolitan France. And, by contrast to other French-controlled parts of North Africa, Algeria had a European population of well over a million, people who regarded themselves as French citizens. So, whereas Tunisia and Morocco had been allowed to achieve statehood without much resistance, Paris chose to fight in order to preserve a French Algeria.

In the years following this decision French forces were able, by and large, to overcome the FLN's guerrilla warfare tactics in the Algerian countryside. The army had learned some lessons from its protracted though losing struggle against the Viet Minh in Southeast Asia. What the French military could not do, despite the extensive use of torture, was completely destroy the FLN's urban terrorism apparatus in the major cities of Algiers (as depicted in the Gillo Pontecorvo film *The Battle of Algiers*) and Oran.[13] The pressures from the European settler population, the target of an indiscriminate FLN bombing campaign, and their sympathizers in the military became so intense that by 1958 the government in Paris was willing to grant virtually complete power to Charles de Gaulle, hero of the Free French during World War II.

At first de Gaulle gave the impression he sympathized completely with the cause of a French Algeria, that he would provide the military with whatever they needed to defeat the FLN. But within a year, during which the French constitution was rewritten to create the Fifth Republic with its strong presidential system, de Gaulle announced his government's decision to enter into negotiations with the FLN. And despite a pro-settler terrorist campaign waged by the Secret Army Organization (SAO) and supported by elements within the military, Algeria won its independence from France in 1962 following extended negotiations between de Gaulle's government and FLN representatives. The FLN then assumed the responsibility for governing the newly independent country. In the Algerian case, then, we are dealing with a conflict in which terrorism played, if not a decisive, certainly an important role in the insurgents' victory and the withdrawal of the colonial power.

Algeria, though, represented more the exception than the rule. By and large terrorism was more an annoyance or a subsidiary tactic than a central factor in the various national independence struggles from 1947 to 1965. Terrorism became a major factor in political conflicts beginning during the second half of the 1960s, as the world entered what Walter Laqueur has labeled "the Age of Terrorism."

We need to ask ourselves first what general conditions existed around the world during the 1960s that helped precipitate this new age of terrorist violence? Some physical conditions played a role. It seems easy to forget but the 1960s witnessed the development of the satellite-assisted transmission of television images around the world. For the first time it became possible for millions of people to see live pictures of events occurring on the far side of the globe in real time, i.e. as they happened. The world, to use a phrase from the era, was becoming a "global village." To the extent that terrorism ("propaganda by deed") is a kind of violence whose purpose is to send a message to an audience, the prospective size and composition of that audience became infinitely larger and more diverse thanks to this technological development. The 1972 Munich Olympic Games had an audience of close to one billion people, an almost irresistible target for the Black September commandos who seized Israeli athletes at the Olympic Village with the purpose of publicizing the Palestinian cause.

The first half of the 1960s was also a time when commercial jet airliner traffic became a regular means of transportation for large numbers of people. It seems obvious but worth reminding ourselves that commercial jet airliners now as then follow printed and public schedules from one destination to another at regular time intervals. Among other things, this made it possible for terrorists to "skyjack" planes carrying large numbers of passengers and hold them hostage until various demands were met. It also made it possible to kill large numbers of passengers by detonating explosives while planes were in mid-air if bombs could secretly be placed on board the flight before its departure. Jet travel also made the lives of terrorists somewhat easier by permitting them to move from one place to another, from the locale where they carried out their attack to a host country that would offer them sanctuary.

The 1960s witnessed at least two events that had worldwide consequences and which served to radicalize the political situation on a worldwide basis. The radicalized atmosphere, in turn, provided the background for the outbreak of terrorism by the end of the decade. First, the Vietnam War, or more precisely opposition to the American involvement in it, set off massive protests throughout much of Western Europe and North America, protests involving hundreds of thousands of demonstrators who engaged not only in direct action but also in various acts of largely peaceful civil disobedience.

Another spin-off from the Vietnam War was a growing belief of young people in various parts of the world that

America's vaunted military prowess might not in fact be what it seemed. The Viet Cong's evidently successful guerrilla campaign in South Vietnam against US forces suggested to many that unconventional warfare on behalf of a revolutionary cause might bring victory over seemingly superior conventional military establishments – and not only the American one.

Another development, also in East Asia, played a role as well. In China Mao Tse-tung's denunciation of the Soviet Union as a "revisionist" power willing to reach an accommodation with the capitalist countries created a schism within the communist bloc and among communist parties throughout the world. New pro-Chinese parties emerged in Latin America, South Asia, and Western Europe which were prepared to pay more than lip service to the cause of violent revolution. In addition, beginning in 1966 Mao unleashed the "Great Proletarian Cultural Revolution" in China, a vast young people's campaign aimed at promoting the cause of permanent revolution. Because of these developments China under Mao became a source of inspiration for a generation of young, anti-Vietnam-War radicals who hoped the cause of social revolution could be pursued in spite of the tired-looking bureaucrats in the Kremlin.

Beyond the impact of Vietnam and Mao there were a number of events of a regional nature that helped cause the advent of the terrorist age. In Latin America, after Fidel Castro came to power in Cuba in 1959, thousands of young people became excited by the possibilities of making a revolution by waging guerrilla warfare as Castro and his "bearded ones" had in the Sierra Maestra mountains against the corrupt and weak-willed government in Havana. Castro's second-in-command, Ernesto "Che" Guevara, became a legendary and romantic figure for all those who dreamed of duplicating Castro's achievement in their own countries. Revolutionaries throughout Argentina, Brazil, Peru, Venezuela, and elsewhere in Latin America embarked on the revolutionary path as followers of either Castro or, in a few cases, Mao. Their efforts achieved little. The long-suffering indigenous people to whom the guerrillas appealed were often indifferent. In other instances the repressive apparatus of the state proved too powerful. In Bolivia, Guevara launched a guerrilla campaign from the Andes which aimed at liberating all the continent's oppressed millions. But in 1967 the Bolivian military (with CIA assistance) overwhelmed Guevara's band and killed its leader.

The defeat of rural-based guerrilla insurgencies led such Latin American revolutionaries as the Brazilian communist Carlos Merighella and the Uruguayan writer Abraham Guillen to contemplate the possibility of urban guerrilla warfare. Though Castro had referred to cities as the "graveyard of revolution," Merighella and Guillen believed otherwise. They reasoned that all over Latin America the countryside was losing population at a rapid pace and the cities were quickly being transformed into vast conurbations with millions of displaced and impoverished slum dwellers who would provide the social base for new urban insurrections. Furthermore, they reasoned that cities were where the mass media were centered. Violent events that in remote locales would hardly be noticed would in urban areas almost surely draw the attention of television stations and other media outlets. As a result of these calculations urban guerrilla bands began their attacks (as we shall see) during the second half of the 1960s.

The Middle East was another region where terrorist violence became of great significance at the end of the 1960s. In this case it was the June 1967 Arab–Israeli war that triggered the terrorism. For a number of years the strategy of such Palestinian groups as Fatah (Yassir Arafat's organization), the Marxist Popular Front for the Liberation of Palestine (PFLP), and the Egyptian-backed Palestine Liberation Organization (PLO) was to provoke a war between Israel, the hated Zionist entity, and the Arab states surrounding it. The presumption was that this war, when it came, would result in Israel's complete defeat and the replacement of the Jewish state by a secular Palestinian one.

In the year before June 1967 Fatah *inter alia* staged a series of raids inside Israel with the aim of provoking retaliation that the Syrian government, in particular, would not tolerate. The strategy worked. In the spring of 1967 first Syria then Egypt and Jordan mobilized their forces for a final showdown with Israel. The result of the ensuing conflict was virtually the opposite of what the various Palestinian struggle groups had hoped. Israeli armed forces scored an overwhelming victory against the Arab armies arrayed against them. When a ceasefire was declared six days after the outbreak of hostilities the Israelis were in control of the Sinai desert (including the Gaza Strip), East Jerusalem, the West Bank, and the Golan Heights. Rather than being destroyed Israel appeared stronger than ever and the Palestinian situation more hopeless.

The Palestinian groups reacted to their predicament by undergoing an organizational transformation and by switching strategies. First, in 1968 the PLO became an umbrella organization for all or almost all the various groups seeking to replace Israel with a Palestinian state (as restated in the 1968 PLO Charter). Yassir Arafat, the head of the largest group, Fatah, became the PLO chairman. Second, given the Vietnam War and the successful struggle against France waged by the FLN in Algeria, the PLO committed itself to a "people's war." Rather than rely on conventional Arab armies, the PLO leadership expressed the intent to engage in self-liberation by conducting guerrilla warfare against the Israelis to a point when the large Palestinian population now under Israeli occupation would make the same kinds of sacrifices as the Vietnamese peasants were making on behalf of the Viet Cong.

In practice this meant a strategy of infiltration into the Israeli-occupied West Bank from PLO bases in Jordan accompanied by efforts to establish a network of supporters in the area. With a handful of exceptions these efforts to launch a guerrilla insurgency were not successful. Among other things, many West Bankers retained their loyalty to Jordan, and the barren terrain on which PLO commandos chose to fight left them exposed to aerial surveillance by Israeli helicopters.

It was against this background that the PLO, the PFLP in particular, shifted to terrorism. In 1969 there was a wave of commercial airliner skyjackings in the skies over Europe. It was these episodes, which received extensive television coverage, more than anything else that won publicity for the Palestinian cause on a worldwide basis.

Western Europe and North America present a different picture. In the advanced industrialized democracies the late 1960s was a period of large-scale mass protest and agitation. Opposition to the Vietnam War was usually the major cause. But in some places the grievances of industrial workers, e.g. in Italy, or the civil rights demands of minorities, e.g. in the United States, were of major significance. Almost always university students played leading roles. Political movements, often based on New Left ideas, arose to mobilize and sustain the discontents into revolutionary directions. But as the level of militancy waned and most of those caught up in the movements contemplated a return to more normal lives, small bands of revolutionary terrorists appeared with names like the Red Brigades, Red Army Fraction, Weather Underground, and Revolutionary Road, whose goal was the violent overthrow of the capitalist system either locally or on a worldwide basis. Commonly the groups claimed inspiration from Mao or Leon Trotsky.

Western Europe in the late 1960s and early 1970s was also the site of nationalist/separatist struggles. Despite or perhaps because of the long-standing policy of repression pursued by the dictatorship of Francisco Franco in Madrid, Spanish Basque nationalism underwent a revival. In particular, university students and other young people formed a group eventually to be known as Basque Homeland and Liberty (ETA) which, after a prolonged period of incubation, launched a terrorist campaign against the Spanish government with the aim of creating a separate state for the country's Basque community. The most dramatic early achievement of ETA was the assassination of Franco's heir-apparent, Admiral Carrero Blanco, in 1972.

At about the same time as the situation of the Basques in northern Spain was giving rise to terrorist violence, the circumstances of Northern Ireland's Catholic population re-ignited the long-standing conflict over that province's political status. By and large the province's Protestant majority were Unionists who wanted to retain its tie to the United Kingdom. Catholics, generally speaking, were Nationalists who wished the region to be merged with the republic in the south to form a united Ireland.

In the north Catholics had suffered from various forms of political and economic discrimination. When these accumulated grievances led to civil rights marches and other, largely peaceful, forms of public protest in 1968 and 1969, the situation soon deteriorated. Protestant and Catholic bands began to battle on the streets of Belfast and Londonderry. It was in this context that the Irish Republican Army (IRA) and its Protestant paramilitary counterparts began to carry out violent attacks on their opponents' population. As the situation deteriorated the government in London suspended Northern Ireland's provincial government in Stormont and sent British troops to restore order. The decision to send troops was regarded as a provocation by the IRA, or more precisely the Provisional IRA, a faction that broke with the parent organization over the question of violence. The Provisionals or "Provos" defined the British forces as an army of occupation whose presence justified an armed struggle to end Northern Ireland's colonial status. The result was "The Troubles," a protracted period of terrorist violence waged by the Provos but also a number of Protestant paramilitary bands committed to the Unionist cause.

The third wave

The events we have described over the last several pages gave rise to an age of terrorism; a period, still with us, during which political terrorism has become a major international problem rather than simply an occasional annoyance. With this transformation in mind we need to describe the results, the terrorist campaigns of the 1970s and early 1980s, a period the political scientist David Rapoport labels the "third wave" of modern terrorism.

Brazil, Uruguay, and Argentina all experienced urban guerrilla campaigns from the late 1960s through the mid 1970s. In all three cases these campaigns were brought to an end by police/military repression, often with the use of "death squads" composed of nominally off-duty military/police personnel dressed in civilian clothes. In all three cases the urban guerrilla bands thought that terrorist attacks, including assassinations, kidnapping, and bank robberies, could be used to provoke the authorities into over-reacting. If the latter could be provoked into acting in a harsh and indiscriminate manner, their behavior would show the masses the "true" nature of the bourgeois capitalist regime that ruled over them, and consequently pave the way for widespread revolutionary upheaval.

In all three instances the theory seemed to work, or at least part of it. The authorities were provoked and did, indeed, become repressive or more repressive than they had been previously. But that was the end of things. No social revolution was forthcoming. Torture, extrajudicial imprisonment, murder, and the violation of the full panoply of human rights by state agencies managed to snuff out the urban guerrilla campaigns and, not uncommonly, the urban guerrillas themselves.

Despite the similarity of response the three cases were far from identical. Uruguay in the late 1960s was one of Latin America's few democracies when the Tupamaros launched a terrorist campaign to topple the government in Montevideo in 1968. Brazil, on the other hand, was already a military dictatorship when three Marxist–Leninist bands began to stage terrorist attacks in Sao Paolo and the other major cities at about the same time.

The situation in Argentina was more complex. A number of groups, of which the Montoneros and People's Revolutionary Army (ERP) were the most significant, carried out a series of attacks. Widespread protests led to the return from exile of the populist dictator Juan Peron. Peron and his wife were quickly elected the country's president and vice-president. The Montoneros, for one, believed that Peron sympathized with their social revolutionary objectives. When this proved not to be the case, urban guerrilla operations escalated significantly. Peron died and his wife Isabel succeeded him as Argentina's head of state. Against this background, the severity of terrorist violence mounted. Attacks were carried out against police and military officers and their families. In 1976 the military intervened by staging a *coup d'état*. The country's armed forces then proceeded to wage a "dirty war" against the urban guerrillas and their presumed sympathizers over the next several years.

Terrorist activity in Latin America was by no means confined to the "Southern Cone" and Brazil. Both Peru and Colombia have had to deal with significant revolutionary insurgencies. In both cases these insurgencies have combined rural guerrilla warfare and urban terrorism. In Peru the Shining Path (Sendero Luminoso), a Maoist movement rooted in the country's impoverished Indian population in the Andes, began to assault outposts of government authority from 1980. Despite the capture of its leader and revolutionary theoretician, Abimael Guzman, in 1992 the challenge to the authorities in Lima persists. A similar scenario applies to Colombia, where the government in Bogotá has had to grapple with at least three sizable Marxist groups: FARC, M19, and the National Liberation Army (ELN).

Particularly FARC has benefited from links with the country's narcotics dealers and other organized crime elements. As in Peru the conflict has persisted into the twenty-first century.

In the Middle East the PLO made a strategic decision in the period 1968–69 to switch from a guerrilla-style insurgency on the West Bank to the prosecution of a terrorist campaign against Israel and that state's sympathizers in other parts of the world, Western Europe most notably. At first these operations were devised and launched from the organization's bases in Jordan. The situation changed radically as the result of an event that took place in the summer of 1970. Commandos from the PFLP skyjacked four commercial airliners in the skies over Europe and flew them to Dawson's Field, a former British air base near Amman. After extended negotiations the PFLP released its hostages but blew up the planes, an act that achieved worldwide press coverage. Neither King Hussein, the Jordanian monarch, nor his armed forces were amused. The PLO groups had begun to act as a state within a state, running Palestinian neighborhoods and refugee camps as if they were sovereign authorities. The Dawson's Field incident was the final straw. In September 1970, later to become known as "Black September," Jordan launched a campaign to disarm the PLO groups on its soil. The result was a humiliating defeat for the PLO and the removal of its headquarters, including the headquarters of the various groups under its umbrella, to Lebanon.

Over the next twelve years from Beirut and southern Lebanon, which came to be known as "Fatahland" (because of its control by Fatah, the largest and most influential of the Palestinian groups), the PLO launched three types of terrorist attacks. First, there were cross-border infiltrations into Israel where "commando" units seized Israeli civilians and demanded the release of Palestinian prisoners in exchange for their captives' lives or, not uncommonly, simply killed outright whichever Israelis they happened to come across. Almost always these assaults resulted in the deaths of the PLO fighters staging them. Second, the PLO groups carried out attacks on Israeli and Jewish targets abroad, most commonly in Western Europe. The most famous of these was the 1972 attack by Black September members on Israeli athletes participating in the summer Olympic Games in Munich. This event attracted a worldwide television audience and perforce an extraordinary volume of publicity for the Palestinian cause.

The third type of PLO operation in these years involved attacks on third parties, installations or people regarded as friendly to Israel. Almost always these terrorist attacks occurred in Western Europe. Airports in Rome, Vienna, Athens, and Zurich were attractive targets, as were airliners flying from these locales to Israel. Unlike the outcomes of the attacks inside Israel, the perpetrators of these terrorist acts often got away with it. If they were held in prison for any length of time the Palestinian groups to which they belonged would seize hostages from the same country and threaten to kill them if their colleagues were not released. The imprisoned terrorists thus became "poisoned pawns." By holding them for their crimes the country involved almost guaranteed further attacks. And so the temptation to let the PLO fighters go with a slap on the wrist became very strong.

In 1982 the PLO was expelled from Lebanon as the result of an Israeli invasion. Despite verbal commitments Arab governments did virtually nothing to prevent the PLO's humiliating defeat at the hands of Israeli forces. The PLO re-established its headquarters in Tunisia, far from the site of its struggle with Israel. It seemed not only geographically but politically marginalized until the outbreak of the first Palestinian Intifada in the occupied territories in December 1987. As this uprising proceeded, the PLO, at least those elements not completely rejecting the possibility of a peace with Israel, began to abandon the bomb and the gun in favor of negotiations with their Israeli enemies.[14]

During these years the wealthy and highly industrialized Western democracies were by no means immune from terrorist violence. In a number of cases revolutionary terrorist bands emerged as the student-centered campaigns of mass protest against Vietnam and other issues subsided. In the United States the far left and short-lived Weather Underground and Symbionese Liberation Army appeared in the early 1970s as the protests were repressed by the authorities or declined because of a waning of emotional energy among their participants. Under similar circumstances more sustained campaigns of terrorism were launched in the Federal Republic of Germany by the Red Army Fraction, June 2 Movement, and other bands. In Italy the trouble-plagued center-left government of Christian Democrats and Socialists was compelled to confront a half dozen revolutionary groups, including the especially powerful Red Brigades (responsible for the 1978 kidnapping and murder of former prime minister Aldo Moro), along with a number of such violent neo-Fascist bands as the New Order and National Vanguard. Turkey, then as now on Europe's periphery, suffered the most serious case (close to four thousand people were killed by the violence in 1979–80 alone). In this case, as in the Italian, far left groups not only sought to make a revolution and, *inter alia*, detach the country from NATO, but engaged in shootouts on the streets of Istanbul and Ankara with right-wing nationalist bands such as the Grey Wolves. France and Belgium as well as Greece and Spain, after the latter restored democratic rule in the 1970s, were all plagued by smaller bands of "communist combatants" which aspired to revolution but only managed to kill a handful of people identified either with NATO or capitalist exploitation. [15]

Except for Turkey, where the military seized power in 1980, all the countries mentioned above retained their democratic institutions. In Germany and Italy the laws were modified to enhance the ability of the police and security services to investigate terrorist acts and arrest those suspected of their commission.

It was not simply defeat at the hands of the authorities that brought an end, or at worst a significant decline, in social revolutionary terrorism in the established democracies during the 1980s. Changes in the international milieu certainly played a role as well. The transformation of China after Mao into a country committed to capitalist forms of enterprise, the complete collapse of communist regimes in Eastern Europe, and the disintegration of the Soviet Union radically reduced the allure of Marxism and Marxist-based ideas for thousands of young people throughout Western Europe and North America. Further, from a more practical perspective, the Soviet Union under the leadership of Mikhail Gorbachev (from 1985 forward), was no longer willing to provide much in the way of covert assistance to the selected revolutionary terrorist groups it had supported during the 1970s as an inexpensive means of disrupting the USSR's Cold War NATO adversaries.

The waning of revolutionary violence in Latin America and the industrialized democracies and the commitment of the PLO to eschew terrorism in favor of diplomatic solutions to its problems may have brought an end to one worldwide wave of terrorism in the 1980s. But the decade of the 1980s did not bring an end to terrorism itself. Rather the decade saw the beginning of a "fourth wave" of modern terrorism, a new upsurge that has proved to be far more lethal than any of the earlier experiences. It is this "new terrorism" to which we now turn our attention.

Further reading

James Billington, *Fire in the Minds of Men: Origins of the Revolutionary Faith* (New York: Basic Books, 1980).

Martha Crenshaw (ed.), *Terrorism in Context* (University Park: Pennsylvania State University Press, 1995).

Walter Laqueur, *Guerrilla* (Boston: Little, Brown, 1976).

Anna Geifman, *Thou Shalt Kill: Revolutionary Terrorism in Russia, 1894–1917* (Princeton: Princeton University Press, 1993).

David Rapoport, "Fear and Trembling: Terrorism in Three Religious Traditions," *American Political Science Review* 78:3 (1984) pp. 658–677.

3

The first war of the twenty-first century

The new terrorism

Many of the bands and organizations that used terrorist violence in the 1960s, 1970s, and early 1980s as a means of igniting social revolution have either passed from the scene or faded into the background. In Europe traces remain here and there, but such groups as the Red Army Fraction, Front Line, and Direct Action have virtually slipped from sight. Marxism-Leninism continues to produce passionate converts in Nepal (a country singularly lacking an urban proletariat) and such Latin American countries as Peru, where the Shining Path is still active. Increasingly though, the handful of social revolutionary terrorist groups remaining appear like the nineteenth-century advocates of "propaganda by deed." History has somehow passed them by. But this hardly means that terrorism itself has disappeared: far from it. Terrorist violence during the first decade of the twenty-first century is far more menacing than it has been at any point in its modern history, and includes the most lethal single event in the history of terrorism, the attacks on the World Trade Center and the Pentagon on September 11, 2001. Some refer to the recent and immensely destructive wave of terrorism as "the first war of the twenty-first century" or as the "new terrorism." In either case, we ought to begin our analysis of it by describing what events or series of events ignited the current wave of terrorism. Following this account we proceed to specify the dominant traits of this new terrorism and how they distinguish it from earlier waves of terrorist violence. Finally we need to discuss the major organizations, the al Qaeda network especially, presently waging the first war of the twenty-first century.

Three developments are exceptionally important in helping us to understand the appearance of the new wave of terrorism from the 1980s to the present. First, the Iranian Revolution of 1979–80 has been of immense significance.

For much of the Cold War period the West, and the United States especially, regarded Iran under the leadership of Shah Mohammed Reza Pahlavi as an anti-communist bastion and as an island of stability in an otherwise turbulent Middle East. The Shah, the King of Kings, was widely regarded as a modernizing and reform-minded ruler who intended to transform Iran into a thoroughly modern industrialized and largely secular country. Iran had a long border with the Soviet Union as well as a domestic communist movement, the Tudeh Party, which aspired to revolutionary insurrection. To undercut the potential communist threat, the Shah pursued two policies for much of his reign. First, his government bought immense quantities of arms from the United States and other Western suppliers. The Shah also permitted the stationing of American military personnel on Iranian territory, for the purpose of training his armed forces and monitoring developments on the other side of his country's border with the Soviet Union. Believing that the Tudeh Party and other revolutionary opponents of the monarchy would win popular support by exploiting the country's impoverished peasantry, the Shah undertook his own land redistribution program. In the early 1960s this program, known as the "White Revolution," gave land to the landless by taking it away from the large holders – which included the property of Iran's Shiite clergy.[1]

These policies were supposed to set the country on a course of peaceful economic and social development while insulating it from the winds of red revolution blowing from across the

Caspian Sea or, in the case of Soviet-backed Iraq, from the Persian Gulf. But seen in retrospect they had the opposite effect.

What occurred during the 1970s was a massive backlash against the Shah's efforts at modernization. The opposition to the monarchy was led not by followers of Marx and Lenin but by the country's mullahs, its Shiite clergy. From his exile in Iraq and later France the austere but charismatic figure of the Ayatollah Ruhollah Khomeini gave voice to a long list of popular grievances and resentments. He depicted the Shah as a corrupt and ungodly puppet of the United States. He condemned the influence of American culture, e.g. popular music and the use of drugs, on the youth. He denounced the brutality of the SAVAK, Iran's secret police force. He attacked the unfair economic competition the country's bazaar merchants were forced to suffer at the hands of modern department stores.

The Ayatollah's statements were recorded on cassettes and secretly distributed throughout Iran, where they were then played in the mosques and religious schools. Khomeini's speeches fueled resentments that by 1977 were widespread among virtually all segments of society. The result was a series of increasingly tumultuous mass protests in the major cities throughout 1978–79. Neither the Shah nor his advisers, including American ones, knew how to respond to protests that by the end brought more than one million people on to the streets of Tehran.[2]

At the beginning of 1979 the Shah went into exile, leaving a caretaker government in his place. Within a month the Ayatollah Khomeini returned from his exile in France to a near ecstatic welcome in Tehran. Over the next year a new Islamic Republic was established with Khomeini as its "supreme guide" dominating from the top. A major crisis between the United States and Iran was created when the Carter administration allowed the Shah into America in order to receive medical treatment for what was to prove a fatal illness. Iranian radicals, with the Ayatollah's approval, responded by seizing the American embassy in Tehran and holding the Americans inside it hostage for over two years. By defying what Khomeini labeled "the Great Satan" in this way, the clerical regime enhanced its growing prestige at home and excited the admiration of millions of Shiites throughout the Middle East.

Nowhere was the religious and political excitement set off by the Iranian Revolution more intensely felt than in Lebanon. Sections of South Beirut, the Bekka Valley, and parts of southern Lebanon, areas with large Shiite populations, were festooned with posters showing the Ayatollah Khomeini at his most ferocious. The country's large Shiite population tended to be poor and its political influence was rarely commensurate with its numerical presence. Lebanon at the time of the revolution was caught up in its own civil war, a conflict that pitted the country's various sectarian communities against one another. To compound the country's woes, Israeli forces had invaded the country in an effort to expel the PLO. There was also a Syrian presence. And in the period 1983–84 the United States, France, and Italy sent peace-keeping forces to Beirut in an effort to restore order and strengthen the Lebanese government.

In this context the mullahs in Tehran sent revolutionary guards to the Bekka Valley to train local Shiites and transform them into an effective paramilitary force. The result of these developments was the emergence of the "Party of God" or Hizbollah. In addition to becoming thoroughly engaged in the civil war against largely Christian sectarian opponents, this Party of God launched a series of terrorist attacks against the American and French presence. Suicide bombers destroyed the American and French embassies and the US Marine Corps barracks near Beirut's international airport in 1983. Later Hizbollah kidnapped or killed various American and European journalists and academics its leaders suspected of spying for the CIA or the Israelis.[3]

Shiite militancy appeared in other places in the Middle East, along the southern shore of the Persian Gulf especially, but it failed to achieve the same level of intensity as it reached in Lebanon by the mid 1980s.

The second development that contributed to the onset of the new terrorism involved the Soviet invasion of Afghanistan in December 1979. Local communist military officers had seized power in Kabul in 1978 and embarked on a policy of forced social and economic modernization along Marxist-Leninist lines. Their reforms included radical agrarian reform, compulsory literacy, and the imposition of socialism through mass arrests and executions. These Stalinist-style efforts set off a general rebellion in April 1979, led by Afghanistan's religiously devout tribal leaders, who saw the Marxists in Kabul as engaged in the installation of atheism in a strongly Muslim country.

The government's military position quickly deteriorated so that within a matter of months it controlled only the major cities. It was at this point that one faction of the Afghan communist movement invited Soviet intervention. To save the situation leaders in the Kremlin responded by sending the Red Army south across the border. The decision was to lead to the Soviet Union's Vietnam.

Muslim leaders throughout Afghanistan, Pakistan, Saudi Arabia, and elsewhere in the Muslim world called for a jihad, a holy war, aimed at expelling the Russian infidels from the House of Islam. The United States saw an opportunity to embarrass (the Carter administration barred American participation in the 1980 summer Olympic Games held in Moscow) and perhaps defeat its Cold War adversary. Both the US and the Saudis provided help. Money, weapons, and training were forthcoming. Thousands of young men throughout the Arab world flocked to Afghanistan and towns like Peshawar near the Pakistan–Afghan border, to wage a guerrilla-style holy war against the Soviets. With government blessing, young Muslim immigrants were even recruited from New York and other American cities.

The Afghan resistance was successful. The Soviets were caught in a quagmire until Gorbachev withdrew the Red Army in 1989. Holy warriors had compelled one of the world's two nuclear superpowers to abandon the conflict and suffer a humiliating defeat. But this achievement had an unexpected consequence, what became known to American observers as a "blowback" effect.[4]

Thousands of Arab veterans, so-called "Afghans," returned to Algeria, Egypt, Saudi Arabia, and the other Middle Eastern countries from which they had come, imbued with a sense of mission and intent on continuing their jihad on behalf of Muslims suffering throughout the world. One such "Afghan" was the young Saudi millionaire Osama bin Laden.

The third factor that helped set off the fresh wave of terrorism in the 1980s and beyond was the approach of the year 2000. The advent of the third millennium had little meaning for Muslims or followers of other religious traditions around the world. But for Christians, especially those linked to denominations labeled "fundamentalist," as well as adherents of new religious cults (e.g. Japan's Supreme Truth) whose symbolism was adapted from the Christian faith, the year 2000 was fraught with eschatological meaning. For some the beginning of the new millennium would witness the beginning of the End Times, a thousand-year period that would culminate with the Second Coming of Christ but which would be preceded by a cataclysmic struggle between good and evil. For some the Book of Revelation predicted a final reckoning and a "Tribulation." In other words, as the year 2000 approached there was a fair amount of "end of the world" talk in many countries affected by Christian belief.

Among the believers who took this doomsday talk with utmost seriousness the most common response was to begin a process of withdrawal from the surrounding society. In a few instances the mass withdrawal behavior became extreme. In the United States, for example, followers of the Heaven's Gate cult were led to believe that the approach of the Hale-Bopp comet heralded the beginning of the end of life on earth. But their leader also persuaded them they might be "saved" by committing mass suicide. Their spirits would reappear aboard a spaceship hidden behind the comet as it made its way around the Solar System. In southern California over a dozen Heaven's Gate adherents killed themselves in this belief.

In a handful of cases, though, instead of turning inward and preparing for the end, believers (such as members of Supreme Truth) turned outward and perpetrated serious acts of terrorism in order to accelerate the battle of Armageddon, the final conflict between good and evil. They hoped to save the human race by killing many of its members.

The Iranian Revolution, the Soviet invasion of Afghanistan, and the proximity of the year 2000 were the developments that ignited the new terrorism. What are its major characteristics? And how does it differ from the old terrorism that preceded it?

What's new?

First and most obviously the new terrorism has been inspired by religion. Religious motives either by themselves or, in some cases, linked to nationalist sentiments have been behind much recent terrorist activity. Muslims claiming inspiration from Islamic ideas have been responsible for much of the new terrorism in the Middle East, Russia, South and Southeast Asia, the United States, and the West European democracies. But this is hardly the end of the story. In Israel a small band of religious fanatics developed a scheme to destroy the Dome of the Rock and the Al Aqsa Mosque on top of the Temple Mount. They hoped that by so doing they could begin the construction of a Third Temple to replace these Muslim holy sites. In India followers of the Sikh religion carried out a terrorist campaign in an effort to carve an independent state of Khalistan out of the Punjab. In Sri Lanka, Hindu Tamils belonging to the Liberation Tigers have waged a protracted campaign against the Buddhist-dominated government in order to establish an independent homeland. And in Uganda, the Lord's Liberation Army, a Christian-inspired cult, has committed a long list of atrocities to seize control of a section of the country and pave the way for a Second Coming.

What do the groups that employ terrorist violence in the name of religious ideas have in common? Almost always observers apply the term "fundamentalist" to the various groups and organizations involved. But what does this mean exactly?

For the most part it means the following. The groups involved are *reactive* in character in the sense they have emerged in reaction against secularizing trends at work in the modern world. Their religious views are based upon a highly selective reading of the sacred texts of their respective religious traditions. The selections almost always are ones that provide justifications for the use of violence against others identified as the enemy. In keeping with this viewpoint is a *Manichean* outlook that divides the world in dichotomous terms into two camps, the all-good versus the evil: the forces of light versus the forces of darkness. *Absolutism* is another and related characteristic. Sacred texts are not open to debate, discussion, or interpretation. Sacred texts are to be taken literally and accepted without question. Those who challenge this outlook are identified with the forces of darkness, as enemies. Often those who share this fundamentalist outlook hold out *messianic* expectations that an end to human history is imminent and that a messianic figure will arrive to distribute ultimate justice. Finally, virtually all religiously inspired terrorist organizations are highly *authoritarian* in nature, frequently with a charismatic or pseudo-charismatic leader believed to possess special powers of insight and wisdom. Often these powers are used to discern and report to the faithful the existence of widespread conspiracies aimed at eliminating the group and the mass of the faithful more generally.[5]

In addition to their religious orientation practitioners of the new terrorism share an outlook towards the use of violence. Back in the 1970s the Rand Corporation analyst Brian Jenkins noticed that terrorists "wanted a lot of people watching, not a lot of people dead." Attention getting and mass media exposure were primary objectives, not mass murder. For the revolutionary and nationalist terrorist groups of the 1960s and 1970s, murdering large numbers of innocents was often seen as counter-productive. Such killings would likely alienate the very audiences the groups hoped to make sympathetic to their cause. As the attack on the World Trade Center in New York on September 11, 2001 illustrates dramatically, this logic of self-restraint no longer applies. In recent years terrorists wish to see not only a lot of people watching but a lot of people dead as well. The new terrorists are now interested in mass murder.

In the minds of many analysts this second attribute is clearly related to the first. The practitioners of the new terrorism believe themselves to be acting in the name of God. And it is to God that their deeds are directed, often in the hope the violence will accelerate or radically transform the course of human history. They are much less concerned with affecting the opinions of various human audiences than the secular revolutionary groups that preceded them in the business of terrorism. Evidence accumulated by the Rand Corporation and other sources discloses that the number of fatalities per terrorist event have increased substantially since the advent of the new terrorism, the result of its religious dimension.

A third characteristic almost always mentioned in connection with the new terrorism is the use of weapons of mass destruction

(WMD) or chemical, biological, radiological, and nuclear weapons (CBRN). Fears of WMD use by terrorist groups were stimulated by two developments. Followers of the Japanese religious cult Supreme Truth (Aum Shinrikyo), directed by its guru Shoko Asara, dispersed the poison gas sarin in a Tokyo subway in 1995 in the hope of killing thousands. Because of technical problems they only managed to kill a dozen passengers, but this was not from lack of trying. Subsequent investigations by Japanese authorities revealed that the Supreme Truth (whose members included Ph.D. chemists and physicists) had conducted experiments with a number of ways of mass killing. Based on this experience many terrorism analysts reached the conclusion that a threshold had been crossed and that now, to borrow the title of an old Cole Porter song, "Anything Goes."

More worrying still was the problem of "loose nukes." The Soviet Union disintegrated in 1991, leaving in its wake a weak confederation of newly independent states in Eastern Europe (e.g. the Ukraine, Belarus), the Caucuses (e.g. Georgia), and Central Asia (e.g. Kazakstan, Uzbekistan). Russia itself was left with a demoralized and dramatically underpaid military/scientific establishment. Talk was widespread of a breakdown in Russia's command-and-control structure, sometimes leaving unanswered the question of whose hand was on the button – who had the ability to launch, or prevent the launch of, the country's vast arsenal of nuclear weapons. Western analysts fretted about the possibility of terrorists buying or stealing either nuclear weapons or the fissionable material necessary to make them. Concerns were also voiced about the possibility of terrorist organizations hiring ex-Soviet scientists and engineers with the knowledge necessary to manufacture these weapons or to make use of Russia's secret biological weapons stockpile.

These concerns have not been totally supplanted. But in recent years the worries have been expanded to include the possibility that so-called "rogue states," such as North Korea and

Saddam Hussein's Iraq, might provide terrorists with these weapons, or that terrorist organizations might develop their own WMD.

Worrying though the use of WMD by terrorist organizations may be, the reality is that the perpetrators of the 9/11 attacks on the World Trade Center and the Pentagon, the most lethal terrorist attacks in history, employed primitive box-cutters to take over the aircraft involved in the tragedies. In carrying out the 9/11 attacks the perpetrators had to commit suicide. Their actions call to mind the fact that suicide bombing campaigns have become important features of the new terrorism. Most secular practitioners of the old terrorism of the 1960s and 1970s carried out their operations in the belief they would live again to fight another day. Even if they were imprisoned by the authorities, their cohorts on the outside would seize hostages or stage kidnappings aimed at trading the hostages' lives for the terrorists' freedom.

But from the 1980s forward the quintessential act of terrorist violence has become the suicide bombing. These attacks involve the attacker either having explosives strapped to his or her body and walking to the place of detonation, or driving a vehicle loaded with explosives to a destination and then setting them off. Hundreds of such attacks have been carried out over more than two decades now by groups ranging from the Tamil Tigers in Sri Lanka to Hamas in the context of the Israeli/Palestinian conflict to al-Qaeda-related groups in places ranging from Morocco to Bali.

Also, the center of gravity of international terrorism has moved from the Middle East to South and Southeast Asia. Pakistan, India, and Sri Lanka have become major venues for terrorist activity, such issues as the future of Kashmir and the status of the Sikhs in the Punjab and the Tamils in Sri Lanka providing the leading causes. In Southeast Asia the quest for national independence by Muslim groups in the southern part of the predominantly Christian Philippines has fueled a terrorist campaign by the secessionist Moro National Liberation Front and the Abu Sayyaf Group. The newly democratizing country of Indonesia has provided fertile terrain for the growth of violent Islamist organizations.

A final way in which the new terrorism differs from its predecessor is organizational in nature. Compared with the European and Latin American terrorist groups of the 1960s and 1970s the contemporary ones are far more decentralized and loosely structured. Experience indicates it is far easier for the authorities to defeat or roll up hierarchical and highly centralized organizations. If one or a small handful of individuals at the top of an organization are familiar with its operational plans and are able to identify its members and their locations then the apprehension of these same individuals may lead to the organization's quick destruction. These days, however, terrorist groups have learned lessons from the past. Instead of having an organizational pyramid, they tend to develop as networks of small bands or cells operating independently of one another, where members of one cell typically do not know who belongs to other units and where they are operating. In this way, the elimination of one cell need not represent a major disruption of the organization's ability to continue to carry out terrorist attacks. The bombing campaign underway in Saudi Arabia (in 2004) provides an illustration.

Some observers also pay attention to the growing problem of "lone wolves," that is single individuals with idiosyncratic political agendas, such as the American "Unabomber," who carry out assassinations or detonate bombs without having any formal or even informal link to an organization. A conspicuous example is Timothy McVeigh, who, aided by his friend Terry Nichols, was responsible for the single most devastating act of domestic terrorism in American history when he detonated a bomb in front of the Murrah Federal Building in Oklahoma City in April 1995 which killed 169 people and injured many more. McVeigh had a right-wing racist agenda (he was an admirer of the neo-Nazi propagandist William Pierce) and had also attended meetings of various militia groups. But the evidence suggests his actions were largely his own, not part of some wider organizational plan.

Jihadi organizations

In the aftermath of the Iranian Revolution and the Soviet Union's withdrawal from Afghanistan the Muslim world witnessed the growth of a profusion of jihadi or holy war organizations prepared to use terrorist violence in order to achieve their objectives. The latter ranged from relatively restricted ones – the establishment of an Islamic republic to take the place of a secular-nationalist regime, e.g. in Algeria – to al Qaeda's extraordinarily ambitious goal of recreating the caliphate by waging perpetual conflict until a "commander of the faithful" could rule Muslims on a worldwide basis. It makes sense to move from the less to the more ambitious.

In terms of fundraising and the presence of covert operatives in various countries, no group seriously rivals al Qaeda. The one organization, though, that sometimes is mentioned in the same breath is the Lebanese Shiite Hizbollah. In the now more than twenty years of its activity Hizbollah, supported by Syria and revolutionary Iran, has enjoyed substantial success. It employed a wave of suicide-bombing attacks and the kidnapping of Westerners during the 1980s to achieve the expulsion of American and French forces from Lebanon. And during the 1990s Hizbollah, under the political leadership of Hassan Nasralla and spiritual guidance of Sheikh Fadlalla, used a combination of guerrilla attacks and terrorism to convince the Israeli government to abandon its "security zone" in the southern part of the country.

In the context of Lebanese politics, Hizbollah has literally become a political party. It is represented in the country's parliament in Beirut. And it has developed an extensive web of social and educational organizations to promote its popularity with its Lebanese Shiite constituency. But its activities are not confined to Lebanon. Hizbollah fundraisers have been arrested in the United States. Money-raising activity is evidently underway in the tri-border area in South America, the largely lawless region where the borders of Argentina, Brazil, and Paraguay converge. Hizbollah operatives have been suspected of responsibility for bombing attacks on the Israeli embassy and the Jewish community center (1993) in Buenos Aires, attacks that left over one hundred people dead.

No complete inventory seems practicable of all the Sunni Muslim organizations currently engaged in terrorist activities or who regard themselves as waging a holy war against variously defined enemies. These enemies may be divided, roughly at least, into two categories. First, there are governments run by non-Muslims whom the jihad organizations view as oppressing or persecuting the believers. This oppression frequently takes the form of denying Muslims the right of self-determination or national independence. The second kind of enemy is a regime controlled by "false" Muslims, rulers who purport to be Muslims or who claim to be acting in conformity with Islamic principles but who in reality do not.

Examples of the first kind are organizations active in the Philippines, Kashmir, Chechnya, the Xinjiang province of China, and, most especially, Israel/Palestine. The last mentioned represents the most serious confrontation, not because of the size of the territory or the number of people immediately involved (relatively small in both cases) but because of its location and symbolism. Israel is located close to the center of the "House of Islam" and contains in Jerusalem the Dome of the Rock and the Al Aqsa Mosque, sites regarded as holy by Muslims throughout

the world, not to mention the areas of immense religious significance for Jews especially and Christians as well.

During the 1960s and 1970s most of the Palestinian groups
operating under the auspices of the PLO were secular and
nationalist in outlook. Some, e.g. the PFLP, were Marxist
whereas others stressed pan-Arab nationalism. However, beginning in the 1980s these groups were challenged by two organizations that emerged from Egypt's Muslim Brotherhood: Hamas
("Zeal" in Arabic) and Palestinian Islamic Jihad (PIJ). When the
first uprising or Intifada against Israeli occupation of the Gaza
Strip and West Bank broke out in December 1987 it was the
latter groups that appeared to take the lead. Since then and with
the establishment of a Palestinian Authority (a pre-statehood
form of government) in 1994, Hamas especially and PIJ have
sought to displace the older organizations in the hearts and
minds of Palestinians both in what Israelis refer to as "the territories" and among Palestinians living in the surrounding Arab
nations.[6]

In addition to their Egyptian origins and Islamist view of the
conflict, Hamas and PIJ share three other attributes. First,
neither believes in nor wishes to achieve a compromise settlement with the Israelis. Such a compromise is barred as a matter
of religious principle, according to their spokesmen. Next, both
organizations are not simply anti-Zionist but anti-Semitic as
well, in the sense of believing Jews to be behind virtually all the
ills that have befallen the Muslim world. Third, though Hamas
and PIJ are hardly alone in this regard, the prototypical type of
terrorist attack with which they are most commonly identified is
the suicide bombing. Since the outbreak of the second or al
Aqsa Intifada in the fall of 2000 hundreds of suicide bombers
have been sent (some successful, others not) by leaders of both
groups to strike at Israeli targets.

However, the two organizations are hardly identical.
Palestinian Islamic Jihad is smaller and its activities are largely

confined to terrorist violence. Hamas is something else again. It enjoys widespread popular support throughout Gaza and the West Bank. It maintains an extensive network of health clinics, social service units, and educational institutions among the Palestinian population. It is Hamas's specialized military wing, the Qassem Brigade, which typically claims responsibility for the violence.

There are many cases involving Islamist groups waging Jihad against governments claimed to be controlled by "false" Muslims. We may use Algeria as a case in point.

Algeria gained its independence from France in 1962 after a bitter internal war waged by the FLN against both the French government and the large community of European settlers. Following independence and the departure of most Europeans, Algeria was ruled for years as a one-party socialist regime controlled by a mix of corrupt politicians and military officers. By the late 1980s and as the result of colossal mismanagement Algeria was in crisis with a high rate of unemployment and a restive, youthful population. Against this background the government called for new elections, ones based on open, competitive rules.

When local elections were held in 1990 the anti-government Islamic Salvation Front (FIS) took a majority of the vote. The following year FIS won over eighty percent of the seats in the first round of balloting for Algeria's national parliament. In 1992 the government responded to these developments by declaring the election results null and void and by outlawing FIS. The violence was not long in coming.[7]

Over the next few years the Armed Islamic Group (GIA) launched a terrorist campaign aimed at toppling the clearly illegitimate government of "false" Muslims. But the GIA did not confine itself to attacking public officials or government institutions. Ordinary Algerians, e.g. girls who declined to wear headscarves or villagers who seemed unsympathetic to the cause or insufficiently pious, often had their throats cut. European tourists or business people were among the thousands killed by GIA squads. The violence also spilled over into France. Because the French government provided assistance to its Algerian counterpart, GIA militants launched bombing attacks against targets in and around Paris. One GIA band even skyjacked an Air France plane bound from Algiers to Marseilles. The skyjackers, in what some observers regard as a rehearsal for the 9/11 attacks, demanded the plane be refueled for a flight to Paris – where they hoped to crash it into the Eiffel Tower. Fortunately, French commandos stormed the aircraft in Marseilles before this scheme could be realized.

The terrorist violence in Algeria continues. The GIA's campaign has killed so many Algerians and antagonized so many more that a dissident faction has broken away and now carries out attacks under the name "Salafist Group for Call and Combat." It is this group that enjoys a relationship with al Qaeda. It was in fact a cell of the Salafist Group active in Montreal, Canada that sought to send agents across the border into the United States in 1999 with the goal of setting off a bomb at Los Angeles International Airport on or around January 1, 2000.

Al Qaeda

Al Qaeda (the Base) is at the center of an extensive network of groups present, by one estimate, in more than seventy countries. It is, without much question, the most powerful terrorist organization in human history. First, we need to understand what it hopes to achieve, what its goals are. Next, we need to know something about al Qaeda's history. We have already traced its origins to the holy war waged against the Soviet occupation of Afghanistan during the 1980s. We should advance this history to the first years of the twenty-first century. And after reviewing this history we need to consider al Qaeda as an organization and report how it raises money, how it is linked to other jihad organizations, and how it carries out its numerous operations.

The most far reaching of al Qaeda's objectives is the re-establishment of the caliphate, the form of Muslim rule that existed in the centuries following the death of the Prophet Mohammad in A.D. 632 and which was only formally abolished after World War I following the demise of the Ottoman Empire and its replacement by the Turkish Republic. Osama bin Laden and other al Qaeda leaders believe that the division of the Muslim world, the Arab part of it especially, into small countries is an artificial consequence of Western imperialism. What is required, they believe, is a Muslim world, one stretching from the Atlantic to the Pacific, which would resemble the great Muslim empires of the past and which would be ruled by a "Commander of the Faithful" or caliph as existed during the "Golden Age" of Islam.

Al Qaeda statements, as expressed through the World Islamic Front against Jews and Crusaders, repeatedly refer to the goal of expelling Western influence from the House of Islam. This expulsion means a number of things. First and foremost it means compelling the United States and its Western allies to leave the Arabian Peninsula, the location of Islam's two holiest sites at Mecca and Medina. Much of al Qaeda's violence is intended to achieve this aim. Related to this goal is the desire to reduce America's cultural influence in the Middle East, as expressed via the mass media and other forms of social penetration, e.g. popular music.

The Jews occupy a special place in al Qaeda's Islamist demonology. Not only must Israel be destroyed and Palestine restored to its rightful place as part of the House of Islam, but "the Jews" are frequently identified as engaged in a vast conspiracy to undermine Muslim institutions on a worldwide basis.

Consequently, Jews and Jewish institutions are regarded by al Qaeda spokesmen as appropriate targets for retaliation against this anti-Muslim conspiracy: witness recent suicide-bombing attacks on synagogues in Morocco and Turkey, buildings with no obvious connections to the state of Israel.

Then there is the matter of current "false" Muslim regimes, especially those in Saudi Arabia and Egypt, regimes that, among other things, represent means by which the Americans extend their influence in the Middle East. An important objective for al Qaeda, an organization led by Osama bin Laden and Ayman al-Zawahiri, two profoundly alienated members of the Saudi and Egyptian elites, is the replacement of these corrupt regimes with authentically Islamic ones. To that end al Qaeda seeks not merely a political but a spiritual restoration, a return to the "straight path" of human conduct as provided by the Prophet many centuries ago.

Al Qaeda emerged from the Afghan Service Bureau (MAK). The latter was created by Osama bin Laden and Sheikh Abdullah Azzam in 1984 for the purpose of recruiting and training young Muslims, largely Arabs, for waging jihad against the Soviet occupiers of Afghanistan. The organization's base was in Peshawar, but its recruiting effort was virtually worldwide in scope and included offices in New York and other cities in North America and Western Europe. In addition to its recruitment campaign – thousands of young men passed through its training camps – MAK engaged in fundraising activities. Over the 1980s it raised and then dispensed approximately US$200 million for the struggle in Afghanistan. In short, by the late 1980s MAK was an extensive and highly successful organization, one that both bin Laden and Azzam wanted to take on new tasks once the Soviets departed from Afghanistan. The central task, as the two leaders came to identify it, was to provide fighters and render material assistance to Muslims wherever they were the victims of oppression. Kashmir and Chechnya were obvious destinations.

Al Qaeda was the new organization bin Laden and Azzam formed in 1989 to assume this responsibility. It was, in effect, intended to generalize from the Afghan conflict by applying this experience globally. Bin Laden and Azzam fell out over tactical considerations: the Sheikh opposed the use of terrorist violence involving randomized attacks on unarmed civilians as incompatible with Islamic teachings. Egyptian fighters in the emerging organization sided with bin Laden. They hoped to launch a terrorist campaign directed at the despised Mubarak government in Cairo. The Egyptians and bin Laden resolved the dispute with Azzam in November 1989 when the latter was killed (along with his two sons) by a powerful car bomb as he was on his way to Friday prayers in Peshawar.

Following this killing and the Soviet withdrawal from Afghanistan, bin Laden returned to Saudi Arabia. There he was treated with the respect due a leader in the successful jihad against the communists. The situation changed after Iraq's invasion of Kuwait in August 1990. The Saudi kingdom itself was widely seen as threatened by this act of aggression. Bin Laden approached the Saudi government with an offer to use the mujahidin, the "holy warriors," those who had fought so bravely against the Soviet forces, to protect the country against a possible attack from Saddam Hussein's armed forces. This offer was rebuffed. Instead the Saudi princes turned to the United States for help and permitted the stationing of American forces on Saudi soil.

This decision infuriated bin Laden. Not only was his offer to provide holy warriors rebuffed but, more galling still, the government decided to allow the kingdom, with its Muslim holy sites at Mecca and Medina, to be used by the infidel Americans. When the Saudis decided to retain an American military presence on an indefinite basis after they had successfully expelled the Iraqis from Kuwait in March 1991 bin Laden could not contain his anger.

He launched a series of religiously inspired condemnations of the Saudi establishment. Before the authorities could arrest him for giving voice to this opposition he returned to Pakistan briefly. Fearing arrest there as well, since the governments in Islamabad and Riyadh enjoyed close relations, bin Laden responded to an invitation extended by the Sudan's spiritual leader, Hassan al-Turabi, and moved to Khartoum along with some fifteen hundred fighters, most veterans of the campaign in Afghanistan.[8]

The Sudan had become an Islamic republic following the 1989 seizure of power by military forces under the leadership of General Omar Hassan al-Bashir, with the Western-educated al-Turabi playing the role of *éminence grise*. The Sudan became the second Muslim country, following Iran, to identify itself as an "Islamic republic."

In this congenial setting, bin Laden and his al Qaeda organization quickly established a substantial presence. Bin Laden was the heir to a substantial fortune. He used his wealth as well as his business acumen (he had received a degree in business) to create a number of enterprises in the Sudan, an impoverished country then engaged in a costly civil war with dissident and largely Christian communities in the southern part of the country.

From 1991 until Khartoum's decision to expel him (under intense Saudi and American pressure) and his cohorts in 1996, bin Laden's organization provided financial assistance to violent Islamist groups throughout the Muslim world and beyond. In addition, bin Laden and his followers developed an interest in the development and use of chemical and biological weapons during this Sudanese stage of al Qaeda's evolution. We should not forget that it was in this period that an Islamist with ties to al Qaeda, Ramzi Yousef, led the first effort, in 1994, to blow up New York's World Trade Center. Also during this period the organization plotted the assassinations of a number of prominent political leaders including US President Bill Clinton, Philippine

President Fidel Ramos, and Egypt's head of state Hosni Mubarak. The last-mentioned attempt actually came to fruition. Mubarak's motorcade was attacked by al Qaeda operatives as it passed through the streets of Addis Ababa in 1995.

In the aftermath of these terrorist attacks the Sudanese yielded to international pressures and agreed to expel bin Laden and his organization. Apparently neither the United States nor Saudi Arabia sought to bring him into custody. So, instead of being imprisoned and having their organization eliminated, bin Laden and the bulk of al Qaeda's holy warriors returned to Afghanistan, where (as in Pakistan) a substantial infrastructure already existed.

Within six months of al Qaeda's arrival in Afghanistan roughly two-thirds of the country came under the control of the Taliban. The Taliban (or "Students") consisted of young men, either Afghan refugees or Pakistanis, who trained to wage jihad at madrasas in Peshawar and other sites in Pakistan. They aimed first at bringing an end to the Afghan civil war. After the departure of the Soviets this meant armed conflict among the country's various ethnic groups. Second, they aimed to create another Islamic republic according to the most stringent standards of belief and practice. Taliban rule provided a near ideal setting for al Qaeda's extensive activities.

Many of these activities over the next several years captured TV and newspaper headlines on a worldwide basis. The most spectacular were the near simultaneous bombings of the American embassies in Nairobi and Dar-es-Salaam (1998), the suicide attack on the American destroyer USS *Cole* in the port of Aden (2000), and the September 11, 2001 attacks on the World Trade Center and the Pentagon – acts of terrorism that killed over three thousand people. The list could be extended considerably, but these names should be sufficient to rivet our attention on al Qaeda's Afghan operations.

Between bin Laden's arrival in Afghanistan in 1996 under the auspices of the Taliban and the latter's rapid defeat at the hands of American and Northern Alliance forces in the months following the 9/11 attacks, al Qaeda set up and used an extensive array of bases and other training facilities for preparing thousands of young mujahidin from around the Muslim world to wage jihad against a variety of enemies. It was also during this (1998) period that bin Laden and his Egyptian counselor Dr. Ayman al-Zawahiri formed the World Islamic Front for Jihad against the Jews and Crusaders. Leaders of both Egypt's Islamic Group and Islamic Jihad along with representatives of like-minded groups from Pakistan, Bangladesh, and various other countries (whose names were not disclosed because of fears for their security) made an agreement that amounted to a declaration of war against the United States, encompassing its military, government, and citizens. Bin Laden issued a *fatwa* or religious ruling sanctioning holy war on a worldwide basis. It reads in part,

> The ruling to kill the Americans and their allies, civilians and military, is an individual duty for every Muslim who can do it in any country in which it is possible to do it, in order to liberate the al-Aqsa mosque and the holy mosque (Mecca) from their grip, and in order for their armies to move out of all the lands of Islam, defeated and unable to threaten any Muslim.[9]

Some critics challenged bin Laden's authority to issue such a religious edict, since he is not a cleric. But a number of Pakistan's mullahs were willing to be supportive and endorsed bin Laden's call for indiscriminate violence against Americans, Europeans, Israelis, Saudis, and others. The violence was not long in coming, and included multiple attacks on Westerners living in or visiting Saudi Arabia, bin Laden's most immediate concern, as well as Yemen, Egypt, Algeria, Morocco, Indonesia, and a list of other predominantly or even partially Muslim nations. All these assaults were additional to the terrorist spectaculars mentioned above.

How were al Qaeda and al-Qaeda-linked organizations able to carry out these attacks? How is al Qaeda organized? Why does it appear so successful and so resilient compared with so many other terrorist groups, either contemporary or active in the recent past?

A good way to understand al Qaeda's structure is to begin by making a distinction between center and periphery. At its center the organization (circa 2002) was headed by bin Laden as its "emir-general." By issuing pronouncements and public statements (which typically get disseminated on a worldwide basis) from time to time, bin Laden is able to communicate his views to the public and also instruct and inspire a far-flung network of al Qaeda members and various jihadi groups. Immediately below the emir-general there is a consultative council or *shura majlis* whose members form a body of trusted advisors appointed by and loyal to bin Laden.[10]

At the next level the al Qaeda center consists of four committees, each of which is headed by an emir who reports to the consultative council. The committees, with their own extensive responsibilities, are as follows: military; finance and business; *fatwa* and Islamic study; and media and publicity.

Since we are dealing with a terrorist organization, the military is obviously of great importance. It is responsible for recruiting and training new fighters as well as procuring and testing new weapons. The military committee is also asked to develop new "special" weapons including the CBRN ones whose potential use are of such concern to governments around the world. In addition the committee takes on operational tasks including intelligence gathering and the surveillance of potential targets. And once the targets have been chosen the military committee assembles the teams that actually plan and carry out the terrorist attacks. It also provides trainers, weapons, and other assets to Muslim fighters in Chechnya, Kashmir, and elsewhere. Further, the committee plays a liaison role by selecting agents who direct a large network of local support and operational cells. After 9/11 al Qaeda cells were detected in Albania, Italy, Germany, the US, South Africa, Tanzania, Kenya, and Yemen, among other countries.

Most terrorist organizations are not wealthy; most groups have had to rely on bank robberies, ransom for hostages, and various forms of petty crime in order to sustain their operations. A few groups have been rich. The PLO during its terrorist phase was the beneficiary of contributions from both the oil-rich Arab states and private supporters. But few if any terrorist organizations in history come close to al Qaeda in terms of its business acumen and the material resources at its disposal. Overall responsibility for the acquisition of this wealth belongs to the finance and business committee.

The latter oversees the solicitation of funds from wealthy donors in Saudi Arabia, the United Arab Emirates, and the other Persian Gulf sheikdoms. In the Western democracies al Qaeda's appeal is to the growing Muslim communities, whose members are asked to contribute money to private charities for the purpose of helping their impoverished co-religionists in other parts of the world. The "philanthropic" foundations receiving these contributions then channel the funds to al Qaeda. In parts of the developing world with significant Muslim communities, al-Qaeda-owned or-controlled businesses sell products within these communities and then recycle the proceeds for use by the organization. When necessary, dummy corporations and banks in the Gulf states are used to launder the money. All this activity requires considerable business savvy. Intelligence agencies report that al Qaeda's finance and business committee consists of individuals employed in banking and investment.

The committee operates on a decentralized basis through the use of support cells active throughout much of the world. These cells, depending upon the circumstances, either funnel the money to the al Qaeda center or disburse it directly to operational cells planning to carry out terrorist attacks. This calls to mind another feature of the al Qaeda organization, its cell structure. Great emphasis in the "al Qaeda Training Manual" is placed on compartmentalization and secure communications. Accordingly, most al Qaeda members belong to small clandestine cells and are kept unaware of the identities of the members of other cells active in the same country or even the same locality. In the event the authorities are able to arrest or penetrate one cell they will not be able to destroy the entire apparatus. The cellular form of organization is one that communist parties used with considerable success when they were forced to operate on an underground basis in parts of Europe and North America during the Cold War.

And like the communist parties, al Qaeda places great stress on a doctrine and ideology, though obviously the Islamist ideas of al Qaeda are a far cry from Marxism-Leninism. The principal task of the *fatwa* and Islamic studies committee is to offer religiously based justification for each al Qaeda operation. The committee, composed of Islamist clerics, provides a rationale for terrorist attacks by referring members and audience alike to a *fatwa* that may be interpreted as supportive of the violence.

The role of al Qaeda's media and communications committee is to present the organization's activities in a favorable light to a wider Muslim audience. To this end it developed a press office in Europe (closed down shortly after 9/11), has established a number of periodicals, and from time to time issues communiqués to explain why the organization has carried out a particular attack. These efforts seem to have paid off. According to public opinion polls al Qaeda and its leader enjoy widespread popularity throughout the Arab world, even after, or perhaps because of, the World Trade Center and Pentagon attacks.

Al Qaeda is a complex organization. We have described its core or center. Now we need to discuss its periphery, its virtually worldwide network of related organizations.

Most of the terrorist spectaculars that have attracted the attention of worldwide audiences in recent years have been the work of clandestine al Qaeda cells which surface from time to time to carry out suicide attacks on high visibility targets. But radical Islamist groups with links to al Qaeda have been responsible for many more though typically less lethal acts of terrorism. These associated groups receive financial support, tactical advice, and training in terrorism and guerrilla warfare from the al Qaeda apparatus.

Central, South, and Southeast Asia have become important areas of activity for these peripheral groups. Among other things they have the advantage of making the jihad more global, since the organizations involved are composed of non-Arab Muslims.

In Central Asia the end of the Soviet Union in 1991 left in its wake five newly independent successor states: Kazakhstan, Kyrghyzstan, Uzbekistan, Tajikistan, and Turkmenistan. The new countries all had predominantly Muslim populations. By and large these states came to be ruled by former communist officials who brushed a thin veneer of democracy over what continued to be autocratic systems. In this situation a number of violent Islamist groups appeared who appealed to religious values as a means of challenging the autocracies. Such groups as the Islamic Movement of Uzbekistan (IMU) have received support from al Qaeda, particularly when it was free to operate in Afghanistan, in order to carry out attacks on their countries' secular and usually corrupt rulers.

In Indian-controlled Kashmir (a state with a large Muslim majority) al Qaeda helped to recruit and arm such groups as Lashkar e-Tayba and Harakat ul Mujahidin for the purpose of carrying out attacks on representatives of Indian authority, e.g. state legislators, as well as Hindu villagers who happened to be in the wrong place at the wrong time. The long-term goal of this terrorist campaign, which included an attack on the Indian national parliament itself in New Delhi, was to detach Kashmir from India and merge it with an Islamic Republic of Pakistan. These terrorist operations have been sufficiently provocative to the Indian government that the two countries involved, both equipped with nuclear weapons, have almost gone to war.

Al Qaeda has come to enjoy a substantial presence in Southeast Asia as well thanks to an array of affiliated groups. The governments of most of the countries of the region, especially those with large Muslim communities – Malaysia, Singapore, the Philippines, and Indonesia – have arrested violent Islamists either before or after they carried out large-scale terrorist attacks. The Moro Liberation Front and the Abu Sayyaf Group in the Philippines have embarked on terrorist campaigns with two aims in mind: first, they are committed to separating Mindanao and other southern islands, an area with a Muslim-majority population, from the government in Manila and establishing an independent country; second, Abu Sayyaf especially is interested in attacking Americans and the substantial American presence in the Philippines as part of the worldwide jihad al Qaeda has undertaken.

It is Indonesia, however, the country with the largest Muslim population in the world, which has the most menacing of all the al-Qaeda-affiliated organizations in Southeast Asia: Jemaah Islamiyah (JI). This is itself a network or subnetwork of al Qaeda; an organization with its own intricate sources of funding and means for the recruitment and training of Islamist youth. Furthermore, JI militants are present not only in Indonesia but also in Malaysia and Singapore. Its long-run goal is the establishment by violence of a Daulah Islamiyah or Islamic State throughout the entire region. Either JI or groups linked to JI were responsible for the horrendous nightclub bombings on the island of Bali in 2002 which killed more than one hundred Australian tourists and injured many others. Subsequently, JI has carried out car bomb attacks on American-owned hotels and other facilities in Jakarta, the country's capital. Other planned attacks were thwarted by the Indonesian authorities (along with their Singaporean and Malaysian counterparts) before they could be brought to fruition.

Conclusion

The majority of terrorist campaigns in the past (see chapter 2) were confined to a single country, or certainly a single region of the world, and most often could be quelled through the use of conventional law enforcement agencies of the countries affected. There were a few exceptions to this limited reaction, e.g. Peru, where in confronting a combined terrorist/guerrilla insurgency the authorities have tended to employ their armed forces on either a regular or irregular basis.

The Book of Ecclesiastes tells us "there is no new thing under the Sun." But contemporary terrorism does seem to be a "new thing" because of its worldwide scope, its thousands of practitioners, or would-be practitioners, and their willingness to use any means at their disposal, including unconventional weapons, to kill as many people as possible. It seems fair to conclude this account then by indicating that many countries are confronted by what amounts to the "first war of the twenty-first century," in which the perpetrators' goals are virtually without limit as are the means they hope to use in order to achieve them.

In this chapter and in the preceding one we have largely been *describing* terrorist groups and their activities. In the following chapter we seek explanations. What causes terrorism? Is it poverty? Is it a lack of liberty? Why do some people join terrorist organizations? Who are they? Are they "normal?" Where do they come from? What is life like inside terrorist organizations? How do terrorists decide what targets to strike? These are some of the important questions we seek to answer in chapter 4.

Further reading

Daniel Benjamin and Steven Simon, *The Age of Sacred Terror* (New York: Random House, 2002).

John Esposito, *Unholy War: Terror in the Name of Islam* (Oxford and New York: Oxford University Press, 2002).

Rohan Gunaratna, *Inside al Qaeda* (New York: Beverly Books, 2002).

Simon Reeve, *The New Jackals* (Boston: Northeastern University Press, 1999).

Jessica Stern, *The Ultimate Terrorists* (Cambridge, MA and London: Harvard University Press, 1999).

4

Who they are, where they come from, and why they do it

For anyone interested in understanding contemporary political terrorism, four questions need to be answered or at least posed. The efforts to answer these questions have ignited considerable controversy among those journalists, public officials, and academics who have studied the matter over any length of time. Here are the principal questions.

- First, under what circumstances do campaigns of terrorist violence begin? What social and political conditions give rise to terrorism?
- Second, what types of individuals commit acts of terrorism? Where do they come from? Do they come from the lower rungs of society or do they emerge from middle class backgrounds, or both, depending on the circumstances?
- Third, why do certain individuals commit acts of violence directed against perfect strangers who happen to be at the wrong place at the wrong time? Are the perpetrators of attacks on civilian targets, e.g. airline passengers or customers strolling through a shopping mall, unbalanced? Or sadistic? Are they crazy? Or driven by commitments to a misunderstood and insufficiently appreciated political cause?
- Fourth, the final question we need to pose concerns not individuals but organizations. There are exceptions but most

acts of terrorism are carried out not by lone wolves, single individuals acting by themselves, but by members of organizations. Where do such organizations come from? How large are they? How do they function?

What conditions give rise to terrorism?

At first glance, identifying the social and political conditions from which terrorist campaigns emerge seems straightforward enough. Virtually everyone with an opinion on the subject knows that poverty and economic deprivation are the breeding grounds for terrorism. If you drain the swamp, the mosquitoes will disappear; that is, if governments or international agencies promote economic development, providing people with hope for the future, terrorism will go away. Likewise, terrorism is encouraged by the absence of democracy. In countries where citizens are denied the right to participate peacefully in the political process, they naturally turn to political violence. If all channels of open political expression are blocked, aggrieved individuals will turn to terrorism as the only means available to make themselves heard. Promote freedom and you will reduce or even eliminate terrorism.

The conditions that cause terrorism are readily discernible then and so, consequently, are the means for bringing these activities to a peaceful conclusion. Unfortunately, these generalizations do not conform to reality. Consider the following.

The poorest countries in the world, those in sub-Saharan Africa for example, suffer from a myriad of problems but terrorist violence is rarely one of them. Their citizens may have to endure horrendous living conditions, astronomical rates of violent crime, and protracted campaigns of guerrilla and inter-tribal warfare but rarely do they experience terrorism – as we defined the concept in chapter 1. The same observation applies to the impoverished regions of wealthier countries. Italy, to take another example, experienced Western Europe's most severe campaign of revolutionary terrorism during the 1970s. The Red Brigades and Front Line, the most significant revolutionary organizations, conducted most of their terrorist operations in the prosperous northern cities of Milan and Turin. Rarely did these bands carry out attacks in the Mezzogiorno, impoverished southern Italy. The same might be said about the Basque struggle in northern Spain.[1] The Basque provinces from which ETA militants have typically been drawn are among the most prosperous parts of Spain. On the other hand, Andalusia, one of the country's poorest regions has experienced virtually no terrorist violence.

Studies carried out by economists for the World Bank following the infamous 9/11 attacks on the World Trade Center and the Pentagon reported a modest but positive relationship between the incidence of terrorist violence and gross domestic product (GDP). Wealthier countries were somewhat more likely to serve as venues for terrorist attacks than poorer ones.[2] Countries inhabited by the wretched of the Earth were somewhat less susceptible to terrorism than better-off locales.

If readers find the above difficult to believe, they will find the following even more so. The absence of democracy need not be a root cause of terrorism. Here are some cases to consider.

The People's Republic of China (PRC) following the repression of the student protest movement in Tiananmen Square in 1989 seemed ripe for terrorism. Young, enthusiastic, freedom-seeking university students (advocates of what the regime described as "bourgeois liberalism") had been brutally repressed by the communist government's armed forces. Similar peaceful protests had met the same fate in other parts of China. Despite the denial of peaceful forms of protest no terrorist campaign followed. Why not? The answer is not all that hard to deduce. The government retained its monopoly control over all the channels of mass communication, making "propaganda by deed" virtually impossible to accomplish. Furthermore, the entire coercive apparatus of the PRC could be deployed to make sure that those contemplating terrorism were arrested, or worse, before they could initiate their operations.

Or, consider the case of the Soviet Union (1917–91). This clearly represented a situation in which almost all forms of popular opposition to the government and the leadership role of the Communist Party in it were blocked. No freedom of expression. No right of peaceful assembly. And no terrorism either, at least of the type committed by private groups and organizations. As in the case of the PRC so too with the Soviet Union, the reasons for the absence of terrorist violence are not all that hard to deduce: monopoly control of the mass media, and the extensive system of surveillance and the coercive forces available to those in power.

Notice, though, what happens after the Soviet Union disintegrates in 1991 and Russia plus newly independent states emerge in Eastern Europe and Central Asia. Under these circumstances terrorist campaigns are launched in various regions, including and most obviously Chechnya. The secessionist movement in this largely Muslim area of the North Caucuses has engaged in widely publicized acts of terrorism in Moscow and other Russian cities. Where once there was none, there are now suicide bombers blowing themselves up in Grozny and surrounding Chechen communities.

Spain offers another case worth our attention. The Basque nationalist organization ETA was formed in the 1960s during the right-wing Franco dictatorship. It carried out a modest number of terrorist attacks, including the 1972 assassination of Franco's hand-picked successor, before the dictator's death in 1975 and Spain's subsequent transition to democracy. The installation of democracy coincided with a sharp increase in ETA terrorism: the greater the opportunity for free expression in Spanish political life, seemingly the more terrorist violence occurred.

More recently and at almost the other end of the world, there is the example of Indonesia. Under the military dictatorship of General Suharto, for many years Indonesia experienced, whatever the country's other woes, relatively little terrorism. After Suharto was forced to resign his office and Indonesia underwent a tentative transition to parliamentary democracy, the Islamist terrorism of Jemaah Islamiyyah appeared, most dramatically in the case of the Bali nightclub bombings of 2002.

Using a series of anecdotes or individual cases to make a judgment about how things are in general is certainly fraught with difficulty. In this instance we have used examples to suggest that democracy is not necessarily a cure for terrorism. Democracy, though, is a large concept. If we consider some constituent parts, the relationship changes somewhat.

Some observers have stressed that it is the transition to democracy that is crucial. Countries undergoing a transformation to democratic rule are vulnerable to the outbreak of terrorist campaigns because the rules of the new system are not clear or widely understood. When they are understood and accepted, terrorism tends to dissipate. Other observers emphasize the rule of law. The latter is simply one attribute of democratic government. For some analysts, though, it seems to be crucial in inhibiting serious campaigns of terrorist violence. The "rule of law" interpretation – where the rule of law prevails there is little terrorism – is vulnerable to the problem of cause and effect. It may be that the authorities in countries subject to terrorist campaigns suspend at least some of the rule of law by imposing various emergency measures (e.g. holding people in preventive detention without benefit of habeas corpus protections) as a means of defeating the terrorists. It is the terrorism that has brought about a decline in rule-of-law protections rather than the latter inhibiting the former.

If neither economic deprivation nor the absence of democracy constitutes terrorism's root causes, what does? For some, history offers a powerful cause. By citing history as a cause, writers have in mind the experiences of various countries where terrorism has become a significant problem in recent years. The generalization is that those countries subject to contemporary terrorist activity have long histories of violent political conflict frequently accompanied by earlier and repeated terrorist episodes. In Latin America, Colombia, a country with an exceptionally bloody history, is often cited as an example. Political violence was a serious matter in Northern Ireland well before the onset of the Troubles in the late 1960s. In Algeria in the 1950s the National Liberation Front carried out waves of terrorist attacks on Europeans aimed at achieving national independence from French rule. In the 1990s thousands of Algerians were killed by the Armed Islamic Group and other Islamist bands hoping to transform the country into an Islamic republic. The message is from Ecclesiastes: "What has been shall be, for there is no new thing under the Sun."

The problem with using historical experience as an explanation is not much different than identifying economic deprivation and the absence of democracy as terrorism's root causes. In all three instances the explanation fits some cases but not others. What appear to be the same economic, political, and historical conditions that give rise to terrorism in some settings do not in others. If this is true, are we then compelled to throw up our hands and claim no general explanation or root cause is available?

Some observers have made this assertion. Unlike mass insurrections and other forms of collective violence, terrorist attacks usually involve relatively few individuals. Nineteen people carried out the 9/11 attacks on the World Trade Center and it appears that about the same number of Islamists were responsible for the March 11, 2004 attacks on the Spanish rail system that killed close to two hundred Madrid-bound commuters. The point is that there is simply too great a discrepancy between the small number of perpetrators and the large-scale variables employed to explain their conduct for the latter to be useful in understanding the former.

Another way of putting it is to maintain that terrorism has been used to advance so many different goals – religious and secular, left-wing revolutionary and right-wing reactionary, nationalist and anti-nationalist – that it is unreasonable to expect the same conditions that gave rise to one type of terrorist campaign to also apply to the others. There is a need to narrow our focus and pursue explanations plural rather an explanation singular. In addition to narrowing our focus, there is a need to pay attention to subjective perceptions as well as objective economic and political conditions. For groups to launch campaigns of terrorist violence their supporters, members, and leaders need to translate prevailing conditions in such a way as to make them sufficiently intolerable (and correctable) to propel the groups towards terrorism. We are in search, then, of what triggers terrorist campaigns.

If terrorist attacks are typically carried out by relatively small groups with high ambitions (e.g. national liberation, the re-establishment of the caliphate, proletarian insurrection), its members must believe they have a large audience of at least potential supporters (and usually of antagonists as well). If there is no perceived constituency (and no enemy, no dragon to be slain), the violence becomes largely pointless or, at best, a form of self-therapy. Second, there needs to be some means of communicating with this audience. Access to the mass media is crucial. In much of the world today's terrorists operate in a media-rich environment. Such cable television networks as CNN and Sky News operate twenty-four hours a day on a worldwide basis. Furthermore, enterprising terrorist organiza-tions need not rely exclusively on these channels and their reporters to get their messages across. Many of the organizations now have their own websites fully capable of explaining what they did, why they did it, and what they hope to accomplish in the future.

If we can now assume (1) the perceived existence of a constituency to be aroused by acts of terrorist violence and (2) available channels of mass communication to convey messages to it, the next problem is to identify the specific conditions that have triggered terrorist campaigns over the last several decades of the twentieth century and first years of the twenty-first.

In the advanced industrialized democracies of Western Europe and North America left-wing revolutionary terrorism appeared in the 1970s as the cycles of mass protest set off by the Vietnam War declined. In Germany, Italy, Japan, the United States, and a few other places terrorist groups emerged as mass protest movements and then lost their momentum as the result of either internal reasons – excessive factionalism, widespread exhaustion – or external considerations, e.g. repression by the authorities. In these circumstances, small groups of the most militant among the movement activists split away and embarked on an armed struggle. The origins of such groups as the Italian Red Brigades, German Red Army Fraction, United Japanese Red Army, and American Weathermen can be traced to the waning of mass protest.[3]

The economic and the social circumstances of Latin America's poor were far worse than those of the working class in the advanced industrialized countries, but it was not these conditions, not directly at any rate, that triggered the terrorism. Rather it was the failure of guerrilla insurgencies. Rural-based guerrilla campaigns modeled after Castro's success in Cuba failed to achieve the same results elsewhere. It was in the wake of Che Guevara's defeat in Bolivia in 1967 that many of Latin America's revolutionaries turned to urban terrorism as a means of igniting mass insurrections against the ruling classes. The origins of revolutionary terrorist bands in Uruguay, Brazil, Argentina, Peru, and elsewhere are to be found in their leaders' disillusionment with the tactics of guerrilla warfare.

Terrorist violence need not be directed at the achievement of some revolutionary objective. Not uncommonly it has been employed by groups in Europe, the United States, and Latin America with racist, anti-Semitic, neo-Nazi, and neo-Fascist goals.[4] We ought not to forget that the most lethal act of domestic terrorism in the United States, the April 18, 1995 bombing of the Murrah Federal Building in Oklahoma City, was carried out by an individual inspired by the works of the late neo-Nazi figure William Pierce. Or that the worst act of domestic terrorism in Western Europe following World War II was the bombing of the Bologna railroad station in August 1980, an attack carried out by Italian neo-Fascists that killed almost ninety vacation-bound passengers. And in Latin America over the years right-wing death squads have been responsible for the deaths of hundreds if not thousands of landless peasants, land reformers, and trade union organizers. What circumstances seem to ignite this type of far right terrorism?

Unlike revolutionary terrorist activity, terrorism from the far right is typically directed, at least initially, against private groups and individuals rather than the government. In the United States, for example, the Ku Klux Klan launched a terrorist campaign in the southern states during the early 1960s aimed at preventing African-Americans from voting or exercising other constitutionally protected rights. What appears to trigger right-wing terrorism, more generally, is the effort by a minority group, e.g. Catholics in Northern Ireland, to assert claims of equality of status or conditions in relation to dominant segments of the population. Attempts to modify the distribution of wealth, power, and status in a society often create a politics of backlash. Within this context right-wing terrorism emerges as an effort to maintain or return to the *status quo ante*.

If the government involved favors or is perceived as favoring the groups seeking to improve their situation and modify the *status quo*, the racist, anti-Semitic, neo-Nazi, or other far right groups will come to regard it as an enemy. They will see the government as having betrayed the cause of the dominant race, religion, or class and may then launch terrorist attacks against its representatives and institutions. The late William Pierce's widely circulated and highly popular racist novel *The Turner Diaries* provides its readers with just such a scenario.

The case of the Palestinians probably deserves to be treated *sui generis* but it makes sense to discuss the roots of other nationalist terrorism in general terms. Protracted campaigns of terrorist violence on behalf of nationalist causes begin with the assertion of claims by territorially distinct ethnic/religious minorities for greater control over their own affairs. What happens next often depends upon the reactions of the governments involved. If the government responds to demands for greater autonomy with offers of power sharing and guarantees of greater local control over the affected group's territory, the result will be a compromise agreement likely to satisfy much of the relevant population. If instead the government reacts to demands for greater local control with threats and conspicuous acts of repression, the chances for terrorist violence will mount correspondingly. Rather than simply seeking autonomy and local control, spokespersons for the affected group will demand secession and the establishment of a wholly separate country (e.g. Tamils in Sri Lanka, Muslims in the Philippines) or amalgamation with another country, e.g. Kashmir's transfer from Indian to Pakistani control.

Terrorism committed by Palestinian groups aimed at bringing about the destruction of the state of Israel has gone on for many decades and has attracted worldwide attention. Its perpetrators have been driven by a mix of nationalist and religious motives. In this sense the case is not dramatically unlike other

Third World conflicts, ones often involving far more people and much bigger territory than those at stake between the Mediterranean and the Jordan river. What distinguishes this particular struggle is the fact that it is waged over the "Holy Land," i.e. territory containing sites regarded as sacred by Jews, Christians, and Muslims around the world. As a result millions of followers of these religions believe they have an important stake in the conflict's outcome.

But to say that the Palestinian–Israeli struggle has been protracted and that it has captured massive attention does not tell us why terrorism became an important tactic for the groups championing the Palestinian cause. Other conflicts that bear some resemblance to this one have not resulted in comparable levels of terrorism. For example, some have seen a parallel between the situation of the Palestinians and that of indigenous Africans during the apartheid era in South Africa. Yet even if we accept the parallel, apartheid was ended via a negotiated settlement and in the absence of much terrorism by the African National Congress or other groups seeking an end to the country's system of racial domination. Why the difference? Is it sufficient to note that Yassir Arafat is not Nelson Mandela?

While the answer to this question is self-evident, it is not sufficient to explain the use of terrorism by various Palestinian groups against Israeli civilians over so long a period. The explanation rests neither with the particular conditions of the Palestinians (whose material conditions at least would have improved substantially if there had been less not more terrorism), nor in the character of a single individual leader. Rather the explanation has to do with a series of strategic decisions made by different Palestinian groups, often in competition with one another, to use terrorism as the most effective way of advancing their cause.

Three strategic decisions seem especially important. First, following the defeat of the Arab armies in June 1967, the PLO underwent a process of re-assessment and reorganization. One of the results of this process was a decision, undertaken first by the PFLP, to begin waging a terrorist campaign, by among other things sky-jacking commercial airliners, in an effort to bring their cause to the attention of a large audience and to show both sympathizers and their Israeli antagonists that their cause could not be ignored. The result of this strategic decision was a protracted terrorist campaign. But there have been at least two other decisions we need to consider. (1) During the first Palestinian uprising or Intifada against Israeli rule of the West Bank and Gaza Strip which began in December 1987 new religiously grounded organizations emerged. Leaders of both Hamas and PIJ decided that the use of terrorism was the best way to attack Israel and to challenge the substantially secular PLO for a dominant place in the Palestinian struggle. (2) Following the breakdown of the Camp David peace talks between the Israelis and representatives of the Palestinian Authority (PA) in the summer of 2000, Arafat and other leaders made a strategic decision to abandon the negotiating process and resume the use of terrorism, thereby improving their negotiating position for later talks. The resulting second or al Aqsa Intifada has spun out of control and, if anything, weakened the PA's overall position *vis-à-vis* Hamas and PIJ, not to mention the Israelis.

The strategic choices were not made in a vacuum. More often than not, decisions made by the Israeli government served to provoke the Palestinian groups and inflame the situation (e.g. Ariel Sharon's visit to the Temple Mount in September 2000). And the choices in favor of terrorism were reinforced by financial subsidies, weapons deliveries, and expressions of solidarity from well-wishers in the Arab world and beyond.

For most people these days when the word 'terrorism' is mentioned on television or used in the other mass media the first thoughts and images that normally come to mind are of Osama bin Laden, his deputy Dr. Ayman al-Zawahiri, and the al Qaeda network of organizations scattered around the world. In terms of the scope of their operations, the number of people attracted to the cause, and the amount of damage inflicted, al Qaeda, really more a movement of loosely connected groups than a tight-knit organization, is an unprecedented operation; far more extensive, for example, than the Assassins, the medieval band of *fidayeen* out to purify Islam at the time of the Crusades.

Why and when did al Qaeda and the numerous groups with which it has been linked appear?

Commentaries stress three sources. First, al Qaeda and the other groups are intellectually rooted in the writings of a number of Islamic philosophers. The teachers and writers who are almost always included on the list of the most influential are Hasan al Banna (1906–49), founder of the Egyptian Muslim Brotherhood, the Pakistani Mawlana Mawdudi (1903–79), and, most significant of all, Sayyid Qutb (1906–66), al Banna's successor as leader of the Muslim Brotherhood.[5] What these writers had in common was a radical rejection of Western civilization and the values, e.g. crude materialism, sexual license, female equality, they associated with it. Qutb regarded the impact of these values on the Muslim world as an infection that needed to be extirpated by jihad, by which he meant armed struggle. Furthermore, the governments of most Muslim but especially Arab countries had become infected with the Western disease. These political regimes, whatever the rhetoric of their rulers, had become un-Islamic and needed to be replaced, also via jihad, by authentic Muslims committed to the establishment of a social and political order as existed in the years immediately following the death of the Prophet in A.D. 632. Accordingly, the writers looked forward to the re-establishment of a caliphate, a Commander of the Faithful to rule over the entire Muslim world. We should take note that Qutb's younger brother was one of Osama bin Laden's teachers in Saudi Arabia.

In addition to the growing attractiveness of the teachings of Qutb and the other Islamist thinkers in the last decades of the twentieth century there was also growing disenchantment with alternative worldviews. The appeal of pan-Arabism, the idea that all Arabs should belong to a single nation from the Atlantic to the Persian Gulf, waned as the result of the Arabs' defeat by the Israelis in the June 1967 war. It was the Egyptian champion of the pan-Arab cause, Gamel Nasser, whose leadership was most discredited by the defeat. Marxism, a Western import but also an anti-imperialist ideology, had made some inroads in the Middle East. But it too became discredited because of its atheism and its association with the Soviet Union after the latter's 1979 invasion of Afghanistan, part of the House of Islam.

Abstract ideas are one thing, broad social support for them is something else. What made Islamist ideas so attractive to so many young Muslims in the waning years of the twentieth century? One way to respond is by suggesting they answered a personal need. For many young Muslims living in Western Europe or exposed to Western culture growing in their home countries, Islamist ideas provided a way of overcoming feelings of estrangement and inferiority. Islamist preachers, especially Saudi-based advocates of Wahhabism, provided these young people with a vocabulary that stressed their superiority to and justified their contempt for the West and its various attractions. The ensuing hostility could be manifested through jihad, war against the perceived enemies of the faith.

Enemies abounded. There were the Israelis with their mistreatment of the Palestinians, along with the West's indifference to the latter's plight. There were the corrupt and un-Islamic regimes ruling in much of the Middle East. But it was the Soviet Union's invasion of Afghanistan in 1979 that was most influential in stimulating the formation of al-Qaeda. Thousands of young men from all over the Muslim world were recruited to serve as mujahidin in the holy war to expel the infidels from the House of Islam. It was in the context of this successful struggle that al Qaeda made its appearance in the mid 1980s, initially as a means of channeling funds, weapons, and recruits to the Afghan war effort. As this effort proved increasingly successful, and Soviet forces left the country in 1989, the ambitions of al Qaeda's leaders expanded. The targets shifted from the Soviets to the United States, the other superpower, and its client "crusader" countries in Europe, the Jews (perceived in increasingly world-conspiratorial terms), and the un-Islamic regimes in Egypt, Saudi Arabia, and Algeria

Bin Laden and his followers, many of whom initially were veterans of the Afghan campaign, were able to forge a loose alliance, the World Islamic Front for Jihad against Jews and Crusaders, for the purpose of launching religiously sanctioned terrorist attacks on the organization's numerous enemies. With the victory of the Taliban in Afghanistan in 1998, al Qaeda and its affiliates acquired a valuable though temporary sanctuary and training center for would-be holy warriors from all over the world.

What kind of people become terrorists?

Now we have identified the circumstances that gave rise to terrorist campaigns over the last three decades of the twentieth century, it is appropriate to ask where the terrorists themselves come from. And who they are.

Bearing in mind we are dealing with matters of central tendency rather than perfect uniformity, the following answers may be derived from evidence scholars have accumulated over the years. First, since many who join terrorist organizations or who help turn already existing political groups towards terrorism are young people (the average age of Palestinian *shahids* or suicide bombers is slightly under twenty-three), it should not be all that surprising to learn that terrorists or would-be terrorists come from school settings. Given the predominance of Islamist terrorism in recent years this frequently means that recruits are drawn from madrasas or Muslim religious schools in Pakistan, Indonesia, the West Bank and Gaza Strip, and elsewhere around the Muslim world. But the scholastic or academic origins of terrorists are not confined to Islamists. Many left-wing revolutionary terrorists in the 1960s and 1970s were drawn from university student populations. In Italy, for instance, the founders of the Red Brigades came from the University of Trent; in Germany students at the Free University of Berlin provided a pool from which members of the June 2nd Movement were drawn. In the United States many members of the Symbionese Liberation Army were or had been students at the University of California at Berkeley.

Jails and prisons also offer a nurturing environment for terrorists. Non-political inmates are frequently already experienced in the use of violence for criminal ends before their confinement. If they have not done so before they arrive, they may learn to use violence as a means of surviving in a brutal and brutalizing environment. The missing ingredient is political education. The latter may be provided by already politicized inmates committed to converting others to their cause or by groups on the outside engaged in prison outreach programs that correspond with and offer sympathy to elements of the prison population, e.g. Aryan Warriors, Ku Klux Klan, and other racial supremacist bands in the United States. Alternatively, the jailers may play a role through their mistreatment of the inmates. Young Palestinians in Israeli prisons for relatively minor offenses, e.g. stone throwing, may be so radicalized by their experiences that they turn to terrorist violence after their release.

It is not commonly mentioned in the literature on the subject but true nonetheless that the youth organizations of political parties often furnish a milieu from which terrorists and terrorist groups appear.[6] A far-left, far-right, or militantly nationalist/separatist political party typically attracts followers strongly committed to the party's ideological, religious, or territorial aims and objectives. By engaging in the mundane world of practical politics, party leaders are often compelled to compromise with other contestants in national political life. It is also not uncommon for even a radical political party's leaders to become full-time office holders or professional staff members of the party organization. They become wedded to their careers. These developments often come with a price.

The price is that members of the party's youth wing, e.g. Young Communists, Young Fascists, reach the conclusion that the parent organization has betrayed the cause and that the underlying reason for the betrayal has been the adults' willingness to work within the system. The result is that the youth wing breaks away from the political party and embarks on a terrorist campaign as a means, often perceived as the only means, of achieving their revolutionary or secessionist objectives. In much of Latin America during the 1960s and 1970s, for example, the youthful admirers of Fidel Castro, Mao Tse-tung, and other Marxist-Leninists, turned to terrorism and guerrilla warfare after they had reached the conclusion that their country's conventional communist party had abandoned the cause of revolution in exchange for a comfortable place in the bourgeois world of conventional party politics.

Another way in which terrorism and political parties are tied to one another occurs in democratic settings when the military stages a *coup d'état*. If, as in Brazil in 1964, high-ranking military officers intervene in politics in order to forestall economic and social reforms of which they disapprove, they often dissolve the political parties they regard as the sources of these changes. Although the parties may be placed outside the law and barred from further participation in open electoral competition, their leaders may transform them into underground organizations and transform their struggle from one of winning votes to conducting campaigns of terrorist violence against the powers that be. The origins of the prolonged and frequently gruesome terrorist violence in Algeria during the 1990s conform to this pattern. Its outbreak occurred after the government cancelled parliamentary elections out of fear the Islamic Salvation Front (FIS) would win them. But instead of simply going away, militants from FIS chose to conduct politics by other means.

Terrorists may also emerge from certain neighborhoods whose residents are known for their sympathies to the relevant causes. In Northern Ireland certain areas of Belfast had reputations for their support of the Republican and Loyalist causes and here the IRA and the Protestant paramilitaries did much of their recruiting. Likewise in Rome and Milan during the 1970s some neighborhoods and public squares became known as scenes where violent neo-Fascist youth gathered and others were well known as hangouts for the far left. A similar process may have been at work in Baghdad in the months following the April 2003 American occupation of that city.

Who are the terrorists? Is it possible to provide a meaningful answer to this question beyond noting that most people arrested for terrorism-related crimes or otherwise identified as terrorists have tended to be young people, for the most part individuals under the age of thirty? Some have responded to these questions by throwing up their hands, arguing that terrorism is a tactic that has been used to achieve so many different goals by so many different groups over the years that it is virtually impossible to arrive at a coherent social profile. Beyond noting that terrorists are largely young and fanatical, there is not much more to be said about their backgrounds.

Take the problem of social class. In the 1970s Latin America abounded with revolutionary urban guerrilla organizations that employed terrorist techniques – bombing, kidnapping, and hostage taking – aimed at making socialist revolutions in Brazil, Uruguay, Argentina, Venezuela, and elsewhere. Many members of these urban guerrilla bands were subsequently identified as university students of middle class background rather than the peasants and workers who were the intended beneficiaries of revolutionary upheaval. This led analysts to dismiss the terrorists by concluding they were really dilettantes who dabbled in revolutionary politics for reasons having more to do with generational rebellion or personal ennui than material self-interest.

But this dismissive generalization quickly encountered other cases and more evidence. In Northern Ireland, members of the IRA's "active service units" were discovered to be predominantly of working class background. The Italian Red Brigades, an organization that defined itself as a party of fighting proletarians, were composed to a significant extent of, well, fighting proletarians, young workers from the plants and factories of Milan, Turin, and Genoa. Facile generalizations about dilettantes needed qualification. But the observations themselves pointed to the diverse social composition of terrorist organizations.

To indicate social diversity, though, does not mean that generalizations about the social composition of terrorist groups are impossible any more than the diverse social composition of all voluntary political organizations, peaceful as well as violent, means that efforts to generalize about their members are destined to fail. As with all political organizations, we need to pay attention to what the terrorist groups hope to achieve, the internal relationships between leaders and followers, and the age of the organizations.

Take the matter of leadership. Those who assume leadership roles within most voluntary political organizations tend to be drawn from the educated middle classes. The same seems to apply in general to terrorist groups, ranging from the

Russian People's Will in the 1870s, through the Socialist Revolutionaries in the early years of the twentieth century (see chapter 2), to al Qaeda at the beginning of the twenty-first century. Those young men who received training at al Qaeda bases in Taliban-controlled Afghanistan may have come from impoverished backgrounds in various parts of the Muslim world, but this was decidedly not true of al Qaeda's founders and leaders: bin Laden and al-Zawahiri came from exceptionally prosperous family backgrounds. Similarly, in the Israeli–Palestinian conflict, whereas the suicide bombers who destroyed themselves and so many others from 1993 onward tended to come from the impoverished Palestinian refugee camps on the West Bank and Gaza Strip, the leaders of such organizations as Hamas, PIJ, the al Aqsa Martyrs' Brigade, and the PFLP who recruited and then sent them on their missions came from other social strata. The present (2004) leaders of both Hamas, the physician Dr. Abdel Aziz Rantisi, and PIJ, the former professor of Middle Eastern studies Dr. Ramadan Abdallah Shallah, come from different circumstances than most of their followers. The same may be said about the pediatrician Dr. George Habash, the founder and long-time leader of the PFLP, and Yassir Arafat, the founder of Fatah and long-serving chairman of the PLO, who comes from a prominent Palestinian family and received a university degree in engineering in Cairo.

The membership of a terrorist organization or a political group that includes terrorist violence in its tactical repertoire bears some relationship to its admission standards as well as its aims and objectives. Consider the role of women.

A significant percentage of left-wing revolutionary organizations in Latin America, Western Europe, and the United States during the 1960s and 1970s were women. The same may be said about the Russian revolutionary bands of the late nineteenth and early twentieth century. In a number of these cases women were not merely foot soldiers, following the orders of male commanders, but played leadership roles. The German Red Army Fraction, the Italian Red Brigades, the Weather Underground, and Symbionese Liberation Army were organizations that women either served as important leaders or virtually controlled, making the majority of tactical decisions.

The situation on the far right is very different. Neo-Fascist, neo-Nazi, and racial supremacist groups are largely male preserves. There are exceptions here and there, but right-wing terrorist groups have proportionally smaller numbers of women and far fewer women in positions of leadership than their leftist counterparts. The websites and chat rooms of contemporary right-wing racist bands often include lamentations about the scarcity of Aryan or Nordic women members whose participation might include serving as mothers of racially superior children to be fathered by males conscious of their duty to avoid the extinction of the white race.

The logic here is that the role of women in a terrorist organization is linked to the organization's goals. The left-wing groups, no matter how much they define themselves as the vanguard of revolutionary change, stress egalitarianism and the elimination of class-based privilege. The rightist groups, on the other hand, convey a very different message. The latter tends to stress hierarchy along with macho ideas about the masculine nature of political violence. Commonly, these groups emphasize a traditional role for women as wives and mothers. For the far right, terrorism is often a distinctly male undertaking. In view of these differences in outlook it is hardly surprising to discover gender-based differences in the composition of right-wing and revolutionary terrorist groups.

The status of women in nationalist and religiously driven terrorist organizations presents a mixed picture. Women are conspicuously missing from most of the Islamist-based jihad groups, although organizations active in Chechnya and in Israel's occupied territories have been willing to employ females as suicide bombers. Among other things, women usually wear bulkier clothing and arouse less suspicion than men and as a consequence make effective suicide bombers. But like the far right-wing terrorist organizations the religious groups typically extol the traditional role of women in society and invoke sacred texts to justify this prejudice.

The presence or absence of women in nationalist terrorist organizations seeking secessionist or separatist goals reflects the cultural background of the particular ethnic groups in whose name the organizations wage their campaign of violence. Women have achieved prominence in some, e.g. the Tamil Tigers and ETA, but not others.

This discussion of the role of gender in the composition of terrorist groups calls our attention to another point. The social composition of such groups is not random but bears a relationship to their ideas about the world and their objectives. This points us to another problem in identifying the social composition of terrorist groups, that of over-determining their membership.

In almost all instances the membership of terrorist organizations represents only a tiny fraction of those people who by age and social background might be inclined to join. What explains the difference between the large pool of potential members and the small number of members? One response is that in many cases terrorist groups wish to limit the size of their membership, for a variety of reasons, including fears that increasing size makes the organization more vulnerable to penetration by police spies or *agents provocateurs*. Another is that recruitment often involves an element of chance. Recruits are often individuals whose friends, relatives, and acquaintances are already members. Most often joining involves more a process of gradually getting drawn into the terrorist group's milieu than a single, distinct choice.

Why do people become terrorists?

Now that we have some understanding of how people join terrorist groups and the types of people most likely to embark on a career in terrorism we should turn our attention to another fundamental question. Why do people join? What motivates individuals to become involved in violent attacks on bus, train, or plane passengers, passers-by in shopping malls – perfect strangers, in other words?

One widely discussed response is mental illness. Terrorists, or those who join terrorist organizations (the two are not necessarily the same), have personalities that dispose them to kill the helpless or unsuspecting. A nineteenth-century Italian criminologist, Cesare Lombroso, even went so far as to argue that terrorists' brains and head shapes differed from those of ordinary people. Explanations based on head bumps and mental illnesses appear reassuring. Among other things, they transform perpetrators into freaks radically different from most people; whose political ideas, if any, need not be taken seriously. The fundamental problem in using mental illness as a response to the 'why?' question is that it is not supported by the facts. Few studies or clinical interviews with terrorists or ex-terrorists have detected serious signs of mental disturbance. Apparently there is no such thing as a terrorist personality. Profoundly disturbed individuals who hear voices speaking to them from inanimate objects or live in a delusional world are unlikely to be admitted into terrorist organizations because, among other things, their peculiarities would make them so unreliable they would endanger the lives of other members.

The reason terrorists are sometimes regarded as mentally ill may have more to do with the character of the organizations to which they become attached than their own internal mental processes. Among other things, through the dynamics of these groups terrorists or would-be terrorists are likely to be exposed to a process of moral disengagement through which they learn techniques for de-humanizing and demonizing the enemy in such a way as to make he, she, or them easier to kill. Or, they may learn that it is the will of God that the enemy be destroyed by any means possible. Once inside the group the member's understanding of the outside world is filtered through the group's (and its leaders') view of what constitutes reality. Not uncommonly the latter will appear substantially distorted to those on the outside.

In addition, there is the phenomenon of "groupthink." Individuals are often more likely to take greater risks on behalf of a group with which they strongly identify than they would if they acted alone. Loyalty to the group shapes the conduct of individual members. Terrorist bands are often able to exploit this natural affinity for the group to encourage members to undertake extremely hazardous or even suicidal missions.

Why people join terrorist groups may have more to do with the attractions they offer than the internal mental states of those who join. With few exceptions (e.g. the Lord's Liberation Army in Uganda), terrorist organizations are voluntary. Rarely are people compelled to join. So the question becomes: What incentives or inducements do such groups possess that attract recruits?[7]

The obvious answer is their strong commitment to a cause of one kind or another. Belief in the cause serves as the principal incentive for joining. Still, we would be jumping to conclusions if we accepted the group's goal as the only incentive for joining. One qualification is that there are typically far more people who believe in a goal than actually join the terrorist group committed to achieving it. Why do some join and others not? Another reservation is that in some cases individuals have joined a terrorist group without a clear understanding of what its objectives are. There are still other cases when a group's goals change depending on the circumstances in which it finds itself. For instance, the late Abu Nidal's Fatah Revolutionary Council began as an organization in 1974 because its leader rejected any means other than violence of bringing about Israel's destruction. Over time Nidal's organization became willing to carry out a terrorist attack on behalf of any cause willing to pay for its commission.

Other incentives: Often people join terrorist groups because doing so offers them or seems to offer them an opportunity for action. Not uncommonly, those drawn to terrorist bands are individuals who have grown weary of empty rhetoric about the need to do something about a cause. Bars, coffee houses, bookstores, school cafeterias, and other gathering sites frequently abound with individuals engaged in seemingly endless discussions about their social and political grievances. Terrorist organizations provide a way for those who wish, finally, to translate the words into reality. Individuals who wish to take up arms against a sea of troubles may be attracted to organizations that promise something beyond rhetorical condemnations of various enemies.

The fact that terrorist groups often attract individuals based on the opportunity for action comes with a cost. The group may need to engage in exceptionally risky and potentially self-destructive attacks because they risk losing the support of members whose strongest incentive for joining the group is the excitement stimulated by violent action.

Status often serves as another incentive. Superficially membership in a terrorist group seems unlikely to enhance someone's status or social standing. Joining a violent organization does not seem the equivalent of joining an elite social club or illustrious university faculty. However, membership in a terrorist group may well confer heightened social status. For young men especially, walking down a street carrying a gun or grenade launcher, appearing tough and menacing to others, may indeed raise their status in the eyes of their peers.

Suicide bombers or "martyrs" in the Middle East provide examples of the benefits to be gained. The self-sacrificers (*shahids*) are rewarded for their deeds by immediate entry into paradise, a substantial improvement over their terrestrial circumstances. They achieve earthly fame because their pictures appear on posters throughout the area. Before departing on their adventure they are often filmed explaining why they are going to do what they are about to do. Film clips are then shown on television following the suicide bombings. Surviving family members are frequently regarded with enhanced status by the community at large because of their son's or daughter's willingness to die on behalf of the cause.

Material benefits may accrue to those who become involved in terrorism. As with social standing, it is hard to imagine money and other material incentives being significant in decisions to join terrorist organizations. But such may indeed be the case. Some terrorist organizations are quite wealthy. They may be the beneficiaries of major contributions from wealthy donors. In recent years wealthy businessmen from Saudi Arabia and the oil-rich Persian Gulf sheikdoms have contributed vast amounts of money to Islamic charities. The latter, in turn, funnel much of this money to Islamist groups in Pakistan and elsewhere, ostensibly for educational purposes. In reality the money finds its way to jihadi organizations engaged in terrorist activities directed *inter alia* against Indian-controlled Kashmir. Otherwise unemployed young men receive monetary compensation, hazardous duty pay, for carrying out terrorist attacks on Hindu Kashmiri and representatives of Indian authority in the region. The leaders of these groups, although they may be at pains to disguise it, often live lives of some luxury.

This situation is by no means unique to South Asia. During the 1970s the Israelis assassinated a PLO leader in front of his villa on the French Riviera. Yassir Arafat is the personal beneficiary of funds intended to benefit the Palestinians; he siphons off enough to maintain substantial banking accounts, some reportedly in Israeli banks.

On reflection the significance of money as an incentive should hardly be a surprise. Terrorists often support themselves by staging bank robberies, holding hostages for ransom, and participating in various money-making schemes. In Northern Ireland both the IRA and the Protestant paramilitaries are heavily involved in petty racketeering. And in Latin America, Shining Path and FARC have become major beneficiaries of the cocaine business.

The longer a terrorist group endures, the more likely its existing membership as well as new inductees are to find material incentives of growing importance. In some instances, such as the Muslim separatist Abu Sayyaf Group (ASG) in the Philippines (which specializes in kidnapping Westerners and holding them for ransom), it becomes hard to tell where political terrorism stops and organized criminal activity begins.

The opportunity to gain revenge for previous sufferings and humiliations may also serve as a powerful incentive for joining groups engaged in terrorism. If you or a person in your family or circle of friends has suffered at the hands of a perceived enemy the ability to retaliate may become a very powerful attraction. Women suicide bombers in the Chechen "Black Widows" and Sri Lankan "Birds of Paradise," for instance, are widely believed to have been the victims of rape at the hands of their Russian and Sinhalese antagonists.

Where do terrorist organizations come from?

In moving from the individual to the organizational aspects of the terrorist problem the first question we need to ask ourselves is: What is a terrorist organization? Some political organizations include the use of terrorism as one of several tactics they employ in order to achieve their goals. In addition to terrorist violence such groups as Hamas and Hizbollah operate schools and provide various social services for residents of the Gaza Strip and southern Lebanon. On the other hand, some groups are engaged exclusively on terrorism; have no other arrows in their quivers. The Italian Red Brigades of the 1970s, the current ASG, and PIJ do little else than carry out terrorist attacks. It makes sense to attach the label "terrorist organization" to both types of groups, but bearing in mind though that some are substantially more complex than others.

Where do terrorist organizations come from? There is another distinction to be made here. Some are pre-existing organizations or parts of organizations whose members make a strategic decision to employ terrorist violence. Basque Homeland and Liberty went through a gestation of more than a decade before launching terrorist attacks against the Spanish authorities. In other cases, however, the group is formed for the purpose of carrying out terrorist attacks. Algeria's Armed Islamic Group (GIA) is a case in point.

Political parties and religious societies often provide the settings from which terrorist groups appear. Dissident factions, often rooted in the youth wings or extreme fringes of the respective organizations, secede from the parent organization, dissatisfied with a presumed turn towards accommodation with opponents, and launch terrorist campaigns in the hope of achieving maximal objectives. The histories of Egypt's Muslim Brotherhood and Italy's neo-Fascist Italian Social Movement are illustrative.

In many instances new groups are formed specifically for the purpose of launching terrorist campaigns, without the benefit of an intermediary step. These groups are usually event driven, formed as the result of negative or even catastrophic events such as acts of government repression, crushing electoral defeat instead of an expected victory, a lost civil war, foreign invasion, and the waning of enthusiasm for a movement of mass protest.

For example: The Israeli invasion of Lebanon in 1982 put in motion a series of events that led to the formation of Hizbollah. The decision by the Algerian government to cancel national elections and deny the Islamic Salvation Front a share in power created the circumstances for the appearance of the Armed Islamic Front.

Terrorist organizations also vary in their visibility. Some operate on a clandestine basis. They become visible to the public only when they carry out an operation. The Italian Red Brigades or German Red Army Fraction of the 1970s were composed of members who assumed new identities and lived the life of underground fighters. On the other hand some terrorist groups receive sanctuary from friendly governments and, as a result, are able to operate openly, at least within the confines of the host country. In recent years, both Hamas and PIJ have maintained their headquarters in Damascus.

Terrorist organizations also vary in size and shape. Some groups, like the nominally revolutionary Weather Underground and the Symbionese Liberation Army in the United States or the Angry Brigade in Great Britain, consisted of no more than a few dozen members and well-wishers at the height of their operations in the late 1960s and 1970s. At the other extreme are groups like Argentina's Montoneros, active at about the same time as the above groups, which was able to attract several thousand young people to its ranks. Al Qaeda, appears to be in a class of its own with thousands of members scattered around the Muslim world and with "sleeper cells" in Western Europe and other places. Some observers have claimed that for terrorist organizations size and effectiveness were opposed. The bigger the group the easier it became for the authorities to plant or recruit informants, thereby making the organization easier to dismantle. This does not seem to be the case with al Qaeda, but in this instance it may be more the shape than the size of the terrorist organization that matters most in forecasting its durability.

Unlike most groups organized during the third wave of terrorist activity (see chapter 3), al Qaeda is not structured along hierarchical lines. Rather, observers stress its network-like horizontal form of organization, with semi-autonomous nodes of activity and little day-to-day supervision from the top.[8] This arrangement, much like other post-modern forms of enterprise, permits the organization to flourish even if leaders or constituent groups are eliminated by the United States and their other numerous enemies. Osama bin Laden or Ayman al Zawahiri may provide cues through the media, but it becomes the responsibility of the semi-autonomous bands to interpret them and transform the rhetoric into violent reality. In this way the authorities may strike at the center but in so doing may not be able to destroy the entire apparatus.

This is the nature of the problem confronting intelligence and law enforcement agencies in the United States and other nations that have embarked since 9/11 on a "war" aimed at defeating al Qaeda and bringing an end to terrorist violence more generally. The response to terrorism is the subject to which we now turn our attention.

Further reading

John Arquilla and David Ronfeldt (eds.), *Networks and Netwars* (Santa Monica: Rand, 2001).

Boaz Ganor (ed.), *Countering Suicide Terrorism* (Herzliya, Israel: International Policy Institute for Counter-Terrorism, 2001).

Walter Laqueur, *The New Terrorism* (Oxford and New York: Oxford University Press, 1999).

Walter Reich (ed.), *Origins of Terrorism* (Cambridge and New York, Cambridge University Press, 1990).

Jessica Stern, *Terror in the Name of God* (New York: HarperCollins, 2003).

5

Reacting to terrorism

The focus of our discussion to this point has been on the natural history of and circumstances surrounding outbreaks of terrorist violence. In chapter 4 we turned from this descriptive undertaking to an analysis of the who and why of terrorism: who the terrorists are and why they do it. In this chapter we turn our attention again to the impact of terrorism on the public and the vital role played by the mass media in shaping popular perceptions. We are also interested in understanding how governments and, increasingly, transnational and international organizations have reacted to threats posed by terrorism. In seeking to understand these reactions we also need to be aware that in addition to countering terrorism there are some governments and various transnational non-governmental organizations that actively promote terrorist activity.

As we are aware by now terrorism is a kind of violence or threatened violence intended to send a message to a wider audience. The immediate victims of the violence, then, represent the means to an end. Pictures of the beheading of a journalist or a businessman shock or excite various audiences but the victims themselves are of only incidental interest to their killers. Nonetheless any discussion of terrorism would be incomplete if it failed to pay attention to those most immediately affected by the violence.

Impact on the victims

In seeking to understand the nature of terrorist victimization we need first to introduce a few fundamental distinctions. The UN counter-terrorism official Alex Schmid suggests we employ the following ones.[1] First, there are the deeds themselves: some terrorist attacks are carried out against specific individuals, often prominent figures of one kind or another, whereas other attacks are indiscriminate, directed against individuals who happen to be in the wrong place at the wrong time when the bomb goes off, a nightclub in Bali or a commuter train in Madrid for example. Terrorist events may also be classified according to their duration. Some events involve only a single phase: a bomb is detonated in a public place or an individual is assassinated by a gunman. On the other hand, there are terrorist events that last for a while. These occur when an individual or individuals are held hostage or kidnapped. In some cases these episodes are quite prolonged. In 1978 the Red Brigades kidnapped Italy's former prime minister Aldo Moro and held him captive for fifty-five days before executing him. In 1996 Members of Peru's Tupac Amaru Revolutionary Movement (MRTA) took over the Japanese embassy in Lima and held dozens of visiting diplomats hostage for more than two months.

Schmid also calls our attention to the fact that there are two kinds of victims of terrorist attacks: immediate and proximate. The former refers to individuals who are killed, maimed, tortured, and psychologically harmed as a result of being targeted by the terrorists. Individuals who have survived terrorist attack, e.g. Kenyans in the vicinity of the 1998 bombing of the US embassy in Nairobi, report a variety of psychological difficulties and physical symptoms: insomnia, memory lapses, diffuse fear, free-floating anxiety, apathy, depression, and the syndrome of problems diagnosed as post-traumatic stress disorder. Beyond the circle of immediate victims there are others who may be harmed by acts of terrorism. These proximate victims include, most obviously, the family, friends, and colleagues of the immediate victims. But this category should also be expanded to include those who have reason to fear – e.g. their names appear on "death lists" – that they may become the next targets of terrorist attack, or those who suffer significant damage to property either as the result of an attack or as the consequence of government retaliation for such an attack, e.g. when Palestinian home owners on the West Bank have their houses destroyed by the Israeli army because of their proximity to the hideouts or alleged hideouts of Hamas or Islamic Jihad bands.

Is it possible to measure the magnitude of terrorist victimization? Our answer is that it is possible but the measures are highly imperfect approximations of the reality. There are at least three reasons why such indicators almost of necessity are flawed. First, there is the matter of reporting. Terrorist events that occur in Western Europe or the Middle East or events involving Americans or Britons, for example, are widely reported by the mass media, sometimes in great detail. On the other hand, terrorist attacks carried out by bands in Uzbekistan or some other locale in Central Asia rarely receive much publicity. Press reports are the usual sources from which terrorist event databases are composed. As a result, events in out-of-the way places are less likely to appear in these compilations, thereby distorting the reality. Second, there is the related problem of measuring terrorist events that take place in the middle of general violent conflicts. For instance, Lebanon suffered a truly horrifying civil war between 1975 and 1988. Thousands were killed in fighting between various sectarian militia groups. Private armies representing Maronite Christian, Druze, Sunni, Shiite, and Palestinian communities fought each other and, at times, the armed forces of Syria and Israel. In the midst of this combat were embedded hundreds, perhaps thousands, of terrorist attacks, e.g. politically motivated bank robberies, revenge assassinations, and suicide bombings. However, because these attacks occurred in the middle of more general fighting, which included mass executions of whole villages, it became difficult to disentangle terrorist events from other horrors committed during the civil war. Third, the extent of psychological injury is exceptionally difficult to calculate. Among other things, victims need to report their feelings to responders and care-givers before their difficulties can be entered into the calculations of those attempting the measurements. Not all those suffering psychological problems come forward to receive help. And not all those injured by a terrorist event experience the injury in the immediate aftermath of the event.

Despite these limitations such private organizations and government agencies as the Rand Corporation and the US Department of State have created databases in which terrorist events are recorded on a continuing basis.[2] Normally, these chronologies report when and where the event occurred, along with information regarding its perpetrators' backgrounds (e.g. citizenship, age, gender) and the victims (e.g. how many, the extent of injury or damage). In this way it becomes possible for analysts to detect patterns in a wave of events which escape the eye of those who rely for their understanding on the snapshots provided by television or newspaper reports of individual attacks. If we review at least some of the findings concerning terrorist victimization, what do we discover?

According to data collected and reported by the Oklahoma City National Memorial Institute for the Prevention of Terrorism (an organization created by the US Congress in the wake of the 1995 bombing of the Murrah Federal Building in that city), between December 26, 1997 and March 8, 2003 there were a total of 7053 terrorist incidents worldwide. These acts of terrorism resulted in 9856 deaths, including the fatalities resulting from the 9/11 attacks on the World Trade Center and the Pentagon, as well as physical injuries to 19,129 other victims.

It is not uncommon in reporting evidence about the magnitude of terrorist victimization to note that the number of deaths and injuries pales when it is compared with the number of casualties involved in conventional armed conflicts: the Iran–Iraq war of the 1980s for example. In the latter cases, however, a high proportion of the casualties is suffered by combatants, individuals organized into military formations of one kind or another. In the case of terrorism virtually all the victims are "noncombatants": individuals unaware they are involved in some violent struggle until the bomb goes off. In fact, that is what gives terrorism its shock value, its "multiplier effect."

Table 5.1 provides us with some information about where the terrorist events occurred and how many were exclusively domestic in nature or were international in character (meaning they were committed by citizens of one country against targets of another or were carried out on territory foreign to either the perpetrators or the victims). One attribute of the distribution

Table 5.1 Terrorist incidents by region from December 26, 1997 to March 8, 2003[3]

	International	Domestic (= national)	Total * (= global)
North America	4	33	37
Western Europe	182	1853	2035
Eastern Europe	43	555	598
Latin America	77	1103	1180
East and Central Asia	13	43	56
South Asia	61	1122	1183
Southeast Asia and Oceania	35	241	276
Middle East and Persian Gulf	333	1209	1542
Africa	29	117	146

* Total incidents 7053; total fatalities 9856; total injuries 19,128

that draws our attention immediately is that domestic terrorist events are far more common than international ones. Even during a period that included the 9/11 attacks, quintessential acts of international terrorism, domestic terrorist attacks were far more common: the National Memorial Institute recorded 5,067 of them versus 777 acts of international terrorism.

The table also shows us in which regions of the world terrorist attacks were most prevalent and least prevalent. At the end of the twentieth century and early years of the twenty-first the Middle East and Western Europe stand out as the regions where both domestic and international terrorism were most common. The Middle East is hardly a surprise here. Western Europe, though, requires some explanation; it is after all composed exclusively of democracies and prosperous ones for the most part. The explanation has to do with the fact that the region is the locus of long-standing domestic terrorist campaigns in Spain and Northern Ireland. And by virtue of its porous borders, open societies, and proximity to the Middle East and North Africa the countries of the region are highly vulnerable to terrorism from organizations having international agendas.

We also need to consider the possibility of reporting bias when considering the regional distribution of terrorist events. The 1990s were a decade in which the countries of South Asia – Sri Lanka, India, and Pakistan – suffered very serious episodes of terrorist violence involving *inter alia* secessionist struggles waged by the Tamil Tigers in Sri Lanka, by Sikh groups in the Punjab of India, and by Islamist bands seeking to separate the state of Jammu Kashmir from Indian control. Events unfolding in Northern Ireland and in Spain's Basque region tended to receive more extensive coverage in the British and American media than the probably more numerous and in all likelihood more lethal terrorist attacks occurring in far-off South Asia.

Another characteristic of the table that may seem surprising is the comparative rarity of terrorist attacks in North America.

Despite 9/11 and the threats made against the United States by Osama bin Laden and his colleagues and admirers, along with the heightened fears about additional attacks, the US and Canada have only rarely been the site of terrorist violence, domestic or international. It is when Americans travel abroad and when American institutions are located on foreign soil that they become frequent terrorist targets.

The above represents a recent snapshot of terrorist attacks. But we should also be curious about trends in the characteristics of terrorist violence. How are things changing, if indeed they are changing?

The major chronologies of terrorist events date from the late 1960s, a time when the terrorist phenomenon became a matter of interest to Western governments. So there are now close to forty years' worth of evidence to consider. When we do consider it, some intriguing developments appear. First, terrorist attacks are becoming more lethal. The number of people killed per event has increased over this time span (see Table 5.2). In the early years of the "Age of terrorism" practitioners were often satisfied with the assassination or kidnapping of one or two individuals as a way of drawing attention to their cause and of extracting some cash by way of ransom. The overall sense was that the indiscriminate killing of large numbers of people would do the terrorists' cause more harm than good. If the latter's goal was to win the hearts and minds of some constituency for a political cause, an exemplary killing or two might help, but mass murder was unlikely to achieve this objective. However, since religiously inspired terrorism, what David Rapoport refers to as the "fourth wave" of modern terrorism, has swept through much of the world the per event death rate has increased. The suicide bombing has replaced plane skyjacking as the prototypical terrorist act. The conventional explanation for terrorism's growing lethality is that religiously motivated terrorists lack the inhibitions imposed by the need to win over a mass constituency.

Table 5.2 Decline in incidents and rise in lethality of international terrorism[4]

	No. incidents international	No. fatalities	No. injured
1989	376	411	385
1990	437	218	682
1991	565	102	242
1992	363	91	636
1993	431	109	1393
1994	322	314	663
1995	440	177	6277
1996	296	314	2915
1997	304	221	693
1998	273	741	5952
1999	392	233	706
2000	423	405	791

For the religious terrorists God is their constituency. This observation may not hold up to closer inspection.

Mass killing and popularity do not seem to be necessarily incompatible. For example, the level of popular support for al Qaeda throughout the Middle East and elsewhere increased substantially in the aftermath of the 9/11 attacks. In markets throughout much of the Arab world figurines are sold depicting planes embedded in the sides of miniature World Trade Centers. Public-opinion surveys in the same region suggest Osama bin Laden has achieved the status of a folk hero, comparable in some ways to the mythical figure of Robin Hood in Britain and America. On the West Bank and Gaza Strip rival Palestinian organizations, e.g. Hamas, Islamic Jihad, al Aqsa Martyrs' Brigade, often compete with one another in claiming credit for suicide attacks that involve multiple fatalities; the more fatalities the more intense the competition. Furthermore, no matter the level of religious enthusiasm felt by the suicide bombers themselves, the organizations that train and send them on their missions often display a high level of political sophistication. If causing multiple fatalities seems to advance their cause and win popular support, terrorist leaders persist in the campaigns of mass killing, e.g. the Madrid train bombings of March 11, 2004, but if not, they don't.

Cultural rather than religious factors may be at work in influencing terrorist practices. The evidence suggests that over the years, including recent years, Latin American terrorist groups have been far more likely to kidnap victims than their counterparts in any other region of the world. Suicide bombings, on the other hand, appear to be the weapon of choice among terrorists in the Middle East and South Asia, including the Tamil Tigers in Sri Lanka, a Hindu/nationalist rather than Muslim organization.

How have terrorist methods changed over the years? This question has stimulated extensive discussion. With suicide car bombings making the headlines on an almost daily basis and fears about the terrorist use of chemical, biological, radiological, and even nuclear weapons becoming widespread it is easy to believe that terrorists have become highly innovative in their methods of attack. Perhaps this is the case or increasingly the case. But before reaching this conclusion we should keep in mind that the vast majority of terrorist attacks still involve the bomb and the gun, precisely the types of weapons the anarchists and the Russian revolutionaries used more than a century ago. The weapons technology may have become far more sophisticated, e.g. miniaturized, but by and large we are still dealing with the same types of weapons. Compared with the kinds of innovations developed by the armed forces of various countries over the same period, terrorist methods have been relatively slow to change.

From the point of view of the perpetrators terrorist operations are relatively inexpensive. This is certainly the case when they are compared with conventional warfare. To take one contemporary example: it costs very little for an al-Qaeda-related group to send suicide car-bombers to detonate their explosives against American or coalition targets in Baghdad. By contrast it costs the United States billions of dollars to sustain its military presence in Iraq. Terrorist violence is a cheap means of making governments and private organizations pay a high cost in terms of both property damage and budgetary outlays for counter-terrorism. Government expenditures on security measures typically increase significantly when a country becomes the target of a terrorist campaign. Public funds that might otherwise be spent on education or health care are diverted to improved airport security and expanded intelligence services.

The role of mass media

Despite the human and material damage inflicted on its victims, we need to bear in mind that terrorism is above all a means of communication, a highly dramatic way of sending a message.[5] To the extent this is true, terrorist organizations are highly sensitive to the role of the mass media, television especially. We need to be aware as well that the relationship is reciprocal. Just as the terrorists need to convey their often symbolic messages to various audiences, so too television networks and newspaper organizations have a general need to capture large numbers of viewers and readers in order to advance their own largely material self-interests. Concomitantly, journalists, print or electronic, have their careers to think about. These careers are often enhanced, by higher salaries or more prestigious jobs, when they gain exclusive access to a terrorist chieftain or on-the-spot coverage to a breaking terrorist event. Terrorism sells newspapers or, to use a contemporary idiom, "if it bleeds it leads."

This sanguinary observation about the mass media is supported by a number of illustrations. From August 12, 1998, the date on which the US embassies in Nairobi and Dar-es-Salaam were bombed by al Qaeda operatives through the end of December 2000, the *New York Times* printed 304 stories on the subject. The major American television networks – CBS, NBC, and ABC – were equally lavish in their coverage. In the three months between the October 2000 attack by suicide bombers on the American destroyer USS *Cole* in Aden harbor and the end of the year, the same networks devoted respectively 252, 109, and 163 news stories to this terrorist incident.[6]

Not only do terrorism stories win extensive coverage by the mass media, they often do so at the expense of other subjects. For example, Brigitte Nacos reports the figures shown in Table 5.3, compiled from Lexis/Nexus and the *New York Times* online Archive.

Table 5.3 News coverage January 1, 1999 through December 31, 1999 (numbers of news items)

	ABC News	CBS News	NBC News	National Public Radio	New York Times
Terrorism	216	434	191	85	948
Health insurance	176	389	274	269	2177
Medicare	94	285	157	134	756
Poverty	45	76	39	79	1256
Social security	100	310	119	145	1551

The table reports the volume of news coverage by subject over the course of 1999 by the major American media. What the table reveals is a significant difference between the television networks news programs and the *New York Times* and the non-profit National Public Radio network. Domestic social policy issues, health insurance, Medicare, poverty-related issues, and social security received extensive coverage in the two latter outlets whereas, with one exception, terrorism is the single most frequently covered topic for the television networks.

It seems indisputable that terrorist events receive extensive coverage (on American TV networks) both absolutely and relative to other problems, but is this coverage accurate? Some years ago analysts sought to answer this question in a systematic way. Gabriel Weimann and Conrad Winn compared the distribution of international terrorist events from 1972 through 1980, employing one of the major chronologies of terrorist events, with the amount of coverage accorded terrorist events by the CBS, NBC, and ABC networks over the same period.[7] Their principal findings were these. First, there was virtually no association between the number of terrorist events during a year and the volume of coverage terrorism received on the networks. Some years in which terrorist attacks were frequent, there was relatively little television coverage. Conversely, some years when there were few events television coverage was extensive. Over the period covered in the Weimann and Winn study a citizen who relied exclusively on the American television networks for their understanding of the terrorist threat would have gotten a distorted picture of the situation. Weimann and Winn observed the same distorting affect based on where terrorist events occurred. For instance, terrorism was relatively common in Latin America in these years but incidents there received little attention from the networks. The Middle East, also another major locale for terrorism, received more coverage than the number of events occurring in that region would seem to warrant. Approximately the same may be said about the victims of the violence. Terrorist attacks aimed at business people and public officials tended to receive less attention than attacks directed against members of the general public. Weimann and Conrad conclude from the latter finding that the network coverage may have made ordinary citizens more fearful about the likelihood of their becoming the victims of terrorist attack than the evidence would warrant.

Nacos make a similar observation about television coverage of anti-globalization protests around the world. When representatives of the World Trade Organization (WTO), International Monetary Fund, World Bank, and G8 have met in recent years, they have typically been confronted by popular protests, often involving individuals and groups who believe that economic integration on a worldwide basis is having a negative effect on Third World countries and workers in the advanced industrialized ones as well. The television coverage of these gatherings has not only virtually ignored the meetings themselves (what was actually going on inside the buildings where the conferences were being held) but also paid little attention to the vast majority of the protestors. For the most part the latter consisted of peaceful individuals, marching, waving placards, and speaking on behalf of their various causes. Instead the television networks have chosen to focus almost exclusively on the small number of "anarchists" who have smashed store windows, set fire to automobiles, and engaged in violent confrontations with the police.

The mass media often help to win sympathy for terrorist organizations. In the case of the Palestinian suicide bombers, Nacos reports that American television coverage has tended to garner more sympathy for the *shahids* and their families than their victims. The suicide bombers are frequently depicted as they would have preferred to depict themselves, as martyrs on behalf of a sacred cause who were acting out of desperation. The school children or senior citizens who were blown apart on the bus when the act of martyrdom occurred often receive little attention or sympathy.

Terrorist recruitment is not a function we ordinarily associate with the mass media. Yet they do appear to perform this task in a variety of cases. Recruitment takes a variety of forms. During the 1980s Colonel Gadhafi's Libyan government used to place advertisements in German newspapers offering bonuses and good pay to young Germans willing to move to the Middle East and engage in the struggle against the Zionist enemy. The glamorous treatment accorded leaders of the Red Brigades by the Italian press during their trials in the mid 1970s led dozens of young people to phone their defense attorneys asking how they could go about joining the organization. More recently al-Jazeera, the independent Arab television station, has evidently structured its coverage of the American and British occupation of Iraq in such a way as to win recruits for the shadowy groups using terrorist violence as a means of bringing a premature end to this occupation.

Not uncommonly spokespersons for the mass media assert that all they do is report the news. If the news is bad so be it. All that the television networks and newspapers do is inform the public about important events no matter how distressing they may be. The press is neutral and objective. Despite these claims, on numerous occasions the media have played a more active role in terrorist operations than they would suggest, sometimes endangering the lives of victims along the way. For instance, in 2000 the ASG, active in the southern Philippines, seized a number of Western hostages and demanded ransom for their release. But the leader of this Islamist band had more than money on his mind. He told two of his captives, a middle-aged German couple, that he was waiting for the arrival of Western journalists before making his demands public. Holding the German couple hostage guaranteed extensive television coverage even on a remote island in the Philippine archipelago. No expectation of television coverage, likely no terrorist event.

There have even been instances where the reporting of terrorist events has endangered the lives of victims. In 1985 three members of Hizbollah skyjacked a TWA airliner bound from Rome to Cairo. They had it flown to Beirut, then Algiers, and eventually back to Beirut again. As part of the extensive television coverage provided by the networks for this spectacular (thirty-nine Americans were among the passengers), a CNN reporter standing on the deck of an American aircraft carrier somewhere in the Mediterranean pointed to a group of armed men standing behind him. The reporter told his audience that this was a group of American Special Forces training to stage an attack on the TWA plane once it landed in hopes of freeing Hizbollah's hostages. This CNN story was carried live throughout the world, including the Middle East. In other words, the skyjackers' confederates were able to see the counter-terrorist preparations underway and alert their confederates accordingly, thereby making it more likely the latter would kill their hostages.

In another case, in November 1974 a British Airways flight from Dubai to Tripoli, Libya was skyjacked. The skyjackers demanded the release of thirteen terrorists held in Egyptian prisons. The Egyptian authorities informed the skyjackers they would comply with their demands by flying the thirteen from Cairo to Riyadh, where the British Airways flight had been compelled to land. Instead, the Egyptians sent a plane containing commandos prepared to attempt a rescue operation to free the hostages aboard the plane. But a local journalist suddenly went on the radio to report that the Egyptians were attempting a ruse. Though they were telling the skyjackers the plane carried the thirteen terrorists it really had a highly trained commando team on board. The skyjackers were able to hear this announcement over the radio and responded by executing a German banker from among the hostages to show the Egyptians they meant business: no more tricks.

In recent years terrorist groups have taken to taping their own performances. For example, video cassettes showing Osama bin Laden and Ayman al-Zawahiri making their way down hillsides in Afghanistan or reclining in caves are made available to television stations in the Middle East and, within a short time, worldwide. Audiotape recordings are used for the same purpose. Bin Laden, al-Zawahiri, et al. are thus able to convey their hair-raising messages to the public without the editing normally practiced by radio or television news directors or government censors. According to some counter-terrorism officials these self-produced shows serve a dual use. They convey open messages to various audiences – threats, reassurances, etc. – but they may also contain hidden signals to terrorist cells giving them the go-ahead to launch new attacks.

Then there is the matter of televised executions, videotapes showing the beheading of hostages by al-Qaeda-related bands in Pakistan and Iraq. These displays arouse disgust among most civilized observers. The latter, however, may not constitute a majority of viewers, many of whom may regard the spectacle as both fully justifiable and exciting. After all, revolutionary mobs were enthralled by the guillotining of thousands in revolutionary France.

Some terrorist organizations – particularly those with a stable territorial base, Hizbollah in Lebanon for example – have been able to create their own radio and television stations. In these instances the organizations are able to broadcast their views without having to be concerned about the editorial discretion exercised by independent media outlets.

The internet offers yet another means by which terrorist organizations can communicate without having to rely on intermediaries (e.g. television news directors) to convey their messages in the way they wish them to be presented.

Sophisticated encryption technology, encoding messages for dissemination on the internet, now makes it possible for members of terrorist organizations to communicate with one another instantaneously and at great distances. Security agencies like the National Security Agency in the United States devote substantial resources to attempting to decipher these messages, to comprehend what is often described in the press as terrorist "chatter." The terrorists, alert to the problem of detection, often disseminate false messages in order to throw the detectors off-track in what amounts to a continuing game of move and counter-move.

But it is the easily accessible websites of terrorist organizations that enable them to reach a wide audience. Most of the major contemporary terrorist groups, e.g. Hizbollah and Hamas, have their own websites. These are typically used to convey the groups' messages in a number of different languages. Those who log on to these sites will also notice almost all of them display exceptionally menacing or threatening images, e.g. eagles or buzzards resting on the top of human skulls, indicating what the group does or hopes to do to its enemies.

The websites may be hacked into by enemies, however. Israeli hackers have had fun disrupting Hamas and Islamic Jihad websites, and pro-Palestinian hackers have reciprocated against various Israeli government sites, as this never-ending conflict has become digitized.

Models of government response

How do or should governments respond to the challenges posed by terrorist violence? Simple questions but unfortunately the answers to them are necessarily a bit complicated. We should probably begin by making a distinction between democratic and authoritarian governments. The former are characteristically bound by the rule of law whereas the latter are not. This difference is often of considerable importance in determining how states respond to terrorist threats.

If an authoritarian state ruled by the military or some civilian strongman regards a terrorist campaign as posing a serious challenge it rarely has much trouble eliminating the groups it believes responsible for posing the threat. A few examples will illustrate the point.

Argentina from the late 1960s through the mid 1970s was plagued by a particularly brutal terrorist problem. The Montoneros, the People's Revolutionary Armed Forces, and a number of smaller revolutionary groups waged an urban guerrilla campaign in the major cities. "Proletarian expropriations," i.e. bank robberies, multiplied. Bankers, business people, and politicians were abducted and held for ransom. Police officials and military officers along with members of their families were targeted for assassination. By 1976 the leaders of Argentina's armed forces had had enough. They replaced the country's inept but democratically elected government with a military junta, which ruled for the next half-dozen years. The military took off the proverbial kid gloves and waged what became known as a "dirty war" against the revolutionaries. Individuals suspected of belonging to or even sympathizing with the relevant groups were taken from their homes or off the streets by figures dressed in civilian clothes and driving unmarked cars. The suspects, sometimes entire families, were seized and taken to prisons where they were subject to excruciating torture before, not uncommonly, being killed. Thousands of Argentines "disappeared" in this way. The repression worked. By the time the military relinquished its hold on power in 1982 the terrorism (at least as practiced by the insurgent groups) had come to an end.

Another example may be taken from the Iranian experience. When the Ayatollah Khomeini and his followers sought to impose theocratic rule in Iran following the departure of the Shah in 1980, they were confronted by a violent challenge by other radicals opposed to religious domination. Revolutionary groups of fedayeen and mujahidin who had participated in the insurrection against the Shah objected to the direction in which Khomeini and his followers wished to lead the country. Hundreds of fedayeen and mujahidin launched terrorist attacks against the forces loyal to Khomeini. Among other operations, they blew up the national headquarters of the Islamic Republican Party as well as the prime minister's office during a meeting of the National Security Council. The newly elected president of Iran was killed along with members of the Majlis (parliament) and leading figures within the pro-Khomeini Revolutionary Guards. The new regime responded to these attacks with great brutality. Fedayeen and mujahidin militants were tortured and summarily executed after they had provided Khomeini loyalists with information they demanded concerning the whereabouts of their confederates. Fedayeen and mujahidin wounded in gun battles with Revolutionary Guardsmen were dragged from hospitals in Tehran on the grounds they were not entitled to medical treatment. Within a few months of this type of reaction, Khomeini's followers had brought the terrorist campaign to an end by the almost total destruction of the challenging organizations.

In his Pulitzer Prize winning volume *From Beirut to Jerusalem* Thomas Friedman describes the 1982 response of the Syrian government to a terrorist campaign directed against it by the country's Muslim Brothers.[8] This fundamentalist organization gave voice to the distress apparently felt by many Sunni Muslims over the secular direction that the infidel Baathist dictatorship in Damascus was taking the country. Among other things the new constitution proposed by the dictator Hafez al-Assad failed to mention the name of God and the country's Muslim character. It also extended equal status to women. In reaction to these affronts the Brothers staged a series of terrorist attacks. A bomb was detonated in Damascus which killed sixty-four passers-by. Students at the Syrian military academy in Aleppo were murdered in their barracks. President al-Assad himself was the target of an almost successful assassination attempt.

As in the Argentine and Iranian cases the Syrian regime reacted with great brutality. Simple membership in the Brotherhood was made a capital crime. According to an Amnesty International report, following the attempt on al-Assad soldiers entered the Tadmur prison and, following instructions from their superiors, executed an estimated six hundred to one thousand Muslim Brothers being held in that facility. Their bodies were then dumped in a common grave immediately outside the prison. Other prisoners were tortured into disclosing the whereabouts of other militants. Finally, in 1982, following word that the Brothers were planning an uprising, government forces moved into position on the outskirts of Hama, long a center of Brotherhood activity. The Syrian military then proceeded to bombard those neighborhoods in the city believed to house many of the fundamentalists. Somewhere between fifteen and twenty thousand people were killed as the result of this largely indiscriminate shelling of Hama. Uncomfortable though it may be to admit, the repression worked. Hafez al-Assad was not bothered by Islamist terrorism for the duration of his life.

If brutal repression appears to work, why not do it? The answer of course is that for democracies at least the cure may very well be worse than the disease. The repression may itself cause the democracy to abandon the very qualities that distinguish it from dictatorships. In Latin America during the 1970s Argentina was not the only country where the military seized power in order to suppress terrorist activity. Next door in Uruguay a democratically elected government proved incapable of defeating another revolutionary group, the Tupamaros. The country's military became sufficiently frustrated that it staged a *coup d'état* in 1972 and held power over the next decade. In other words the price Uruguay paid for the defeat of the Tupamaros was the suspension of its democracy for an extended period. In Western Europe and North America no democracy, as yet, has fallen to dictatorship as the result of efforts to repress terrorism. But defenders of civil liberties on both sides of the Atlantic have voiced alarm, particularly after 9/11, over measures governments have adopted to root out al Qaeda cells and those of other terrorist groups. The American government launched a "war on terrorism" in Iraq and Afghanistan in order to extend and to protect democracy. Thus disclosures about the use of torture and extrajudicial punishments by US forces operating in both countries have discredited the cause in whose name the war was launched. The key question becomes: How can democracies defend themselves against terrorist attacks without losing the very qualities that distinguish them from police states?

First and foremost of these qualities is the maintenance of the rule of law, meaning that the government cannot do whatever it wants whenever it feels like doing it.[9] Democratic governments must act in accordance with constitutional limitations and legal restrictions. In practical terms this means that the establishment of special courts not bound by conventional rules of evidence, the suspension of the right of habeas corpus to those suspected of involvement in terrorist activity, and the creation of special security forces, e.g. "death squads," outside the normal chain of command or not responsible to democratic authorities should be avoided at almost all costs.

In thinking about how democracies should respond to the threat of terrorism, analysts have suggested the use of one of two models: the criminal justice model and the warfare model. In the former case, democracies should regard terrorism as a type of criminal activity comparable to the operations of the Mafia and other criminal organizations.[10] In all democracies blowing up buildings, kidnapping individuals, taking hostages, assassinating public officials, robbing banks, and killing large numbers of citizens are crimes. Those who commit such acts for reasons of material gain or private vengeance are normally prosecuted under regular criminal statutes. Why not those who carry out the same deeds for political or religious motives? In other words, individual terrorists should be held criminally responsible for their acts and tried in open courts much like Mafia dons, cocaine barons, and more prosaic criminals. Ramzi Yousef, a Pakistani citizen and the man responsible for the 1993 attack, the first attack, on the World Trade Center, was eventually captured abroad and returned to the United States, where he was tried and convicted in a federal court in a manner not terribly unlike Manuel Noriega, the erstwhile Panamanian dictator and drug lord.

Other analysts view the criminal justice model as inappropriate or inadequate. They prefer to think of terrorism as a kind of warfare. For years military strategists in Britain and the United States have regarded terrorism as a kind of low-intensity or unconventional war. Some military theorists, reacting to the al Qaeda threat, have gone so far as to argue that international terrorism has replaced conventional wars in which massed armies confront each other along front lines and even the guerrilla insurgencies of the anti-colonial era as the new dominant type of armed conflict in the twenty-first century. The terrorists themselves seem to agree. They routinely issue statements defining themselves as engaged in a war with, variously, the West, the crusaders, the Zionist entity, the British occupiers of Northern Ireland. When they are arrested or captured, terrorists routinely issue statements demanding to be treated as prisoners of war rather than common criminals. Following 9/11 George Bush, the President of the United States, declared war on international terrorism. If the warfare model is adopted the emphasis turns from the police to specially trained military forces and from the criminal justice system to the rules and laws of war.

Which of the two models seems most appropriate? In terms of protecting the rule-of-law principle, the criminal justice model is the better alternative. Nonetheless, it has serious problems. For instance, evidence based on the experience in Northern Ireland suggests it is much harder to convict people for the commission of terrorism-based than common crimes. Most serious physical assaults and murders are committed by and against people who know each other. Witnesses are often willing to come forward and testify. This is not the case with terrorism. Terrorists frequently carry out attacks against random members of the public or specific individuals they have never met. As a consequence the trail of evidence linking perpetrator to victim is often missing or exceptionally hard to come by. Witnesses, fearing retribution from a terrorist's confederates, are often reluctant to tell the authorities and the courts what they have seen. As a result in Northern Ireland during the Troubles the conviction rate of individuals accused of murder etc. for terrorism-related reasons was much lower than that of those tried for similar acts who were motivated by private reasons.

The greater difficulty in responding to terrorist crimes than common ones encourages affected governments to employ special measures. Terrorists may be accused of such political crimes as membership in a group seeking to overthrow the state by violent means or treason. Also, democratic governments are often tempted to loosen their procedural protections for those accused of crimes. The right of trial by jury, for example, may have to be suspended in cases where prospective jurors are threatened with death if they vote to convict a terrorist.

If the level of terrorist violence can be kept at a relatively low level, most democracies will choose to react in approximately the same way as they do to organized criminal activity. They will employ the criminal justice model, modifying the criminal law to some extent, e.g. the rules treating criminal conspiracy, but will avoid more serious steps, such as the declaration of martial law. If the level of violence escalates and governments are confronted by a serious breakdown of public order, democratic leaders will seriously consider the application of the warfare model. The case for the latter option becomes more compelling when the terrorist organizations involved are international in scope and aim *inter alia* at acquiring WMD. We should bear in mind that responding to a terrorist threat by applying the warfare model does not mean that the government involved acquires *carte blanche* − can act without legal restraints of any kind. Anything does not go, because there are established rules of war; even internal wars are governed or are supposed to be governed by legal restraints.

The Hague and Geneva Convention provisions apply. Among other things, these rules make a distinction between combatants and non-combatants. Government forces may not carry out indiscriminate attacks on civilians uninvolved in the fighting even if the authorities believe they sympathize with the terrorists' cause. Such attacks constitute war crimes. They may also be self-defeating because they often win supporters for the terrorists. Similarly the terrorists, by the very nature of the acts they commit against non-combatants, are almost by definition war criminals. As a consequence, when captured they may be prosecuted for their actions. Torture of prisoners by either side is prohibited under the law of war. Under almost all circumstances torture is not only immoral but also ineffective. Individual captives subject to a torture regimen will usually tell their captors whatever they believe the latter want to hear simply to get them to stop. As a result the torturers may pass on erroneous information to their superiors, who, in turn, may make egregious mistakes in acting on it.

In practice most democracies confronted by serious terrorist threats employ some mix of the criminal justice and warfare models. In the case of Israel, a country targeted by waves of suicide bombers and by terrorist organizations bent on the destruction of the state itself, the mix has been more in favor of the warfare than the criminal justice model. In the United Kingdom, on the other hand, where terrorism has come until recently from Northern Irish Republicans and now from Islamic militants, the balance has been in the direction of the criminal justice alternative.

Among the democracies domestic measures against terrorist activity may be divided into "carrots" and "sticks." The latter have received far more attention than the former. In some cases, though, carrots have proved beneficial in reducing or eliminating terrorist activity.

Carrots

Rewards come in two forms, one provided to terrorists themselves, the other to their presumed constituents. Italy, Spain, Colombia, and a number of other democracies have offered terrorists opportunities to defect from their group in exchange for reduced sentences or even in some cases no punishment at all and an opportunity to return to normal life. The relevant legislation, almost always temporary in nature, extends these offers contingent on the terrorists' willingness to disclose information about their former confederates and the organizations to which they belonged. In the Italian case the opportunity to "repent" and return to a normal life became attractive to many revolutionaries, Red Brigadists and others, at the beginning of the 1980s because they saw their cause as lost and the possibilities of coming in from the cold increasingly attractive. When they turned themselves over to the police, many clandestine revolutionary terrorists reported a sense of profound relief, as if a heavy burden had been lifted from their shoulders.

Carrots may also work in the case of presumed fanatics. The American terrorism specialist Bruce Hoffman reported on the end of Black September, the Palestinian group responsible for the 1972 Munich Olympic massacre and other, less spectacular terrorist attacks. When PLO leaders reached the conclusion that the time had arrived to dissolve Black September they organized a party for its members in Beirut. Attractive young Palestinian women were invited to the festivities. Romances blossomed. Marriages followed and with them the responsibilities that go with family life. Within a relatively short time fanatical Black September fighters were transformed into devoted fathers and husbands, leaving their lives as terrorists behind them.

Benefits may also be awarded to the populations on whose behalf the terrorists claim to be acting. We do not have to accept the "root causes" argument to note that in cases involving nationalist or ethnic grievances reforms that stress greater local autonomy or power sharing may undercut popular support for terrorism, at least in the long run. During the 1950s and early 1960s the Italian government was confronted by a terrorist group active in the northern Alpine part of the country. Its cause was the status of the German-speaking minority in what Italy referred to as "Alto Adige" and Austrians called the "South Tyrol." Italy entered into negotiations with the Austrian government, the result of which was an agreement that provided substantial local self-rule for the German speakers in and around the city of Trent. Terrorist violence came to an end shortly thereafter. The "Good Friday" agreement between all parties involved in the status of Northern Ireland has been less successful. But the application of the principle of power sharing among Protestants and Catholics in ruling the provincial government has succeeded in radically reducing the level of violence throughout Ulster.

Sticks

Most discussions of the policies democracies adopt to stop terrorism focus on sanctions, measures aimed at preventing attacks before they occur and punishing those responsible if they do. Particularly since 9/11 governments in North America and Western Europe have strengthened laws and regulations already in place or enacted new ones to deal with what appears to be an unprecedented challenge posed by the al Qaeda network. Summarizing or synthesizing these measures for all the states involved is not an easy task. Dividing them into constituent parts makes it somewhat easier.

Hardening targets

All the democracies have taken steps aimed at making it more difficult for terrorists to strike at what for them would be attractive targets. Most obviously airport security has been strengthened as has that surrounding monuments and public buildings. Embassies and consulates of the United States in many parts of the world now look more like fortresses than diplomatic offices. Public gatherings such as sporting events – e.g. the Olympic Games, World Cup, Super-Bowl, and outdoor events likely to attract big crowds – are now better secured against terrorist attacks.

Money

Terrorist organizations today are less dependent on bank robberies, ransom payments, and other extortion schemes than their predecessors. Latin American groups, in Colombia most obviously, have gone into the highly profitable cocaine business, often by providing protection to the growers and manufacturers. Such Islamist organizations as Hamas, PIJ, Hizbollah, and al Qaeda rely heavily on philanthropy. Donations flow in from such private charities as the Holy Land Foundation, Third World Relief Agency, and a long list of other organizations. When investigators in the United States, Great Britain, Germany, and other democracies are able to show a link between a charity and a terrorist organization its assets may be frozen or seized; its officers may be prosecuted as well. Terrorist groups deriving benefits from the drug business are now targets of international criminal investigations.

Extradition

In the early years of the modern terrorist era, the late 1960s and early 1970s, governments seeking the extradition from another country of individuals suspected of carrying out terrorist attacks were often blocked by the "political crime" exemption found in many bilateral extradition treaties. This exemption dated from the nineteenth century when such democracies as the United Kingdom and The Netherlands did not want to return fugitives, e.g. revolutionary writers and dissident politicians, from authoritarian countries because they had committed a politically motivated crime according to the latter's decrees. Over time the political exemption principle has been modified, so that today the reigning legal principle is "extradite or prosecute;" governments are obliged to extradite or themselves prosecute individuals accused of terrorist acts.

Some democracies, the United States in particular, have sought to exercise extraterritorial jurisdiction over individuals suspected of planning or carrying out terrorist acts outside the country in question. (The long-standing international legal doctrine is that of "passive personality.") For example, those Saudis and Egyptians who planned the 9/11 attacks from sanctuaries in Taliban-ruled Afghanistan or those who planned the 1998 bombings of the American embassies in Kenya and Tanzania may be apprehended by American agents from the

Federal Bureau of Investigation (FBI) and returned to the US to stand trial.

State sponsorship

Legislation in the United Kingdom, the United States, and other democracies now imposes sanctions on states identified as sponsoring or supporting terrorist groups. In the American case, the Department of State is required to submit an annual report to Congress which lists states found to be supporting or sponsoring terrorist organizations. When these states – e.g. Iran, Syria, and North Korea – are identified, trade and other types of economic and cultural exchanges are cut off; so, for example, no American-based corporation may do business in the countries so identified. These sanctions often work, at least over time. Both Libya and the Sudan, long-time supporters and sponsors of terrorism, have recently found it advantageous to their material self-interest to change policy.

Domestic measures

The "Patriot Act," passed in the wake of the 9/11 attacks, has aroused great controversy in the United States. Civil libertarians have argued this legislation poses a serious threat to personal liberty through an unwarranted expansion of the government's police powers beyond what is absolutely necessary to protect the country against further terrorist attack. Because of the dangers involved the issue should certainly not be trivialized, but it might be placed in a comparative context. Virtually all the democracies confronted by serious terrorist threats have passed laws, usually for a specified period, that give the police greater discretion and somewhat more power. In the United Kingdom, for example, the Prevention of Terrorism Act of 1999 and the Crime and Security Act of 2001 provide the police with enhanced powers to stop and search terrorism suspects. The ability of the police to engage in surveillance of suspects has typically been expanded as well; it has become easier for them to obtain authorization to tap telephones and warrants to search the premises of suspects, particularly when there are grounds to believe the latter may be planning an attack and developing chemical, biological, or radio-logical weapons. Some countries, e.g. Italy, have criminalized simple membership in a terrorist group. Individuals may be prosecuted not because of what they have done or what they are planning to do but because they belong to an organization identified as engaged in terrorism. In the United States the relevant legislation was first employed against organized crime: the so-called "RICO Act." Individuals can be prosecuted for conspiring with or belonging to an organized gang whose criminal enterprises crossed state lines. In 1984–85 members of a right-wing, racist, and anti-Semitic terrorist group known as the Order or Silent Brotherhood were prosecuted in a federal court in Seattle, charged with violations of the RICO Act because some of their associates had robbed a Brinks Armored Car in California and planned other criminal acts.

In addition to anti-terrorism laws and other measures, demo-cratic governments confronted by serious terrorist threats often create new agencies or reorganize old ones in the effort to meet the challenge. Analysts frequently refer to terrorism as a kind of asymmetrical conflict, one in which powerful states with large bureaucracies and military establishments are challenged by relatively small bands with very limited resources. The terrorist bands, though, have the advantages of the flea at war with the elephant. The flea is agile and quick and can strike when and where it chooses. The elephant is slow and ponderous and often has other things on its mind. How then does the elephant defeat the flea?

The answer is that the elephant needs to pay more attention, to acquire better intelligence about when and where the flea is likely to attack. The pachyderm must also learn to act more quickly, perhaps by locating the flea's habitat and destroying it.

This little parable illustrates the fact that the democracies, and the United States in particular, are adapting to meet the terrorist threat. The Department of Homeland Security has been created to coordinate the activities of previously independent agencies. The FBI is apparently undergoing reform in order to focus more on the terrorist threat and somewhat less on normal criminal activity. New units have been established to detect the presence of chemical and biological agents. New counter-terrorist coordinating bodies have been set up to inhibit the various bureaucracies involved from working at cross-purposes.

International cooperation

Beginning in the early 1970s and continuing for many years thereafter United Nations efforts to fight terrorism on an international basis were limited by two factors. First, attempts by the General Assembly and other UN organs to define terrorism proved unsuccessful. The reasons for this difficulty were not exclusively taxonomic but had to do with politics. A number of member states belonging to the Soviet and Third World blocs were reluctant to agree upon a connotative definition because they were actively engaged in helping terrorist groups and did not wish their behavior to receive the international opprobrium likely to follow making "terrorism" a crime under international law, a development likely to follow UN agreement over the meaning of the term. Second, many countries belonging to the Soviet and Third World blocs did not wish anything stipulated that would inhibit national liberation movements, as they defined them, from waging their legitimate struggles against colonialism, racism (usually including Zionism), and imperialism. They believed that if there was "just cause," i.e. the fight against colonialism, racism, and imperialism, then any means employed in its pursuit was justifiable. In fact, despite an extensive record of terrorist violence the PLO was accorded observer status by the UN General Assembly in 1974.

Although the UN member states were, and continue to be (2004), unable to achieve an agreement over the meaning of "terrorism," they were able to draft and in most cases ratify international conventions outlawing various forms of terrorist behavior. Over the 1960s and 1970s UN-sponsored conferences in Tokyo, The Hague, and Montreal agreed upon multinational conventions governing airport safety and the skyjacking of commercial airliners. Another convention was opened for ratification making the kidnapping or killing of "internationally protected persons" (i.e. diplomatic representatives) an international crime. Other conventions were approved governing the unlawful seizure of ships on the high seas, i.e. piracy, and oil platforms. Countries apprehending individuals suspected of committing these crimes were required either to extradite or to prosecute them. Failure to do so made the states involved subject to international economic and political sanctions.

The events of 9/11 had a consciousness-raising effect on virtually all international or transnational organizations. The most significant measure is UN Security Resolution 1373 (September 28, 2001). This measure requires all member states to prevent and suppress the financing of terrorist acts and refrain from providing any form of support to individuals and groups planning terrorist attacks on the territory or citizens of other member states. States are now required to cooperate by, among other things, warning one another of impending terrorist attacks and by preventing their territory from being used by individuals seeking to support such attacks. In addition, Resolution 1373 established a Counter Terrorism Committee (CTC) to monitor the member states' implementation of these provisions. Subsequently in 2001 and 2002 the UN sponsored an International Convention on the Suppression of Terrorism which condemns all "acts, methods and practices of terrorism" and to take practical steps aimed at stopping these "acts, methods and practices."[11]

Following 9/11, NATO, the Organization of American States, the European Union, the Organization for Security and Cooperation in Europe, and other multinational organizations have taken steps to improve cooperation among member states in the struggle against terrorism by, among other things, improved intelligence gathering and information sharing. They have also agreed to harmonize policies and work together to produce a common definition of terrorism in their respective criminal codes.

Conclusion

Our concern in this chapter has been on reactions to terrorist violence. We divided the commentary into three parts. In the first part we examined the impact of terrorism on its immediate victims by reviewing the physical and psychological damage caused by terrorist attacks. We took note especially of terrorism's growing lethality and the enhanced popularity the groups committing exceptionally violent attacks appear to have gained in various parts of the Muslim world. We devoted the second section of this chapter to the complex roles of the mass media in conveying the terrorist drama and noted the serious distortions television coverage imposes on terrorist events. We also noticed the ability of terrorist organizations to produce their own shows thanks to such technologies as the video cassette and the internet. Finally, we sought to summarize the major domestic and international governmental responses to terrorism based on the fundamental distinction between criminal justice and warfare models. We stressed the impact of 9/11 on the intensity and volume of government reactions to the violence.

In the next chapter we conclude the volume by investigating how terrorist campaigns come to an end. Terrorist campaigns are not endless. They do end. In chapter 6 we propose to explain how and why they end.

Further reading

Yonah Alexander (ed.), *Combating Terrorism: Strategies of Ten Countries* (Ann Arbor: University of Michigan Press, 2002).

Jane Boulden and Thomas Weiss (eds.), *Terrorism and the UN Before and After September 11* (Bloomington: Indiana University Press, 2003).

Council on Foreign Relations, *The War on Terror* (New York: W. W. Norton, 2003).

Michael Freeman, *Freedom or Security* (Westport, CT and London: Praeger, 2003).

Brigitte Nacos, *Mass-Mediated Terrorism* (Lanham, MD: Rowman & Littlefield, 2002).

Paul Wilkinson, *Terrorism and the Liberal State* (New York: New York University Press, 1979).

Paul Wilkinson, *Terrorism versus Democracy: The Liberal State Response* (London: Frank Cass, 2001).

6

The end of terrorism

In this final chapter we investigate the end of terrorism and engage in some speculation about its future direction. This sentence is not as contradictory as it may seem at first glance. Terrorism as a tactic employed by disaffected groups of one kind or another seems unlikely to go away. Since terrorism is likely to be with us into the foreseeable future, it makes sense to consider how this type of violence will be used and by whom.

On the other hand, the terrorist violence we observe in the first decade of the twenty-first century in Iraq, Kashmir, Indonesia, and elsewhere is not the same as the terrorism we might have observed during the 1970s or during the first decade of the twentieth century. Today we are dealing with a completely different cast of characters than we were a hundred or even thirty years ago. The individuals, groups, causes, and campaigns have all changed. So much so that we may sensibly review how terrorism has ended in the past. By doing this we might even gain some insight about how terrorism will likely end in the future.

Today many in the West are focused on terrorism emanating from Islamist organizations committed, they tell us, to waging a holy war or jihad against the infidel, specifically Jews and crusaders. There may be truces along the way but their struggle will only end with the re-establishment of the caliphate and eventually the universal triumph of Islam.

Perhaps, but we might contemplate the fact that periods of religious excitement among the world's major monotheistic religions seem to come and go. Christians in North America, for example, have undergone several "Great Awakenings" since the arrival of settlers during the seventeenth century. In the same century many Jews living in Eastern Europe proclaimed the arrival of the Messiah, a man by the name of Shabbetai Zevi (1626–76), and prepared to follow him to the Holy Land, until his conversion to Islam. During the 1880s a Sudanese leader, Muhammad Ahmad, proclaimed himself and was proclaimed by his followers as the *Mahdi*, the one directed by God to restore justice on earth. The Mahdi and his movement managed to inflict a serious military defeat on British forces before the latter managed to subdue him at the end of the decade.[1] Based on the historical record, there is no reason to believe that the present period of Islamist militancy need go on for ever. With this observation in mind, let us identify the ways in which terrorism ends.

The individual

If someone intentionally carries out or helps to commit acts of terrorism it seems fair to call that person a "terrorist." But this need not be a role a person plays for the duration of their lifetime. No one is born a terrorist nor, since most terrorists are young people, should we necessarily expect anyone to perform the role endlessly. Gerry Adams, leader of Sinn Fein in Northern Ireland, was known as the "Big Lad" on the streets of Belfast when he was a key figure in the IRA's violent campaign to end British rule. In Mandatory Palestine, Menachem Begin became the leader of the IRGUN, an organization that employed terrorist tactics to get the British to relinquish control over the territory. Later he became prime minister of Israel and still later a Nobel Peace Prize winner. How then do people stop being terrorists?

The first answer that comes to mind is that they stop when the authorities make them stop. Terrorists are apprehended and put in prison. Terrorists are killed by the authorities in the course of an operation or when the authorities learn of their whereabouts. Terrorists also stop when they kill themselves while carrying out suicide attacks against enemy targets. Such outcomes, however, are not the end of the story.

Another way in which individuals cease being terrorists is when the groups to which they belong stop engaging in terrorist violence and turn their attention to other forms of political behavior (see below). There is no reason why a political organization cannot abandon the gun for the ballot given the appropriate circumstances. Even if the organization continues to prefer the former over the latter, individual members may seek to withdraw from it.

For analytical purposes it makes sense to identify this process of withdrawal as "exit." Terrorists exit a organization, stop being terrorists, when the cost of continuing membership exceeds the cost of leaving it. For example, exit may occur when the fear of being captured or killed by the authorities is greater than the fear of punishment by other members, balanced against the likelihood of the group actually achieving its long-term goals. Other factors are likely to be at work as well.

Defection, as a type of exit, takes place when the terrorist retains his or her belief in the aims of the organization but loses confidence in the ability of the organization to achieve them. The use of terrorist violence may come to seem deplorable, pointless, or counter-productive after a certain point. In these instances the defecting individual may seek out other organizations, political parties for example, that seek the same ends as the terrorist one but attempt to pursue them by non-violent means.

Terrorists may become disaffected not only from the organization to which they belong but from the cause itself. In other words, they may lose faith. Not all that long ago Marxism-Leninism was a revolutionary faith in which members of Germany's Red Army Fraction and Italy's Red Brigades believed. But the events of the 1980s caused many of them to feel disaffected from the ideology itself as well as the organizations conducting terrorist attacks in its name. In the case of disaffection, individuals exiting terrorist organizations may withdraw from politics completely, seeking solace in private life or seeking out another faith in which to invest their emotions.

Individuals typically join a terrorist group as the result of personal contacts and social networks. They become drawn into the group by people – e.g. friends, relatives, co-workers – they know who are already inside it. Exit, whether defection or disaffection, often involves the same process, only in reverse. Terrorists may come to know or re-establish contact with individuals outside the organization in whom they place some trust or for whom they feel genuine affection. These outsiders often help devise an exit strategy for the terrorists and so assist them to turn away from the violent life.

The group

As in the case of individual terrorists so too with the groups to which they belong, the most obvious end is one imposed by those authorities with whom they are in conflict. Many terrorist groups end when they suffer *defeat* at the hands of their enemies.[2] This outcome is hardly surprising, since terrorist bands are often small and weak relative to those they challenge. For instance, during the late 1960s and early 1970s the Brazilian military managed to destroy the various left-wing urban guerrilla bands that had waged a terrorist campaign in Rio de Janeiro, Sao Paolo, and other cities. Some years earlier the Venezuelan armed forces had done likewise and some years later Argentina's military (see chapter 5) used exceptionally brutal means to destroy the Montoneros, the Trotskyite People's Revolutionary Army, and the lesser lights of revolutionary insurgency.

Terrorist groups may also come to an end as the result of a *backlash* by their ostensible constituents. In the case of nationalist/ separatist groups the terrorism may become so egregious that it repels most members of the ethnic community on whose behalf the group claims to be acting. In these situations the continued use of terrorism may prove to be self-defeating in the sense that it discredit's the group's aims in the eyes of the very people intended to benefit by their achievement. It also makes recruitment of new members more difficult and enhances the likelihood that members of their constituency, the relevant ethnic group, may be willing to inform the police or the security services about the terrorist group's plans and membership. Governments may accelerate *backlash* if they promote reforms that are likely to win the support of most members of the affected ethnic community.

Backlash may be at work in other circumstances as well. In Italy, after the Red Brigades (BR) murdered a factory worker in Genoa because he had informed on one of the Brigadisti, the labor unions turned out thousands of workers to demonstrate against the BR; a development that gave the terrorist group's leaders some pause. The BR defined itself as the revolutionary vanguard of the Italian working class. Here were thousands of workers protesting against their own vanguard. It could not help give rise to doubt. In a different context, the fact that members of the al Qaeda network in Saudi Arabia have begun to kill fellow Muslims in their campaign to topple the monarchy may, in the long run, weaken its support among the general Saudi population.

In addition to external pressures that promote *defeat* and *backlash*, terrorist groups may crumble as the result of their own internal dynamics. They may suffer *burnout*. Burnout may occur for a variety of reasons. Terrorist organizations often develop an exaggerated sense of their own power and importance, induced in part by the attention lavished upon them by the mass media and in part by the ego baths provided to members by their leaders as a means of sustaining morale. Most terrorists are young and may be impatient. In fact, it is this very impatience that causes some individuals to become terrorists in the first place. When time passes and the group shows few signs of reaching its goals, members may begin to have second thoughts. At first these may cause the group to redouble its efforts and elevate its violence. But what if the group's goals still appear as distant as ever? Some members, increasingly frustrated, may conclude that the group's tactics are insufficiently radical and break away to form their own terrorist organization. Others, worn out by ceaseless struggle with little likelihood of success, may seek a career change by exiting the organization (see above).

Seen from the outside, life inside a terrorist organization often seems exciting. It is this very perception that often leads young people to join; selfless devotion to a transcendent cause, what could be more exciting for the young? The reality, though, is often quite different. Everyday life within a terrorist organization may turn out to be boring and mundane. If enough members of the group become disillusioned by the prosaic quality of their lives as terrorists, the organization itself may become a *burn-out* case, dissolving as the result not of police crackdowns but of collective ennui.

There are also many cases where the organization persists as a collective entity but undergoes a *strategic shift* away from terrorism. The organization, largely intact, may join or rejoin the normal political process, abandoning the gun for the ballot box. In Mandatory Palestine the IRGUN functioned as a terrorist band under Menachem Begin's leadership. Following the establishment of the state of Israel in 1948, virtually the same organization reappeared as the Herut political party, also under Begin's leadership, which contested elections and managed to win seats in the Knesset, the country's parliament.

After their suppression at the hands of the Uruguayan military the Tupamaros resurfaced a decade later as a democratic party whose nominees proceeded to campaign peacefully for seats in parliament. In other cases, as with Sinn Fein in Northern Ireland, the "political wing" of a terrorist group becomes a conventional political party and comes to represent the whole organization in the political arena.

Campaigns

We should make a distinction between the end of a terrorist group and the end of a terrorist campaign. The two are not necessarily identical. The dictionary (*Webster's New Collegiate*) defines a campaign as a "connected series of operations designed to bring about a particular result." In a democratic election campaign, political parties compete with one another to win popular support and the parliamentary seats that go with it. If one of the contestants dissolves or merges with another party, that does not mean the campaign itself has come to an end. In the case of the Israeli/Palestinian conflict, the defeat of one Palestinian group by the Israelis does not mean the end of the terrorist campaign, because there are many other groups prepared to continue the struggle. We may make similar observations about the campaign to end Indian control over Jammu Kashmir in South Asia and the terrorism committed by ETA in the Basque country of Spain. In the latter case we are dealing with a single group, but one that has experienced multiple factional scissions over the years. For example, in the 1980s ETA's political/military faction broke away in order to participate in the peaceful political process. Nevertheless, "military" diehards within ETA have continued to wage a terrorist campaign into the twenty-first century.

For some of those caught up in a wave of terrorism, the process must seem endless; random killings carried out on a daily basis with no clear or obvious end in sight. When will it stop?

Or, will it ever stop? If we examine the historical record, the evidence suggests that terrorist campaigns like individual terrorist groups certainly do come to an end. Virtually all the revolutionary terrorist operations in Western Europe and North America active in the 1970s have ceased. The same is true, by and large, of the violent campaigns aimed at achieving national independence *inter alia* for Puerto Rico, Quebec, South Molucca, Croatia, the South Tyrol, and other areas. Most of the individuals caught up in these campaigns have long since abandoned the bomb and the gun in order to pursue non-violent career paths. Since it seems apparent that terrorist campaigns do come to an end, the question becomes: How does this happen? How do terrorist campaigns end?

A cliché worth repeating here is that terrorism is a "weapon of the weak." In other words, those able to achieve their social and political objectives by some other means will usually seek to do so. Small groups or numerically limited organizations unable to win much voter support at the polls or to inspire the masses to rebellion may contemplate terrorism as a means of winning attention and gaining the appearance rather than the reality of power. Just how weak are groups that rely on terrorism remains to be seen, but clearly one of the principal ways by which their campaigns have been brought to an end is *repression*. The authorities simply overwhelm and destroy the groups challenging their claims to rule. The historical record abounds with such cases. During the late 1960s and throughout much of the 1970s Latin American revolutionaries waged urban guerrilla warfare against governments in Uruguay, Argentina, Brazil, and later Peru. At about the same time left-wing revolutionaries as well as right-wing nationalists mounted terrorist campaigns in Turkey – directed against each other as well as the government in Ankara.[3] Also, the Baathist regime in Damascus faced a terrorist challenge from the Muslim Brothers during the early 1980s.[4] In these cases, once the level of violence passed a certain threshold, a line based on who the targets were (e.g. military officers and members of their families) or the number of casualties inflicted, the military intervened or was deployed by the civilian authorities and the campaigns were quickly brought to a conclusion. The methods employed by the authorities in these episodes were rarely in accordance with Marquis of Queensbury Rules or international human rights standards. But if the objective was the end of a terrorist campaign the application of repressive techniques seemed to work, and to work without all that much difficulty.[5]

If we are willing to contemplate events moving in the opposite direction, terrorist campaigns have also ended as the result of their *escalation*. Those who launch such campaigns frequently believe that their terrorist activities will serve as a spark with which to ignite more widespread forms of insurrectionary violence, a full-scale "people's war." For advocates and observers of guerrilla warfare, terrorism represents the initial "agitation propaganda" or attention-getting phase of a protracted conflict. Once an audience for the insurgents has been formed the time has arrived to begin a new and more widespread phase of the struggle. Michael Crozier, Thomas Thornton, and others who wrote about the terrorist phenomenon at the end of the 1950s and early 1960s described it in precisely these terms.[6]

In practice, some initiatives from this era, the communist insurrection against British rule in Malaya, for example, never went beyond the agitation propaganda phase, whereas in other instances successful guerrilla struggles were waged in the virtual absence of terrorism: the 1959 victory of Fidel Castro and his "bearded ones" in Cuba, for instance. On the other hand the struggle over Vietnam after the departure of the French offers a case of what Crozier, Thornton, and others had in mind. Walter Laqueur is worth quoting at some length here:

This is not to say that the Vietcong behaved like early Christian martyrs. They had already engaged in individual terror on a massive scale in the first phase of the fighting (1949–1954). Systematic assassination of village leaders, local teachers and other "dangerous elements" played a more important role in Vietnam than other Asian guerrilla wars ... Bernard Fall relates that he returned to Vietnam in 1957 after the war had been over for two years and was told by everyone that the situation was fine. He was bothered, however, by the many obituaries in the press of village chiefs who had been killed by "unknown elements" and "bandits." Upon investigation he found these attacks were clustered in certain areas and that there was a purpose behind them.[7]

In practice, it is not inevitable that political violence that escalates from terrorism to more intense forms of conflict should follow the strict choreography outlined above. In Colombia, Peru, and other Latin American venues terrorism and rural guerrilla warfare have been waged simultaneously. If we add deadly ethnic rioting and vendettas to the mix, about the same may be said of the Lebanese Civil War (1975–89). It seems fair to say that in these instances "escalation" really means an intensification of what is already underway: more frequent attacks, more casualties, and a wider territorial spread in their distribution. Roy Licklider, Louis Krieberg, and other scholars report that compromise settlements to such deadly escalated confrontations are relatively rare: one side or the other typically wins an outright victory.[8] Or, if a compromise outcome is achieved, the result requires the participation of an outside power – as in the case of the civil war in Lebanon.

A terrorist campaign may end when the situation in which it is waged is *transformed*. These transformations occur as a result of either the terrorists' exertions or the efforts of other parties to the conflict. In the case of Israel the IRGUN waged what was widely regarded as a terrorist campaign aimed at making the cost of continued British presence in Palestine so great that the British would feel constrained to leave. For a variety of reasons, including the IRGUN's operations, the British withdrew. After the truce agreement that ended Israel's war of independence in 1949, the IRGUN, or at least its principal figures, reappeared as the Herut, a political party that succeeded in electing fourteen deputies to the first Knesset.[9] Similar observations may be made about the end of the apartheid regime in South Africa. After years in which its leaders were either in exile or in prison, the African National Congress (ANC) formed the "Spear of the Nation" to carry out terrorist attacks on symbols of South Africa's white supremacist rule. These violent actions constituted a relatively small part of the ANC's repertoire of anti-apartheid measures and did little to accelerate the end of the system. As the end of apartheid approached, particularly after South African President F. W. de Klerk expressed his willingness to enter negotiations with the ANC, radical right-wing elements within the country's Afrikaner community formed a number of paramilitary bands that waged their own terrorist campaign designed to sabotage the negotiations and preserve the system of racial domination. For instance, "In 1990 ... 52 acts of right-wing terror were committed and more than 91 right-wingers were arrested. Of these attacks the most serious was an episode near Durban in October 1990 in which three members of the AWB [Afrikaner Resistance Movement] and the Orde Boervolk opened fire on a bus, killing seven blacks and wounding 18. It was a retaliatory action for an earlier attack by young black militants who stabbed whites in a Durban shop."[10] When the negotiations between de Klerk and Nelson Mandela brought an end to apartheid and South Africa became a multi-racial democracy, the situation was transformed. After the ANC became the ruling party and Mandela the country's president, the Spear of the Nation disappeared and the right-wing terrorist campaign aimed at blocking racial change subsided.

A similar transformation has taken place recently in Northern Ireland. After more than two decades of the Troubles, a conflict between Republicans and Unionists, or Catholics and Protestants, over the province's continued link to Great Britain, the situation underwent a painfully slow but radical transformation culminating in the 1998 Good Friday agreement. The transformation was slow for a number of reasons, not least the unwillingness of working class Protestant ultras, led by the Rev. Ian Paisley, to countenance any serious concessions to the aspirations of Ulster's Catholic community. On the other side of the religious/political divide, the Provisional IRA, given British military presence or "occupation" of the province, refused to consider any option other than violence for many years.[11] In the aftermath of the 1981 wave of hunger strikes carried out by IRA prisoners the Provisional's leadership underwent a change of heart. Sinn Fein, the IRA's political wing, promoted the by-election candidacy of Bobby Sands, one of the hunger strikers, for the House of Commons. The purpose was to demonstrate the popularity of the cause among Catholic voters. Sands won the seat. This success convinced the leadership that a duel strategy should be pursued, a mix of bombs and ballots. Sinn Fein contested local elections on a regular basis while the IRA continued to carry out terrorist attacks in Northern Ireland and various parts of England.

Over the years it became clearer to IRA decision makers that the "armed struggle" was stagnating and that most citizens of the province were tired of the incessant violence, whose purpose was becoming increasingly obscure. Against this background a new Labour government under Tony Blair came to power in London. The Blair government committed itself to reviving the negotiating process. The Irish government in Dublin expressed similar commitments. The Clinton administration in Washington also sought to play a constructive role in bringing the conflict to a constructive conclusion and sent former Senator

George Mitchell to London to act as the principal negotiator.[12] The result of these interventions was a complex set of discussions, with multiple breakdowns along the way, that resulted in a settlement agreement and the transformation of a violent conflict into a largely peaceful party-political one based on the principle of power sharing.

Terrorist campaigns may be transformed in another way as well. This one does not lead to a peaceful outcome or a happy ending, however. Unlike al Qaeda and its affiliated groups, many terrorist bands have not been the beneficiaries of large contributions from wealthy supporters or sympathetic philanthropists. As a result they have been compelled to finance their own operations. In practice, this has often meant staging bank robberies and other "proletarian expropriations" along with kidnapping wealthy individuals and corporate executives and demanding cash in exchange for their freedom. In addition, we should note that prisons are among the most common places around the world where terrorists are recruited for a cause.[13] Inspirational lectures by inmates already committed to a political goal, accompanied by the selected reading of a terrorist group's basic texts, sometimes transform common criminals into political warriors. As in the case, for example, of the Italian Nuclei of Armed Proletarians during the 1970s, once out of prison the new converts to the political cause participate in the terrorist campaign. The latter frequently involves bank robberies and kidnapping. On occasion the temptations prove to be too strong. The funds stolen or extorted for political purposes are diverted for private ones.

There is a tendency for groups that have embarked on a campaign of terror in pursuit of a nationalist/separatist cause to transform into straightforward criminal enterprises. The Inner Macedonian Revolutionary Organization (IMRO) began its career in the 1890s as a nationalist/separatist group that employed terrorism in order to free its homeland from Turkish control. But by the 1930s IMRO had "developed into a Mafia-type organization, accepting 'contracts' from the highest bidders and engaging, *inter alia*, in the traffic in narcotics."[14] The trajectory of the recently deceased Abu Nidal's Fatah Revolutionary Council bears some resemblance to IMRO's transformation.

Ostensibly revolutionary groups are not immune either. For instance, FARC retains its rhetorical commitment to Columbia's workers and peasants, but its various violent enterprises seem increasingly to be motivated by private pecuniary considerations rather than the possibility of lifting the yoke of oppression from the backs of the proletariat.

At this point it may be more a hope than a reality. But there is at least some evidence that even members of fanatical religiously driven terrorist groups are responsive to material incentives. Charles Glass, an American journalist held hostage in Beirut by members of Hizbollah during the mid 1980s, reports overhearing a conversation among his captors. Instead of discussing the sermons of Sheik Fadallah or the achievements of the Iranian Revolution, they were complaining about how little they were being paid for the hazardous jobs they were assigned by their leaders.[15] If many jihadis, waging a terrorist campaign on behalf of religious principles, are like Glass's guards, in the long run it may be that their endeavors can be transformed into straightforward criminal activity.

The distinguished political scientist and biblical scholar David Rapoport offers us another way of understanding how terrorist campaigns end.[16] In keeping with his interest in biblical perspectives, we might see Rapoport's view as based on the Book of Ecclesiastes, and in particular the passage that reads, "One generation passes away and another generation arises." Rapoport sees terrorist campaigns ending largely as the result of *generational exhaustion*. But as one generation and one set of causes pass away another generation and new causes warranting the use of terrorist violence arise to take their place. "Since the

1880s, four successive, overlapping, major waves of terror have washed over the world, each with its own special character, purposes, and tactics. The first three lasted approximately a generation each; and the fourth, which began in 1979, is still in process. ... Major unexpected political turning points exposing new government vulnerabilities precipitated each wave."[17]

The first wave, according to Rapoport, was brought on by the major economic and social reforms undertaken by the Russian czars in the 1860s and after. One of the effects of these measures was to raise the hopes of many Russians for economic improvements, democracy, and political autonomy beyond what could be realized under the existing order. The result was the People's Will and a succession of terrorist bands committed *inter alia* to the causes of independence of various ethnic minorities from the Russian and, later, Ottoman Empires. The second wave of modern terrorism began in the 1920s, following World War I, crested in the years following World War II, and had ended by the early 1960s. The cause in this case was national self-determination. The cases that come readily to mind are those of Algeria, Palestine, Cyprus, and Aden (Yemen). In each episode a terrorist organization (FLN, IRGUN, EOKA) played a significant role in persuading the colonial power that the time had come to withdraw its control. The third wave, as Rapoport sees it, was caused by the American participation in the Vietnam War beginning in the mid 1960s. The ability of the Viet Cong to wage a long-term and ultimately successful unconventional war against the United States and its allies inspired large numbers of young people, university students especially, in Europe, North and South America, and elsewhere. The causes were anti-imperialism and anti-capitalist revolution. The Red Brigades, the Red Army Fraction, United Japanese Red Army, Revolutionary Road, Direct Action, Popular Front for the Liberation of Palestine, and a long list of other groups carried out terrorist attacks while invoking the ideas of Marx, Lenin, Trotsky, Mao, and other revolutionary thinkers. "Praxis" was the watchword. But the collapse of the communist enterprise on a worldwide basis during the 1980s, and related disenchantments, led to the end of modern terrorism's third wave. The fourth was brought on by the Iranian Revolution of 1979. This wave represents a reaction to secular and globalizing trends in society and has been inspired by religious ideas, Islamist ones especially. We are currently in the midst of this fourth wave of terrorism with no obvious end to it in sight. But if the past of terrorist violence offers us an insight into its future, this wave will likely subside as the generation that made religion its cause ages or fades from the scene. But, in Rapoport's view, a new cause for terrorism will take its place and a fifth wave will likely ensue.

Governments, particularly when they are called upon to cooperate with one another on a long-term basis, have proven to be largely ineffective in bringing these terrorist waves to an end. "Terrorism is deeply rooted in modern culture ... Terrorism's history shows that organizations can be decimated, and useful institutions like un-uniformed police forces can be created. It shows that terrorism can be made less significant but terrorists also can invent new ways to carry out their activities ... In Cyprus, Jewish Palestine, Algeria, and Ireland, the terrorists were never found, even though the long and costly search was over familiar territory."[18] If this is true of the older groups, Rapoport asks, what about al Qaeda's far-flung and complex network?

The final way in which terrorist campaigns appear to end is really a narrower and less ambitious version of Rapoport's inter- pretation. Some terrorist campaigns, typically ones undertaken at the national level, exhibit a *cyclical* pattern. They start, stop, the immediate problems that brought them into being are seemingly resolved, only to flare up again. Campaigns based on ethnic and racial hatreds, including anti-Semitism, seem particularly susceptible to this pattern.

Ehud Sprinzak's ideas concerning the terrorism of radical right-wing organizations aid our understanding of the cyclical character of these campaigns.[19] To begin, Sprinzak distinguishes between terrorist groups committed to "universal" principles versus those whose outlook is "particularistic." In the former instances the groups' grievances are typically directed against the prevailing economic and political order. Only when monopoly capitalism and its lackeys are brought down will workers and peasants be liberated and an era of true socialism be inaugurated. The intent of the Italian Red Brigades to attack the "heart of the state" illustrates this outlook. The resentments of particularistic or far right-wing groups, on the other hand, are not directed at the state or the prevailing economic or political order *per se*. When these groups initiate their operations they may look upon the state, especially its police and military establishments, with considerable favor. Instead, neo-Fascist, neo-Nazi, and other racial or religious supremacist groups direct their hostility towards "enemy" segments of the national population. The enemy group is defined not by what it does or allegedly does but by who it is. For the particularistic terrorist organization, e.g. the Ku Klux Klan, the enemy population is inherently illegitimate. The campaign of violence is typically triggered when members of the radical rightist group perceive a shift in the status of the affected group; when they perceive its members to be over-reaching and seeking to attain a status to which, given their innate inferiority or wickedness, they are not entitled. "For instance, the Jews may suddenly appear too strong, the Blacks too influential, the Arabs too treacherous and the Communists too close to a Marxist revolution."[20]

At this point terrorist violence will be directed indiscriminately at any person belonging to the despised group who has the misfortune to be in the wrong place at the wrong time. Members of the far right group typically expect their actions to be looked upon with either indifference or sympathy by the government, as in the case of local law enforcement agencies in the American south during the civil rights struggles of the late 1950s and early 1960s. When the government does not react in this way the attitude of the far right group towards it will also undergo a change. If the government comes to be seen as supportive of the concerns and interests of the "enemy" segment in the population, it will then itself likely become a target for terrorist attack. The facts that far right groups and publicists in the United States have come to believe the country is under the control of ZOG (the Zionist Occupation Government) and that right-wing activists in Germany and abroad now refer to the Federal Republic as dominated by "Top Jews" indicates that these governments support the enemy and, consequently, are appropriate targets for terrorist attacks.

When attacks by particularistic terrorist groups occur with some frequency the governments involved are usually able to bring these overt campaigns of racial, ethnic, or religious violence to an end without too much difficulty. Seemingly, the problem is solved. But frequently the problem simply reflects the long-standing and deeply rooted values of a national culture. In other words, the underlying factors that led to the initiation of a terrorist campaign remain after the violence has subsided. In writing about terrorism in the United States, Christopher Hewitt reminds us that apparently small percentages in a population may translate into a significant pool of supporters from which potential terrorists may be drawn. Hewitt points out that according to a Gallup Poll only four percent of Americans had a favorable view of the Ku Klux Klan. The latter was widely disliked by the overwhelming majority of the American public. But in 1965 four percent of the population translated into 1,300,000 sympathizers, a pool large enough from which to recruit militants willing to mount a terrorist campaign.[21] The same logic obtains elsewhere.

The particularistic campaign of terror may be brought to end, and the underlying hatred that brought it into existence may go through a latency period (to borrow from Freud), but a new wave of violence may recur. Predicting when it will seems exceptionally difficult. But if we follow Sprinzak's logic any effort that may be perceived as changing the social status assigned to the target racial, religious, or ethnic group has the potential to offend members of a far right or racist organization and thereby to ignite a new terrorist campaign.

A concluding observation

In reviewing the historical record we have been able to identify five ways in which terrorist campaigns end, either on a permanent basis or at least for some time: repression, escalation, transformation, generational exhaustion, and the downside of a cyclical pattern. What causes some campaigns to end in one way rather than another? The answer to this question involves a complex calculation. All we are able to do at this point is identify a few of the variables likely to be involved in it.

First, the role of the authorities compels our consideration. The particular end of a terrorist campaign will likely depend in part on the "opportunity structure" in which the groups waging it operate.[22] If the government targeted by the campaign provides the right set of opportunities for the opponents, it may create the circumstances for an escalation of the campaign into a full-scale insurrection or guerrilla war. It cures the cold by inadvertently causing pneumonia. If the authorities wish to transform the campaign into non-violent forms, they need to provide an appropriate set of incentives and disincentives to bring about this endgame. The use of repressive state apparatus is a frequent outcome. The cost of its use, at least for the democracies, may be the suspension or weakening of constitutional protections of personal freedom. If the chips are down and the terrorist campaign is sufficiently serious, the cost may be worth paying.

Second, the internal dynamics of the terrorist groups need to be considered. Cynthia Irvin reminds us that such groups are likely to be composed of three types of members: ideologues, radicals, and politicos. "Ideologues are often the 'hard' men and women of militant ... organizations. They are drawn to action more than to political discussion, and they are committed to the belief that organizational goals can only be obtained as a result of the armed struggle of their military wings."[23] Radicals share the ideologues' commitment to action but sense that violence alone will not be sufficient to achieve the group's goals. They support the use of terrorist violence as a tactic not as a means of personal catharsis. "Politicos are far more willing than their more 'militarist' counterparts to acknowledge that acts of political violence, particularly those in which noncombatants are killed, invite both crippling repression and the organization's alienation from all but its core base."[24]

The end of many terrorist campaigns is often the outcome of a dialogue within the group conducting it, between members playing one or other of the three roles Irvin mentions. This dialogue, however, does not occur in a vacuum. It is conditioned by the changing situation in which the group finds itself. The situation itself reflects the responses to the group's operations by the authorities as well as the constituency whose cause the group claims to champion.

The future

Terrorism as a tactic seems unlikely to disappear in the foreseeable future. It may, however, mutate in unpredictable ways. At present most observers are especially concerned about terrorists adopting chemical, biological, radiological, and even full-scale nuclear weapons. These concerns are based on a mix of contemporary reality and doomsday speculations. The reality is that a number of terrorist groups have already employed chemical weapons, e.g. Japan's Aum Sinrikyo's use of Sarin gas in the Tokyo subway system in 1995, and conducted experiments with biological agents. At least one al Qaeda agent has been arrested for attempting to develop a "dirty bomb," a conventional explosive that would spread radioactive material throughout an American city. The barriers to terrorist organizations employing such weapons with the potential to kill thousands are technical rather than moral. According to many analysts the obstacles have to do with the techniques for dispersing the poisonous chemicals, bacteria, and toxins rather than their cultivation or manufacture. The internet abounds with websites where information about the latter is readily available. The effective dispersal of the poisons is more of a challenge, particularly in an environment in which government security organizations and international agencies are increasingly alert. In the case of radioactive material, sabotaging nuclear power plants seems an attractive possibility though one obstructed by the same kind of vigilance.

What about the prospects of terrorists' building or acquiring full-scale nuclear weapons? Such "rogue states" as North Korea have built them, along with the means to deliver them to distant targets. Why not terrorist groups? What if Pakistan, already a nuclear power, were to fall under the control of an Islamist regime along the lines of the Taliban in neighboring Afghanistan? Would such a fundamentalist regime provide nuclear weapons to al Qaeda or some other as yet unformed Islamist organization in the future? To the extent that a fundamentalist government in Islamabad would be responsive to the full array of international pressures brought to bear against it, the chances are that it would not make such weapons available. But given a set of extraordinary circumstances the odds might be reduced and the answer more qualified.

Terrorism is widely believed to be a new kind of warfare and the al Qaeda network and al-Qaeda-inspired groups its foremost exponents. This may be the case, but it is still worth interrogating the historical record on this matter. These Islamist organizations claim to be following the path of the Prophet and his immediate successors, the rightly guided caliphs who spread the faith throughout the Middle East and beyond. The territorial triumphs of the Prophet Mohammad and his successors were almost always achieved by force of arms, by the use of the conventional armies of that era and region of the world. Contemporary Islamist terrorism, i.e. suicide bombers sent to kill large numbers of bystanders in public places, is not the same thing. Others may decide on the religious equivalence, but simply from a tactical perspective they are certainly not the same. Setting off bombs endlessly in various places around the world from New York to Riyadh to Bali may indeed sow terror or elicit other emotions but is not in itself a meaningful military tactic. To achieve military success or a serious revolutionary challenge to government, even a Middle Eastern one, requires al Qaeda and its affiliates and likely descendants to transform what are largely theatrical successes into more conventional forms of combat. In other words, to win, the Islamist terrorists would have to *escalate*. To this point we are still confronted by a vastly expanded version of nineteenth-century "propaganda by deed." Efforts by Islamist groups such as those active in Algeria and Egypt during the 1990s to achieve such an escalation have so far failed. And so this new type of warfare bears a striking resemblance to old forms of terrorism.

Further reading

Christopher Hewitt, *Consequences of Political Violence* (Aldershot, England: Dartmouth, 1993).

Roger Mac Ginty and John Darby, *Guns and Government: The Management of the Northern Ireland Peace Process* (London: Palgrave, 2002).

Paul Pillar, *Terrorism and U.S. Foreign Policy*, rev. edn. (Washington: Brookings, 2003).

Sidney Tarrow, *Power in Movement* (New York: Cambridge University Press, 1994).

Max Taylor and John Horgan (ed.), *The Future of Terrorism* (London: Frank Cass, 2000).

Leonard Weinberg and Ami Pedahzur, *Political Parties and Terrorist Groups* (London and New York: Routledge, 2003).

Significant terrorist incidents, 1961–2007

The following is a partial list of significant terrorist events between 1961 and 2003, compiled by the US State Department. This chronology is intended to be more illustrative than comprehensive.

1961–82

First US aircraft hijacked, May 1, 1961. Puerto-Rican-born Antuilo Ramierez Ortiz forced at gunpoint a National Airlines plane to fly to Havana, Cuba, where he was given asylum.

Ambassador to Brazil kidnapped, September 3, 1969. US ambassador to Brazil Charles Burke Elbrick was kidnapped by the Marxist revolutionary group MR-8.

Attack on Munich Airport, February 10, 1970. Three terrorists attacked El Al passengers in a bus at Munich Airport with guns and grenades. One passenger was killed and eleven were injured. All three terrorists were captured by airport police. The Action Organization for the Liberation of Palestine and the Popular Democratic Front for the Liberation of Palestine claimed responsibility for the attack.

US Agency for International Development (AID) adviser kidnapped, July 31, 1970. In Montevideo, Uruguay, the Tupamaros terrorist group kidnapped AID Police adviser Dan Mitrione; his body was found on August 10.

"Bloody Friday," July 21, 1972. An Irish Republican Army (IRA) bomb attack killed eleven people and injured 130 in Belfast, Northern Ireland. Ten days later three IRA car bomb attacks in the village of Claudy left six dead.

Munich Olympic massacre, September 5, 1972. Eight Palestinian "Black September" terrorists seized eleven Israeli athletes in the Olympic Village in Munich, West Germany. In a bungled rescue attempt by West German authorities, nine of the hostages and five terrorists were killed.

Ambassador to Sudan assassinated, March 2, 1973. US ambassador to Sudan Cleo A. Noel and other diplomats were assassinated at the Saudi Arabian embassy in Khartoum by members of Black September.

Attack and hijacking at Rome Airport, December 17, 1973. Five terrorists pulled weapons from their luggage in the terminal lounge at Rome Airport, killing two people. They then attacked a Pan American Boeing 707 bound for Beirut and Tehran, destroying it with incendiary grenades and killing twenty-nine people, including four senior Moroccan officials and fourteen American employees of the Arab-American Oil Company (ARAMCO). They next herded five Italian hostages into a Lufthansa airliner and killed an Italian customs agent as he tried to escape, after which they forced the pilot to fly to Beirut. After Lebanese authorities refused to let the plane land, it landed in Athens, where the terrorists demanded the release of two Arab terrorists. In order to make Greek authorities comply with their demands, the terrorists killed a hostage and threw his body on to the tarmac. The plane then flew to Damascus, where it stopped for two hours to obtain fuel and food. It next flew to Kuwait, where the terrorists released their hostages in return for passage to an unknown destination. The Palestine Liberation Organization (PLO) disavowed the attack, and no group claimed responsibility for it.

Domestic terrorism, January 27–29, 1975. Puerto Rican nationalists bombed a Wall Street bar, killing four and injuring sixty; two days later the Weather Underground claimed responsibility for an explosion in a bathroom at the US Department of State in Washington.

Entebbe hostage crisis, June 27, 1976. Members of the Baader–Meinhof Group and the Popular Front for the Liberation of Palestine (PFLP) seized an Air France airliner and its 258 passengers. They forced the plane to land in Uganda. On July 3 Israeli commandos successfully rescued the passengers.

Assassination of former Chilean diplomat, September 21, 1976. Exiled Chilean foreign minister Orlando Letelier was killed by a car bomb in Washington.

Kidnapping of Italian prime minister, March 16, 1978. Premier Aldo Moro was seized by the Red Brigade and assassinated fifty-five days later.

Iran hostage crisis, November 4, 1979. After President Carter agreed to admit the Shah of Iran into the US, Iranian radicals seized the US embassy in Tehran and took sixty-six American diplomats hostage. Thirteen hostages were soon released, but the remaining fifty-three were held until their release on January 20, 1981.

Grand Mosque seizure, November 20, 1979. Two hundred Islamic terrorists seized the Grand Mosque in Mecca, Saudi Arabia, taking hundreds of pilgrims hostage. Saudi and French security forces retook the shrine after an intense battle in which some 250 people were killed and six hundred wounded.

Bologna railroad station, August, 1980. Neo-Fascists set off a bomb in the waiting room which killed eighty-five vacation-bound passengers and injured another two hundred, some very seriously.

US installation bombing, August 31, 1981. The Red Army exploded a bomb at the US Air Force Base at Ramstein, West Germany.

Assassination of Egyptian President, October 6, 1981. Soldiers who were secretly members of the Takfir Wal-Hajira sect attacked and killed Egyptian President Anwar Sadat during a troop review.

Murder of missionaries, December 4, 1981. Three American nuns and one lay missionary were found murdered outside San Salvador, El Salvador. They were killed by members of the National Guard; the killers are currently in prison.

Assassination of Lebanese prime minister, September 14, 1982. Premier Bashir Gemayel was assassinated by a car bomb parked outside his party's Beirut headquarters.

1983

Bombing of US embassy in Beirut, April 18, 1983. Sixty-three people, including the CIA's Middle East director, were killed and 120 were injured in a four-hundred-pound suicide truck-bomb attack on the US embassy in Beirut, Lebanon. Islamic Jihad claimed responsibility.

Naval officer assassinated in El Salvador, May 25, 1983. A US Navy officer was assassinated by the Farabundo Marti National Liberation Front.

North Korean hit squad, October 9, 1983. North Korean agents blew up a delegation from South Korea in Rangoon, Burma, killing twenty-one people and injuring forty-eight.

Bombing of Marine Barracks, Beirut, October 23, 1983. Simultaneous suicide truck-bomb attacks were made on American and French compounds in Beirut. A twelve-thousand-pound bomb destroyed the US compound, killing 242 Americans, and fifty-eight French troops were killed when a four-hundred-pound device destroyed a French base. Islamic Jihad claimed responsibility.

Naval officer assassinated in Greece, November 15, 1983. A US Navy officer was shot by the November 17 terrorist group in Athens, Greece, while his car was stopped at a traffic light.

1984

Kidnapping of embassy official, March 16, 1984. Islamic Jihad kidnapped and later murdered Political Officer William Buckley in Beirut. Other US citizens not connected to the US government were seized over the succeeding two-year period.

Restaurant bombing in Spain, April 12, 1984. Eighteen US servicemen were killed and eighty-three people were injured in a bomb attack on a restaurant near a US Air Force base in Torrejon, Spain.

Temple seizure, June 5, 1984. Sikh terrorists seized the Golden Temple in Amritsar, India. One hundred people died when Indian security forces retook the Sikh holy shrine.

Assassination of Indian Prime Minister, October 31, 1984. Premier Indira Gandhi was shot to death by members of her security force.

1985

Trans-World Airlines (TWA) hijacking, June 14, 1985. A TWA Airlines flight was hijacked *en route* to Rome from Athens by two Lebanese Hizbollah terrorists and forced to fly to Beirut. The eight crew members and 145 passengers were held for seventeen days, during which one American hostage, a US Navy sailor, was murdered. After being flown twice to Algiers, the aircraft was returned to Beirut after Israel released 435 Lebanese and Palestinian prisoners.

Attack on a restaurant in El Salvador, June 19, 1985. Members of the Farabundo Marti National Liberation Front (FMLN) fired on a restaurant in the Zona Rosa district of San Salvador, killing four Marine Security Guards assigned to the US embassy and nine Salvadorean civilians.

Air India bombing, June 23, 1985. A bomb destroyed an Air India Boeing 747 over the Atlantic, killing all 329 people aboard. Both Sikh and Kashmiri terrorists were blamed for the attack. Two cargo handlers were killed at Tokyo Airport, Japan, when another Sikh bomb exploded in an Air Canada aircraft *en route* to India.

***Achille Lauro* hijacking, October 7, 1985.** Four Palestinian Liberation Front terrorists seized the Italian cruise liner in the eastern Mediterranean Sea, taking more than seven hundred hostages. One US passenger was murdered before the Egyptian government offered the terrorists safe haven in return for the hostages' freedom.

Airport attacks in Rome and Vienna, December 27, 1985. Four gunmen belonging to the Abu Nidal Organization attacked the El Al and TWA ticket counters at Rome's Leonardo da Vinci Airport with grenades and automatic rifles. Thirteen people were killed and seventy-five were wounded before Italian police and Israeli security guards killed three of the gunmen and captured the fourth. Three more Abu Nidal gunmen attacked the El Al ticket counter at Vienna's Schwechat Airport, killing three people and wounding thirty. Austrian police killed one of the gunmen and captured the others.

1986

Aircraft bombing in Greece, March 30, 1986. A Palestinian splinter group detonated a bomb as TWA Flight 840 approached Athens Airport, killing four US citizens.

Berlin discothèque bombing, April 5, 1986. Two US soldiers were killed and seventy-nine American servicemen were injured in a Libyan bomb attack on a nightclub in West Berlin. In retaliation US military jets bombed targets in and around Tripoli and Benghazi.

Kimpo Airport bombing, September 14, 1986. North Korean agents detonated an explosive device at Seoul's Kimpo Airport, killing five people and injuring twenty-nine others.

1987

Downing of airliner, November 29, 1987. North Korean agents planted a bomb aboard Korean Airlines Flight 858, which subsequently crashed into the Indian Ocean.

Servicemen's bar attack, December 26, 1987. Catalan separatists bombed a Barcelona bar frequented by US servicemen, resulting in the death of one US citizen.

1988

Kidnapping of William Higgins, February 17, 1988. US Marine Corps Lieutenant Colonel W. Higgins was kidnapped and murdered by the Iranian-backed Hizbollah group while serving with the United Nations Truce Supervisory Organization (UNTSO) in southern Lebanon.

Naples USO Attack, April 14, 1988. The Organization of Jihad Brigades exploded a car bomb outside a USO club in Naples, Italy, killing one US sailor.

Attack on US diplomat in Greece, June 28, 1988. The defense attaché of the US embassy in Greece was killed when a car bomb was detonated outside his home in Athens.

Pan American 103 bombing, December 21, 1988. Pan American Airlines Flight 103 was blown up over Lockerbie, Scotland, by a bomb believed to have been placed on the aircraft by Libyan terrorists in Frankfurt, West Germany. All 259 people on board were killed.

1989

Bombing of UTA Flight 772, September 19, 1989. A bomb explosion destroyed UTA Flight 772 over the Sahara in southern Niger during a flight from Brazzaville to Paris. All 170 persons aboard were killed. Six Libyans were later found guilty *in absentia* and sentenced to life imprisonment.

Assassination of Deutsche Bank Chairman, November 30, 1989. The Red Army Fraction assassinated Deutsche Bank Chairman Alfred Herrhausen in Frankfurt.

1990

US embassy bombed in Peru, January 15, 1990. The Tupac Amaru Revolutionary Movement bombed the US embassy in Lima, Peru.

US soldiers assassinated in the Philippines, May 13, 1990. The New People's Army (NPA) killed two US Air Force personnel near Clark Air Force Base in the Philippines.

1991

Assassination of former Indian prime minister, May 21, 1991. A female member of the Liberation Tigers of Tamil

Eelam (LTTE) killed herself, former prime minister Rajiv Gandhi, and sixteen others by detonating an explosive vest after presenting a garland of flowers to the former prime minister during an election rally in the Indian state of Tamil Nadu.

1992

Bombing of the Israeli embassy in Argentina, March 17, 1992. Hizbollah claimed responsibility for a blast that leveled the Israeli Embassy in Buenos Aires, Argentina, causing the deaths of twenty-nine and wounding 242.

1993

World Trade Center Bombing, February 26, 1993. The World Trade Center in New York City was badly damaged when a car bomb planted by Islamic terrorists exploded in an underground garage. The bomb left six people dead and one thousand injured. The men carrying out the attack were followers of Umar Abd al-Rahman, an Egyptian cleric who preached in the New York City area.

Attempted assassination of George Bush by Iraqi agents, April 14, 1993. The Iraqi intelligence service attempted to assassinate former US president George Bush during a visit to Kuwait. In retaliation the US launched a cruise missile attack two months later on the Iraqi capital Baghdad.

1994

Hebron massacre, February 25, 1994. Jewish right-wing extremist and US citizen Baruch Goldstein machine-gunned Muslim worshippers at a mosque in the West Bank town of Hebron, killing twenty-nine and wounding about 150.

Air France hijacking, December 24, 1994. Members of the

Armed Islamic Group seized an Air France flight to Algeria. The four terrorists were killed during a rescue effort.

1995

Attack on US diplomats in Pakistan, March 8, 1995. Two unidentified gunmen killed two US diplomats and wounded a third in Karachi, Pakistan.

Tokyo subway station attack, March 20, 1995. Twelve people were killed and 5,700 were injured in a sarin nerve gas attack on a crowded subway station in the center of Tokyo, Japan. A similar attack occurred nearly simultaneously in the Yokohama subway system. The Aum Shinrikyo cult was blamed for the attacks.

Bombing of the Federal Building in Oklahoma City, April 19, 1995. Right-wing extremists Timothy McVeigh and Terry Nichols destroyed the Federal Building in Oklahoma City with a massive truck bomb that killed 166 and injured hundreds more in what was up to then the largest terrorist attack on American soil.

Kashmiri hostage-taking, July 4, 1995. In India six foreigners, including two US citizens, were taken hostage by Al-Faran, a Kashmiri separatist group. One non-US hostage was later found beheaded.

Jerusalem bus attack, August 21, 1995. Hamas claimed responsibility for the detonation of a bomb that killed six and injured over one hundred people, including several US citizens.

Saudi military installation attack, November 13, 1995. The Islamic Movement of Change planted a bomb in a Riyadh military compound which killed one US citizen, several foreign national employees of the US government, and over forty others.

Egyptian embassy attack, November 19, 1995. A suicide bomber drove a vehicle into the Egyptian embassy compound in Islamabad, Pakistan, killing at least sixteen and injuring sixty people. Three militant Islamic groups claimed responsibility.

1996

Tamil Tigers attack, January 31, 1996. Members of the LTTE rammed an explosives-laden truck into the Central Bank in the heart of downtown Colombo, Sri Lanka, killing ninety civilians and injuring more than fourteen hundred others, including two US citizens.

IRA bombing, February 9, 1996. An IRA bomb detonated in London, killing two people and wounding more than one hundred others, including two US citizens.

Hamas bus attack, February 26, 1996. In Jerusalem, a suicide bomber blew up a bus, killing twenty-six people, including three US citizens, and injuring some eighty people, including three other US citizens.

Dizengoff Center bombing, March 4, 1996. Hamas and the Palestine Islamic Jihad (PIJ) both claimed responsibility for a bombing outside Tel Aviv's largest shopping mall which killed twenty people and injured seventy-five others, including two US citizens.

West Bank attack, May 13, 1996. Arab gunmen opened fire on a bus and a group of Yeshiva students near the Bet El settlement, killing a dual US Israeli citizen and wounding three Israelis. No one claimed responsibility for the attack, but Hamas was suspected.

Zekharya attack, June 9, 1996. Unidentified gunmen opened fire on a car near Zekharya, Israel killing a dual US Israeli citizen and an Israeli. The PFLP was suspected.

Manchester truck bombing, June 15, 1996. An IRA truck bomb detonated at a Manchester shopping center, wounding 206 people, including two German tourists, and caused extensive property damage.

Khobar Towers bombing, June 25, 1996. A fuel truck carrying a bomb exploded outside the US military's Khobar Towers housing facility in Dhahran, Saudi Arabia, killing nineteen US military personnel and wounding 515 people, including 240 US personnel. Several groups claimed responsibility for the attack.

Basque Fatherland and Liberty (ETA) bombing, July 20, 1996. A bomb exploded at Tarragona International Airport in Reus, Spain, wounding thirty-five people, including British and Irish tourists. ETA was suspected.

Bombing of Archbishop of Oran, August 1, 1996. A bomb exploded at the home of the French Archbishop of Oran, killing him and his chauffeur. The attack occurred after the Archbishop's meeting with the French Foreign Minister. The Algerian Armed Islamic Group (GIA) is suspected.

Patriotic Union of Kurdistan (PUK) kidnapping, September 13, 1996. In Iraq, PUK militants kidnapped four French workers for Pharmaciens Sans Frontières, a Canadian United Nations High Commissioner for Refugees (UNHCR) official, and two Iraqis.

Paris subway explosion, December 3, 1996. A bomb exploded aboard a Paris subway train as it arrived at Port Royal station, killing two French nationals, a Moroccan, and a Canadian, and injuring eighty-six people. Among those injured were one US citizen and a Canadian. No one claimed responsibility for the attack, but Algerian extremists are suspected.

Tupac Amaru seizure of diplomats, December 17, 1996. Twenty-three members of the Tupac Amaru Revolutionary Movement (MRTA) took several hundred people hostage at a party given at the Japanese ambassador's residence in Lima. Among the hostages were several US officials, foreign ambassadors and other diplomats, Peruvian government officials, and Japanese businessmen. The group demanded the release of all MRTA members in prison and safe passage for them and the hostage takers. The terrorists released most of the hostages in December but held eighty-one Peruvians and Japanese citizens for several months.

1997

Egyptian letter bombs, January 2–13, 1997. A series of letter bombs with Alexandria, Egypt postmarks were discovered at *Al-Hayat* newspaper bureaus in Washington, New York City, London, and Riyadh. Three similar devices, also postmarked in Egypt, were found at a prison facility in Leavenworth, Kansas. Bomb disposal experts defused all the devices, but one detonated at the *Al-Hayat* office in London, injuring two security guards and causing minor damage.

Tajik hostage abductions, February 4–17, 1997. Near Komsomolabad, Tajikistan, a paramilitary group led by Bakhrom Sodirov abducted four United Nations (UN) military observers. The victims included two Swiss, one Austrian, one Ukrainian, and their Tajik interpreter. The kidnappers demanded safe passage for their supporters from Afghanistan to Tajikistan. In four separate incidents occurring between Dushanbe and Garm, Bakhrom Sodirov and his group kidnapped two International Committee for the Red Cross members, four Russian journalists and their Tajik driver, four UNHCR members, and the Tajik Security Minister, Saidamir Zukhurov.

Israeli shopping mall bombing, September 4, 1997. Three suicide bombers of Hamas detonated bombs in the Ben Yehuda shopping mall in Jerusalem, killing eight people, including the bombers, and wounding nearly two hundred others. A dual US Israeli citizen was among the dead, and seven US citizens were wounded.

Murder of US businessmen in Pakistan, November 12, 1997. Two unidentified gunmen shot to death four US auditors from Union Texas Petroleum Corporation and their Pakistani driver after they drove away from the Sheraton Hotel in Karachi. The Islami Inqilabi Council, or Islamic Revolutionary Council, claimed responsibility in a call to the US consulate in Karachi. In a letter to Pakistani newspapers, the Aimal Khufia Action Committee also claimed responsibility.

Tourist killings in Egypt, November 17, 1997. Al-Gama'at al-Islamiyya (IG) gunmen shot and killed fifty-eight tourists and four Egyptians and wounded twenty-six others at the Hatshepsut Temple in the Valley of the Kings near Luxor. Thirty-four Swiss, eight Japanese, five Germans, four Britons, one French, one Colombian, a dual Bulgarian/British citizen, and four unidentified persons were among the dead. Twelve Swiss, two Japanese, two Germans, one French, and nine Egyptians were among the wounded.

1998

Revolutionary Armed Forces of Columbia (FARC) abduction, March 21–23, 1998. FARC rebels kidnapped a US citizen in Sabaneta, Colombia. FARC members also killed three people, wounded fourteen, and kidnapped at least twenty-seven others at a roadblock near Bogotá. Four US citizens and one Italian were among those kidnapped, as well as the acting president of the National Electoral Council (CNE) and his wife.

Somali hostage-takings, April 15, 1998. Somali militiamen abducted nine Red Cross and Red Crescent workers at an airstrip north of Mogadishu. The hostages included a US citizen, a German, a Belgian, a French, a Norwegian, two Swiss, and one Somali. The gunmen were members of a subclan loyal to Ali Mahdi Mohammed, who controlled the northern section of the capital.

IRA bombing, Banbridge, August 1, 1998. A five-hundred-pound car bomb planted by the Real IRA exploded outside a shoe store in Banbridge, North Ireland, injuring thirty-five people and damaging at least two hundred homes.

US embassy bombings in East Africa, August 7, 1998. A bomb exploded at the rear entrance of the US embassy in Nairobi, Kenya, killing twelve US citizens, thirty-two foreign service nationals (FSNs), and 247 Kenyan citizens. Approximately five thousand Kenyans, six US citizens, and thirteen FSNs were injured. The US embassy building sustained extensive structural damage. Almost simultaneously, a bomb detonated outside the US embassy in Dar-es-Salaam, Tanzania, killing seven FSNs and three Tanzanian citizens and injuring one US citizen and seventy-six Tanzanians. The explosion caused major structural damage to the US embassy facility. The US government held Osama bin Laden responsible.

IRA bombing, Omagh, August 15, 1998. A five-hundred-pound car bomb planted by the Real IRA exploded outside a local courthouse in the central shopping district of Omagh, Northern Ireland, killing twenty-nine people and injuring over 330.

Colombian pipeline bombing, October 18, 1998. A National Liberation Army (ELN) planted bomb exploded on the Ocensa pipeline in Antioquia Department, killing approximately seventy-one people and injuring at least one hundred others. The pipeline is jointly owned by the Colombia State Oil

Company Ecopetrol and a consortium including US, French, British, and Canadian companies.

1999

Ugandan rebel attack, February 14, 1999. A pipe bomb exploded inside a bar, killing five people and injuring thirty-five others. One Ethiopian and four Ugandan nationals died in the blast, and one US citizen working for the US Agency for International Development (USAID), two Swiss nationals, one Pakistani, one Ethiopian, and twenty-seven Ugandans were injured. Ugandan authorities blamed the attack on the Allied Democratic Forces (ADF).

Greek embassy seizure, February 16, 1999. Kurdish protesters stormed and occupied the Greek embassy in Vienna, taking the Greek ambassador and six other persons hostage. Several hours later the protesters released the hostages and left the embassy. The attack followed the Turkish government's announcement of the successful capture of the Kurdistan Workers' Party (PKK) leader Abdullah Ocalan. Kurds also occupied Kenyan, Israeli, and other Greek diplomatic facilities in France, The Netherlands, Switzerland, Britain, and Germany over the following days.

FARC kidnappings, February 25, 1999. FARC kidnapped three US citizens working for the Hawaii-based Pacific Cultural Conservancy International. On March 4 the bodies of the three victims were found in Venezuela.

Hutu abductions, March 1, 1999. One hundred and fifty armed Hutu rebels attacked three tourist camps in Uganda, killed four Ugandans, and abducted three US citizens, six Britons, three New Zealanders, two Danes, one Australian, and one Canadian. Two of the US citizens and six of the other hostages were subsequently killed by their abductors.

Indian Airlines Airbus hijacking, December 24, 1999. Five militants hijacked a flight bound from Katmandu, Nepal, to New Delhi, India, carrying 189 people. The plane and its passengers were released unharmed on December 31.

2000

Car bombing in Spain, January 27, 2000. Police officials reported that unidentified individuals set fire to a Citroen car dealership in Iturreta, Spain, causing extensive damage to the building and destroying twelve vehicles. The attack bore the hallmark of ETA.

Revolutionary United Front (RUF) attacks on UN mission personnel, May 1, 2000. On May 1 in Makeni, Sierra Leone, RUF militants kidnapped at least twenty members of the United Nations Assistance Mission in Sierra Leone (UNAMSIL) and surrounded and opened fire on a UNAMSIL facility, according to press reports. The militants killed five UN soldiers in the attack. RUF militants kidnapped three hundred UNAMSIL peace-keepers throughout the country, according to press reports. On May 15 in Foya, Liberia, the kidnappers released 139 hostages. On May 28 on the Liberia and Sierra Leone border, armed militants released unharmed the last of the UN peace-keepers. In Freetown, Sierra Leone, according to press reports, armed militants ambushed two military vehicles carrying four journalists. A Spaniard and one US citizen were killed in a May 25 car bombing in Freetown for which the RUF was probably responsible. Suspected RUF rebels also kidnapped twenty-one Indian UN peace-keepers in Freetown on June 6. Additional attacks by RUF on foreign personnel followed.

Diplomatic assassination in Greece, June 8, 2000. In Athens two unidentified gunmen killed British defense attaché Stephen Saunders in an ambush. November 17 claimed responsibility.

Kidnappings in Kyrgyzstan, August 12, 2000. In the Kara-Su Valley, the Islamic Movement of Uzbekistan took four US citizens hostage. The Americans escaped on August 12.

Church bombing in Tajikistan, October 1, 2000. Unidentified militants detonated two bombs in a Christian church in Dushanbe, Tajikistan, killing seven people and injuring seventy others. The church was founded by a Korean-born US citizen, and most of those killed and wounded were Korean. No one claimed responsibility.

Attack on USS *Cole*, October 12, 2000. In Aden, Yemen, a small dingy carrying explosives rammed the destroyer USS *Cole*, killing seventeen sailors and injuring thirty-nine others. Supporters of Osama bin Laden were suspected.

Manila bombing, December 30, 2000. A bomb exploded in a plaza across the street from the US embassy in Manila, injuring nine people. The Moro Islamic Liberation Front was likely responsible.

2001

Srinagar airport attack and assassination attempt, January 17, 2001. In India, six members of the Lashkar-e-Tayyba militant group were killed when they attempted to seize a local airport. Members of Hizbul Mujaheddin fired two rifle grenades at Farooq Abdullah, Chief Minister for Jammu and Kashmir. Two people were wounded in the unsuccessful assassination attempt.

British Broadcasting Corporation (BBC) studios bombing, March 4, 2001. A car bomb exploded at midnight outside the BBC's main production studios in London. One person was injured. British authorities suspected the Real IRA had planted the bomb.

Suicide bombing in Israel, March 4, 2001. A suicide bomb attack in Netanya, Israel killed three people and wounded sixty-five. Hamas later claimed responsibility.

ETA bombing, March 9, 2001. Two policemen were killed by the explosion of a car bomb in Hernani, Spain.

Airliner hijacking in Istanbul, March 15, 2001. Three Chechens hijacked a Russian airliner during a flight from Istanbul to Moscow and forced it to fly to Medina, Saudi Arabia. The plane carried 162 passengers and a crew of twelve. After a twenty-two-hour siege, during which more than forty passengers were released, Saudi security forces stormed the plane, killing a hijacker, a passenger, and a flight attendant.

Bus-stop bombing, April 22, 2001. A member of Hamas detonated a bomb he was carrying near a bus stop in Kfar Siva, Israel, killing one person and injuring sixty.

Philippines hostage incident, May 27, 2001. Muslim Abu Sayyaf guerrillas seized thirteen tourists and three staff members at a resort on Palawan Island and took their captives to Basilan Island. The captives included three US citizens: Guellermo Sobero and missionaries Martin and Gracia Burnham. Philippine troops fought a series of battles with the guerrillas between June 1 and June 3, during which nine hostages escaped and two were found dead. The guerrillas took additional hostages when they seized the hospital in the town of Lamitan. On June 12, Abu Sayyaf spokesman Abu Sabaya claimed that Sobero had been killed and beheaded; his body was found in October. The Burnhams remained in captivity until June 2002.

Tel-Aviv nightclub bombing, June 1, 2001. Hamas claimed responsibility for the suicide bombing of a popular Israeli nightclub which caused over 140 casualties.

Hamas restaurant bombing, August 9, 2001. A Hamas-planted bomb detonated in a Jerusalem pizza restaurant, killing fifteen people and wounding more than ninety. The Israeli response included occupation of Orient House, the PLO's political head-quarters in East Jerusalem.

Suicide bombing in Israel, September 9, 2001. The first suicide bombing carried out by an Israeli Arab killed three people in Nahariya. Hamas claimed responsibility.

Death of the "Lion of the Panjshir," September 9, 2001. Two suicide bombers fatally wounded Ahmed Shah Massoud, a leader of Afghanistan's Northern Alliance, which had opposed both the Soviet occupation and the post-Soviet Taliban government. The bombers posed as journalists and were apparently linked to al Qaeda. The Northern Alliance did not confirm Massoud's death until September 15.

Terrorist attacks on US homeland, September 11, 2001. Two hijacked airliners crashed into the twin towers of the World Trade Center. Soon thereafter the Pentagon was struck by a third hijacked plane. A fourth hijacked plane, suspected to be bound for a high-profile target in Washington, crashed into a field in southern Pennsylvania. The attacks killed 3025 US citizens and other nationals. President Bush and cabinet officials indicated that Osama bin Laden was the prime suspect and that they considered the United States in a state of war with international terrorism. In the aftermath of the attacks the United States formed the Global Coalition Against Terrorism.

Attack on the Jammu and Kashmir legislature, October 1, 2001. After a suicide car bomber forced the gate of the state legislature in Srinagar, two gunmen entered the building and held off police for seven hours before being killed. Forty people died in the incident. Jaish-e-Muhammad claimed responsibility.

Anthrax attacks, October–November 2001. On October 7 the US Centers for Disease Control and Prevention (CDC) reported that investigators had detected evidence that the deadly anthrax bacterium was present in the building where a Florida man who had died of anthrax on October 5 had worked. Discovery of a second anthrax case triggered a major investigation by the Federal Bureau of Investigation (FBI). The two anthrax cases were the first to appear in the United States in twenty-five years. Anthrax subsequently appeared in mail received by television networks in New York and by the offices in Washington of Senate Majority Leader Tom Daschle and other members of Congress. Attorney General John Ashcroft said in a briefing on October 16, "When people send anthrax through the mail to hurt people and invoke terror, it's a terrorist act."

Assassination of an Israeli cabinet minister, October 17, 2001. A Palestinian gunman assassinated Israeli Minister of Tourism Rehavam Zeevi in the Jerusalem hotel where he was staying. The PFLP claimed to have avenged the death of PFLP leader Mustafa Zubari.

Attack on a church in Pakistan, October 28, 2001. Six masked gunmen shot up a church in Bahawalpur, Pakistan, killing fifteen Pakistani Christians. No group claimed responsibility, although various militant Muslim groups were suspected.

Suicide bombings in Jerusalem, December 1, 2001. Two suicide bombers attacked a Jerusalem shopping mall, killing ten people and wounding 170.

Suicide bombing in Haifa, December 2, 2001. A suicide bomb attack aboard a bus in Haifa, Israel, killed fifteen people and wounded forty. Hamas claimed responsibility for both this attack and those on December 1 to avenge the death of a Hamas member at the hands of Israeli forces a week earlier.

Attack on the Indian Parliament, December 13, 2001.
Five gunmen attacked the Indian Parliament in New Delhi
shortly after it had adjourned. Before security forces killed them,
the attackers killed six security personnel and a gardener. Indian
officials blamed Lashkar-e-Tayyiba and demanded that Pakistan
crack down on it and other Muslim separatist groups in Kashmir.

2002

Ambush on the West Bank, January 15, 2002. Palestinian
militants fired on a vehicle in Beit Sahur, killing one passenger
and wounding the other. The dead passenger had US and
Israeli citizenship. The al Aqsa Martyrs' Brigades claimed
responsibility.

Shooting incident in Israel, January 17, 2002. A Palestinian
gunman killed six people and wounded twenty-five in Hadera,
Israel, before being killed by Israeli police. The al Aqsa Martyrs'
Brigades claimed responsibility as revenge for Israel's killing of a
leading member of the group.

Drive-by shooting at a US consulate, January 22, 2002.
Armed militants on motorcycles fired on the US consulate in
Calcutta, India, killing five Indian security personnel and
wounding thirteen others. The Harakat ul-Jihad-I-Islami and
the Asif Raza Commandos claimed responsibility. Indian police
later killed two suspects, one of whom confessed to belonging to
Lashkar-e-Tayyiba as he died.

Bomb explosion in Kashmir, January 22, 2002. A bomb
exploded in a crowded retail district in Jammu, Kashmir, killing
one person and injuring nine. No group claimed responsibility.

Kidnapping of Daniel Pearl, January 23, 2002. Armed
militants kidnapped *Wall Street Journal* reporter Daniel Pearl in
Karachi. Pakistani authorities received a videotape on February

20 depicting Pearl's murder. His grave was found near Karachi on May 16. Pakistani authorities arrested four suspects. Ringleader Ahmad Omar Saeed Sheikh claimed to have organized Pearl's kidnapping to protest Pakistan's subservience to the United States, and had belonged to Jaish-e-Muhammad, an Islamic separatist group in Kashmir. All four suspects were convicted on July 15. Saeed Sheikh was sentenced to death, the others to life imprisonment.

Suicide bombing in Jerusalem, January 27, 2002. A suicide bomb attack in Jerusalem killed one other person and wounded one hundred. The incident was the first suicide bombing performed by a Palestinian woman.

Suicide bombing in the West Bank, February 16, 2002. A suicide bombing in an outdoor food court in Karmei Shomron killed four people and wounded twenty-seven. Two of the dead and two of the wounded were US citizens. The PFLP claimed responsibility.

Suicide bombing in the West Bank, March 7, 2002. A suicide bombing in a supermarket in the settlement of Ariel wounded ten people, one of whom was a US citizen. The PFLP claimed responsibility.

Suicide bombing in Jerusalem, March 9, 2002. A suicide bombing in a Jerusalem restaurant killed eleven people and wounded fifty-two, one of whom was a US citizen. The al Aqsa Martyrs' Brigades claimed responsibility.

Grenade attack on a church in Pakistan, March 17, 2002. Militants threw grenades into the Protestant International Church in Islamabad, Pakistan, during a service attended by diplomatic and local personnel. Five people, two of them US citizens, were killed and forty-six were wounded. The dead Americans were State Department employee Barbara Green and her daughter Kristen Wormsley. Thirteen US citizens were among the wounded. The Lashkar-e-Tayyiba group was suspected.

Car bomb explosion in Peru, March 20, 2002. A car bomb exploded at a shopping center near the US embassy in Lima. Nine people were killed and thirty-two wounded. The dead included two police officers and a teenager. Peruvian authorities suspected either the Shining Path rebels or the Tupac Amaru Revolutionary Movement. The attack occurred three days before President George W. Bush visited Peru.

Suicide bombing in Jerusalem, March 21, 2002. A suicide bombing in Jerusalem killed three people and wounded eighty-six more, including two US citizens. The PIJ claimed responsibility.

Suicide bombing in Israel, March 27, 2002. A suicide bombing in a noted restaurant in Netanya, Israel killed twenty-two people and wounded 140. One of the dead was a US citizen. Hamas claimed responsibility.

Temple bombing in Kashmir, March 30, 2002. A bomb explosion at a Hindu temple in Jammu, Kashmir killed ten people. The Islamic Front claimed responsibility.

Suicide bombing in the West Bank, March 31, 2002. A suicide bombing near an ambulance station in Efrat wounded four people, including a US citizen. The al Aqsa Martyrs' Brigades claimed responsibility.

Armed attack on Kashmir, April 10, 2002. Armed militants attacked a residence in Gando, Kashmir, killing five people and wounding four. No group claimed responsibility.

Synagogue bombing in Tunisia, April 11, 2002. A suicide bomber detonated a truck loaded with propane gas outside a historic synagogue in Djerba, Tunisia. The sixteen dead included eleven Germans, one French citizen, and three Tunisians. Twenty-six German tourists were injured. The Islamic Army for the Liberation of the Holy Sites claimed responsibility.

Suicide bombing in Jerusalem, April 12, 2002. A female suicide bomber killed six people in Jerusalem and wounded ninety others. The al Aqsa Martyrs' Brigades claimed responsibility.

Car bombing in Pakistan, May 8, 2002. A car bomb exploded near a Pakistani Navy shuttle bus in Karachi, killing twelve people and wounding nineteen. Eleven of the dead and eleven of the wounded were French nationals. Al Qaeda was suspected of the attack.

Parade bombing in Russia, May 9, 2002. A remotely controlled bomb exploded near a May Day parade in Kaspiisk, Dagestan, killing forty-two people and wounding 150. Fourteen of the dead and fifty of the wounded were soldiers. Islamists linked to al Qaeda were suspected.

Attack on a bus in India, May 14, 2002. Militants fired on a passenger bus in Kaluchak, Jammu, killing seven people. They then entered a military housing complex and killed three soldiers and seven military dependents before they were killed. The al Mansooran and Jamiat ul-Mujahedin claimed responsibility.

Bomb attacks in Kashmir, May 17, 2002. A bomb explosion near a civil secretariat area in Srinagar, Kashmir wounded six people. In Jammu a bomb exploded at a fire services headquarters, killing two and wounding sixteen. No group claimed responsibility for either attack.

Hostage rescue attempt in the Philippines, June 7, 2002. Philippine Army troops attacked Abu Sayyaf terrorists on

Mindanao Island in an attempt to rescue US citizen Martin Burnham and his wife Gracia, who had been kidnapped more than a year ago. Burnham was killed but his wife, though wounded, was freed. A Filipino hostage was killed, as were four of the guerrillas. Seven soldiers were wounded.

Car bombing in Pakistan, June 14, 2002. A car bomb exploded near the US consulate and the Marriott Hotel in Karachi. Eleven people were killed and fifty-one were wounded, including one US and one Japanese citizen. Al Qaeda and al Qanin were suspected.

Suicide bombing in Jerusalem, June 19, 2002. A suicide bombing at a bus stop in Jerusalem killed six people and wounded forty-three, including two US citizens. The al Aqsa Martyrs' Brigades claimed responsibility.

Suicide bombing in Tel Aviv, July 17, 2002. Two suicide bombers attacked the old bus station in Tel Aviv, Israel, killing five people and wounding thirty-eight. The dead included one Romanian and two Chinese; another Romanian was wounded. Islamic Jihad claimed responsibility.

Bombing at the Hebrew University, July 31, 2002. A bomb hidden in a bag in the Frank Sinatra International Student Center of Jerusalem's Hebrew University killed nine people and wounded eighty-seven. The dead included five US citizens and four Israelis. The wounded included four US citizens, two Japanese, and three South Koreans. Hamas claimed responsibility.

Suicide bombing in Israel, August 4, 2002. A suicide bomb attack on a bus in Safed, Israel killed nine people and wounded fifty. Two of the dead were Philippine citizens; many of the wounded were soldiers returning from leave. Hamas claimed responsibility.

Attack on a school in Pakistan, August 5, 2002. Gunmen attacked a Christian school attended by children of missionaries from around the world. Six people (two security guards, a cook, a carpenter, a receptionist, and a private citizen) were killed and a Philippine citizen was wounded. A group called al Intigami al Pakistani claimed responsibility.

Attack on pilgrims in Kashmir, August 6, 2002. Armed militants attacked a group of Hindu pilgrims with guns and grenades in Pahalgam, Kashmir. Nine people were killed and thirty-two were wounded. Lashkar-e-Tayyiba claimed responsibility.

Assassination in Kashmir, September 11, 2002. Gunmen killed Kashmir's Law Minister Mushtaq Ahmed Lone and six security guards in Tikipora. Lashkar-e-Tayyiga, Jamiat ul-Mujahedin, and Hizb ul-Mujahedin all claimed responsibility. Other militants attacked the residence of the Minister of Tourism with grenades, injuring four people. No group claimed responsibility.

Ambush on the West Bank, September 18, 2002. Gunmen ambushed a vehicle on a road near Yahad, killing an Israeli and wounding a Romanian worker. The al Aqsa Martyrs' Brigades claimed responsibility.

Suicide bomb attack in Israel, September 19, 2002. A suicide bomb attack on a bus in Tel Aviv killed six people and wounded fifty-two. One of the dead was a British subject. Hamas claimed responsibility.

Attack on a French tanker, October 6, 2002. An explosive-laden boat rammed the French oil tanker *Limburg*, which was anchored about five miles off al Dhabbah, Yemen. One person was killed and four were wounded. Al Qaeda was suspected.

Car bomb explosion in Bali, October 12, 2002. A car bomb exploded outside the Sari Club Discotheque in Denpasar, Bali, killing 202 people and wounding three hundred more. Most of the casualties, including eighty-eight of the dead, were Australian tourists. Seven Americans were among the dead. Al Qaeda claimed responsibility. Two suspects were later arrested and convicted. Iman Samudra, who had trained in Afghanistan with al Qaeda and was suspected of belonging to Jemaah Islamiya, was sentenced to death on September 10, 2003.

Chechen rebels seize a Moscow theater, October 23–26, 2002. Fifty Chechen rebels led by Movsar Barayev seized the Palace of Culture Theater in Moscow, Russia, to demand an end to the war in Chechnya. They seized more than eight hundred hostages from thirteen countries and threatened to blow up the theater. During a three-day siege they killed a Russian policeman and five Russian hostages. On October 26, Russian Special Forces pumped an anesthetic gas through the ventilation system and then stormed the theater. All of the rebels were killed, but ninety-four hostages (including one American) also died, many from the effects of the gas. A group led by Chechen warlord Shamil Basayev claimed responsibility.

Assassination of a US AID Official, October 28, 2002. Gunmen in Amman assassinated Laurence Foley, executive officer of the US AID mission in Jordan. The Honest People of Jordan claimed responsibility.

Suicide bombing in Jerusalem, November 21, 2002. A suicide bomb attack on a bus on Mexico Street in Jerusalem killed eleven people and wounded fifty more. One of the dead was a Romanian. Hamas claimed responsibility.

Attack on temples in Kashmir, November 24, 2002. Armed militants attacked the Reghunath and Shiv temples in

Jammu, killing thirteen people and wounding fifty. The Lashkare-e-Tayyiba claimed responsibility.

Attacks on Israeli tourists in Kenya, November 28, 2002. A three-person suicide car bomb attack on the Paradise Hotel in Mombasa, Kenya killed fifteen people and wounded forty. Three of the dead and eighteen of the wounded were Israeli tourists; the others were Kenyans. Near Mombasa's airport, two SA-7 shoulder-fired missiles were fired as an Arkia Airlines Boeing 757 took off carrying 261 passengers back to Israel. Both missiles missed. Al Qaeda, the Government of Universal Palestine in Exile, and the Army of Palestine claimed responsibility for both attacks. Al Ittihad al Islami was also suspected of involvement.

Attack on a bus in the Philippines, December 26, 2002. Armed militants ambushed a bus carrying Filipino workers employed by the Canadian Toronto Ventures, Inc. Pacific mining company in Zamboanga del Norte. Thirteen people were killed and ten wounded. Philippine authorities suspected the Moro Islamic Liberation Front (MILF), which had been extorting money from Toronto Ventures. The Catholic charity Caritas-Philippines said that Toronto Ventures had harassed tribesmen who opposed mining on their ancestral lands.

Bombing of a government building in Chechnya, December 27, 2002. A suicide bomb attack involving two explosive-laden trucks destroyed the offices of the pro-Russian Chechen government in Grozny. The attack killed over eighty people and wounded 210. According to a Chechen website run by the Kavkaz Center, Chechen warlord Shamil Basayev claimed responsibility.

2003

Suicide bombings in Tel Aviv, January 5, 2003. Two suicide bomb attacks killed twenty-two and wounded at least one hundred people in Tel Aviv. Six of the victims were foreign workers. The al Aqsa Martyrs' Brigades claimed responsibility.

Nightclub bombing in Colombia, February 7, 2003. A car bomb exploded outside a nightclub in Bogotà, killing thirty-two people and wounding 160. No group claimed responsibility, but Colombian officials suspected the FARC of committing the worst terrorist attack in the country in a decade.

Assassination of a Kurdish leader, February 8, 2003. Members of Ansar al Islam assassinated Kurdish legislator Shawkat Haji Mushir and captured two other Kurdish officials in Qamash Tapa in northern Iraq.

Suicide bombing in Haifa, March 5, 2003. A suicide bombing aboard a bus in Haifa, Israel killed fifteen people and wounded at least forty. One of the dead had US as well as Israeli citizenship. The bomber's affiliation was not known.

Suicide bombing in Netanya, March 30, 2003. A suicide bombing in a cafe in Netanya, Israel wounded thirty-eight people. Only the bomber was killed. Islamic Jihad claimed responsibility and called the attack a "gift" to the people of Iraq.

Unsuccessful hostage rescue attempt in Colombia, May 5, 2003. The FARC killed ten hostages when Colombian special forces tried to rescue them from a jungle hideout near Urrao, in Colombia's Antioquia State. The dead included Governor Guillermo Gavira and former defense minister Gilberto Echeverri Mejia, who had been kidnapped in April 2002.

Truck bomb attacks in Saudi Arabia, May 12, 2003. Suicide bombers attacked three residential compounds for foreign workers in Riyadh. The thirty-four dead included nine attackers, seven other Saudis, nine US citizens, and one citizen each from the United Kingdom, Ireland, and the Philippines.

Another American died on June 1. It was the first major attack on US targets in Saudi Arabia since the end of the war in Iraq. Saudi authorities arrested eleven al Qaeda suspects on May 28.

Truck bombing in Chechnya, May 12, 2003. A truck bomb explosion demolished a government compound in Znamenskoye, Chechnya, killing fifty-four people. Russian authorities blamed followers of a Saudi-born Islamist named Abu Walid. President Vladimir Putin said he suspected that there was an al Qaeda connection.

Attempted assassination in Chechnya, May 12, 2003. Two female suicide bombers attacked Chechen administrator Mufti Akhmed Kadyrov during a religious festival in Iliskhan Yurt. Kadyrov escaped injury, but fourteen other people were killed and forty-three were wounded. Chechen rebel leader Shamil Basayev claimed responsibility.

Suicide bomb attacks in Morocco, May 16, 2003. A team of twelve suicide bombers attacked five targets in Casablanca, Morocco, killing forty-three people and wounding one hundred. The targets were a Spanish restaurant, a Jewish community, a Jewish cemetery, a hotel, and the Belgian consulate. The Moroccan government blamed the Islamist al Assirat al Moustaquim (the Righteous Path), but foreign commentators suspected an al Qaeda connection.

Suicide bomb attack in Jerusalem, May 18, 2003. A suicide bomb attack on a bus in Jerusalem's French Hill district killed seven people and wounded twenty. The bomber was disguised as a religious Jew. Hamas claimed responsibility.

Suicide bombing in Afula, May 19, 2003. A suicide bomb attack by a female Palestinian student killed three people and wounded fifty-two at a shopping mall in Afula, Israel. Both Islamic Jihad and the al Aqsa Martyrs' Brigades claimed responsibility.

Suicide bombing in Jerusalem, June 11, 2003. A suicide bombing aboard a bus in Jerusalem killed sixteen people and wounded at least seventy, one of whom died later. Hamas claimed responsibility, calling it revenge for an Israeli helicopter attack on Hamas leader Abdelaziz al-Rantisi in Gaza City the day before.

Truck bombing in North Ossetia, August 1, 2003. A suicide truck bomb attack destroyed a Russian military hospital in Mozdok, North Ossetia and killed fifty people. Russian authorities attributed the attack to followers of Chechen rebel leader Shamil Basayev.

Hotel bombing in Indonesia, August 5, 2003. A car bomb exploded outside the Marriott Hotel in Jakarta, Indonesia, killing ten people and wounding 150. One of the dead was a Dutch citizen. The wounded included an American, a Canadian, an Australian, and two Chinese. Indonesian authorities suspected Jemaah Islamiah, which had carried out the October 12, 2002 bombing in Bali.

Bombing of the Jordanian embassy in Baghdad, August 7, 2003. A car bomb exploded outside the Jordanian embassy in Baghdad, killing nineteen people and wounding sixty-five. Most of the victims were apparently Iraqis, including five police officers. No group claimed responsibility.

Suicide bombings in Israel and the West Bank, August 12, 2003. The first suicide bombings since the June 29 Israeli–Palestinian truce took place. The first, in a supermarket at Rosh Haayin, Israel, killed one person and wounded fourteen. The second, at a bus stop near the Ariel settlement in the West Bank, killed one person and wounded three. The al Aqsa Martyrs' Brigades claimed responsibility for the first; Hamas claimed responsibility for the second.

Bombing of the UN headquarters in Baghdad, August 19, 2003. A truck loaded with surplus Iraqi ordnance exploded outside the United Nations headquarters in Baghdad's Canal Hotel. A hospital across the street was also heavily damaged. The twenty-three dead included UN Special Representative Sergio Viera de Mello. More than one hundred people were wounded. It was not clear whether the bomber was a Baath Party loyalist or a foreign Islamic militant. An al Qaeda branch called the Brigades of the Martyr Abu Hafz al Masri later claimed responsibility.

Suicide bombing in Jerusalem, August 19, 2003. A suicide bombing aboard a bus in Jerusalem killed twenty people and injured at least one hundred, one of whom died later. Five of the dead were American citizens. Hamas and Islamic Jihad claimed responsibility, although Hamas leader al-Rantisi said that his organization remained committed to the truce while reserving the right to respond to Israeli military actions.

Car bomb kills Shiite leader in Najaf, August 29, 2003. A car bomb explosion outside the shrine of the Imam Ali in Najaf, Iraq killed at least eighty-one people and wounded at least 140. The dead included the Ayatollah Mohammed Bakir al Hakim, one of four leading Shiite clerics in Iraq. Al Hakim had been the leader of the Supreme Council for the Islamic Revolution in Iraq (SCIRI) since its establishment in 1982, and SCIRI had recently agreed to work with the US-sponsored Iraqi Governing Council. It was not known whether the perpetrators were Baath Party loyalists, rival Shiites, or foreign Islamists.

Suicide bombings in Israel, September 9, 2003. Two suicide bombings took place in Israel. The first, at a bus stop near the Tsrifin army base southeast of Tel Aviv, killed seven soldiers and wounded fourteen soldiers and a civilian. The second, at a café in Jerusalem's German Colony neighborhood, killed six people and wounded forty. Hamas did not claim responsibility until the next day, although a spokesman called the first attack "a response to Israeli aggression."

Assassination of an Iraqi Governing Council member, September 20, 2003. Gunmen shot and seriously wounded Akila Hashimi, one of three female members of the Iraqi Governing Council, near her home in Baghdad. She died on September 25.

A second attack on the UN headquarters in Baghdad, September 22, 2003. A suicide car bomb attack on the UN Headquarters in Baghdad killed a security guard and wounded nineteen other people.

Suicide bombing in Israel, October 4, 2003. A Palestinian woman made a suicide bomb attack on a restaurant in Haifa, killing nineteen people and wounding at least fifty-five. Islamic Jihad claimed responsibility for the attack. The next day, Israel bombed a terrorist training camp in Syria.

Attacks in Iraq, October 9, 2003. Gunmen assassinated a Spanish military attaché in Baghdad. A suicide car bomb attack on an Iraqi police station killed eight people and wounded forty.

Car bombings in Baghdad, October 12, 2003. Two suicide car bombs exploded outside the Baghdad Hotel, which housed US officials. Six people were killed and thirty-two wounded. Iraqi and US security personnel apparently stopped the cars from reaching the hotel.

Bomb attack on US diplomats in the Gaza Strip, October 15, 2003. A remote-controlled bomb exploded under a car in a US diplomatic convoy passing through the northern Gaza Strip. Three security guards, all employees of DynCorp, were killed. A fourth was wounded. The diplomats were on their way to interview Palestinian candidates for Fulbright scholarships to study in the United States. Palestinian President Arafat and Prime Minister Qurei condemned the attack, and the major Palestinian militant groups denied responsibility. The next day, Palestinian security forces arrested several suspects, some of whom belonged to the Popular Resistance Committees.

Rocket attack on the al Rashid Hotel in Baghdad, October 26, 2003. Iraqis using an improvised rocket launcher bombarded the al Rashid Hotel in Baghdad, killing one US Army officer and wounding seventeen people. The wounded included four US military personnel and seven American civilians. Deputy Secretary of Defense Paul D. Wolfowitz, who was staying at the hotel, was not injured. After visiting the wounded, he said, "They're not going to scare us away; we're not giving up on this job."

Assassination of a deputy mayor in Baghdad, October 26, 2003. Two gunmen believed to be Baath Party loyalists assassinated Faris Abdul Razaq al Assam, one of three deputy mayors of Baghdad. US officials did not announce al Assam's death until October 28.

Wave of car bombings in Baghdad, October 27, 2003. A series of suicide car bombings in Baghdad killed at least thirty-five people and wounded at least 230. Four attacks were directed at Iraqi police stations, the fifth and most destructive was directed at the International Committee of the Red Cross headquarters, where at least twelve people were killed. A sixth attack failed when a car bomb failed to explode and the bomber was wounded and captured by Iraqi police. US and Iraqi officials suspected that foreign terrorists were involved; the unsuccessful bomber said he was a Syrian national and carried a Syrian passport. After a meeting with Administrator L. Paul Bremer, President Bush said, "The more successful we are on the ground, the more these killers will react."

Suicide bombing in Riyadh, November 8, 2003. In Riyadh a suicide car bombing took place in the Muhaya residential compound, which was occupied mainly by nationals of other Arab countries. Seventeen people were killed and 122 were wounded. The latter included four Americans. The next day, Deputy Secretary of State Armitage said al Qaeda was probably responsible.

Truck bombing in Nasiriyah, November 12, 2003. A suicide truck bomb destroyed the headquarters of the Italian military police in Nasiriyah, Iraq, killing eighteen Italians and eleven Iraqis and wounding at least one hundred people.

Synagogue bombings in Istanbul, November 15, 2003. Two suicide truck bombs exploded outside the Neve Shalom and Beth Israel synagogues in Istanbul, killing twenty-five people and wounding at least three hundred more. The initial claim of responsibility came from a Turkish militant group, the Great Eastern Islamic Raiders' Front, but Turkish authorities suspected an al Qaeda connection. The next day, the London-based newspaper *al-Quds al-Arabi* received an email in which an al Qaeda branch called the Brigades of the Martyr Abu Hafz al-Masri claimed responsibility for the Istanbul synagogue bombings.

Grenade attacks in Bogotà, November 15, 2003. Grenade attacks on two bars frequented by Americans in Bogotà killed one person and wounded seventy-two, including four Americans. Colombian authorities suspected FARC. The US embassy suspected that the attacks had targeted Americans and warned against visiting commercial centers and places of entertainment.

More suicide truck bombings in Istanbul, November 20, 2003. Two more suicide truck bombings devastated the British HSBC Bank and the British consulate general in Istanbul, killing twenty-seven people and wounding at least 450. The dead included Consul General Roger Short. US, British, and Turkish officials suspected that al Qaeda had struck again. The US consulate in Istanbul was closed, and the embassy in Ankara advised American citizens in Istanbul to stay home.

Car bombing in Kirkuk, November 20, 2003. A suicide car bombing in Kirkuk killed five people. The target appeared to be the headquarters of the PUK. PUK officials suspected the Ansar al Islam group, which was said to have sheltered fugitive Taliban and al Qaeda members after the US campaign in Afghanistan.

Attacks on other Coalition personnel in Iraq, November 29–30, 2003. Iraqi insurgents stepped up attacks on nationals of other members of the Coalition. On November 29 an ambush in Mahmudiyah, Iraq killed seven out of a party of eight Spanish intelligence officers. Iraqi insurgents also killed two Japanese diplomats near Tikrit. On November 30 another ambush near Tikrit killed two South Korean electrical workers and wounded two more. A Colombian employee of Kellogg Brown & Root was killed and two were wounded in an ambush near Balad.

Train bombing in southern Russia, December 5, 2003. A suicide bomb attack killed forty-two persons and wounded 150 aboard a Russian commuter train in the south Russian town of Yessentuki. Russian officials suspected Chechen rebels; President Putin said the attack was meant to disrupt legislative elections. Chechen rebel leader Aslan Maskhadov denied any involvement.

Suicide bombing in Moscow, December 9, 2003. A female suicide bomber killed five other people and wounded fourteen outside Moscow's National Hotel. She was said to be looking for the State Duma.

Suicide car bombings in Iraq, December 15, 2003. Two days after the capture of Saddam Hussein, there were two suicide car bomb attacks on Iraqi police stations. One at Husainiyah killed eight people and wounded twenty. The other, at Ameriyah, wounded seven Iraqi police. Guards repelled a second vehicle.

Office bombing in Baghdad, December 19, 2003. A bomb destroyed the Baghdad office of the Supreme Council of the Islamic Revolution in Iraq, killing a woman and wounding at least seven other people.

Suicide car bombing in Irbil, December 24, 2003. A suicide car bomb attack on the Kurdish Interior Ministry in Irbil, Iraq killed five people and wounded 101.

Attempted assassination in Rawalpindi, December 25, 2003. Two suicide truck bombers killed fourteen people as President Musharraf's motorcade passed through Rawalpindi, Pakistan. An earlier attempt on December 14 caused no casualties. Pakistani officials suspected Afghan and Kashmiri militants. On January 6, 2004, Pakistani authorities announced the arrest of six suspects who were said to be members of Jaish-e-Muhammad.

Suicide bombing in Israel, December 25, 2003. A Palestinian suicide bomber killed four people at a bus stop near Petah Tikva, Israel. The Popular Front for the Liberation of Palestine claimed responsibility for the attack in retaliation for Israeli military operations in Nablus that had begun two days earlier.

Restaurant bombing in Baghdad, December 31, 2003. A car bomb explosion outside Baghdad's Nabil Restaurant killed eight people and wounded thirty-five. The wounded included three *Los Angeles Times* reporters and three local employees.

2004

Suicide bombing in Israel, January 29, 2004. A suicide bomber on a bus in Arlozorov, Jerusalem, killed eleven people and wounded fifty. Both the al–Aqsa Martyrs' Brigades and Hamas claimed responsibility.

Suicide bombing in Kurdistan, February 1, 2004. Coordinated attacks on the offices of the Kurdistan Democratic Party and the Patriotic Union of Kurdistan in Irbil killed seventy and wounded more than two hundred people who had gathered to celebrate the Edi al–Adha festival. Among the dead were high ranking officials in the regional government, including the deputy prime minister, the minister of agriculture, the governor of Irbil and the chief of police. Al Qaeda and Ansar al-Islam were suspected.

Attack on the Moscow metro, February 6, 2004. Thirty-nine people were killed and one hundred and twenty-nine others wounded in an attack on the Moscow metro. Chechen separatists were suspected, although their leader Aslan Maskhadov denied responsibility.

Truck bombing in Iraq, February 10, 2004. A truckload of explosives was detonated outside a police station in Iskandariyah, a small town outside Baghdad, killing fifty-three people. Al Qaeda were suspected.

Suicide bombing in Iraq, February 11, 2004. An explosives-laden car was driven into an army recruitment centre in Baghdad, killing forty-seven people and wounding fifty. Ansar al-Islam were suspected.

Boat attack in the Philippines, February 27, 2004. One hundred and sixteen people were killed when a fire broke out on board Superferry 14, which had earlier left the port at

Manila. The fire was found to have been caused by an explosive device. The group Abu Sayyaf claimed responsibility.

Ashura attacks in Iraq, March 2, 2004. In a series of attacks at major Shiite shrines in Baghdad and Karbala, at least one hundred and forty-five people were killed and hundreds of others wounded as they gathered to commemorate the religious festival Ashura. Al Qaeda were suspected.

Suicide bombing in Pakistan, March 2, 2004. A Shiite procession to commemorate the religious festival Ashura was attacked by three men in Quetta. The men threw grenades and opened fire into the crowd before blowing themselves up. Forty-two people were killed and more than one hundred wounded. Sunni extremists were suspected.

Train bombs in Spain, March 11, 2004. In a series of coordinated attacks, ten bombs were detonated in four trains at three stations during the morning rush hour in Madrid. One hundred and ninety-one people were killed and one thousand eight hundred and twenty-four wounded. The attack was linked to al Qaeda and to a group known as Abu Nayaf al-Afgani. Following the attack, the Spanish government was voted out of power and the country's troops were withdrawn from Iraq.

Car bombing in Iraq, March 17, 2004. A car bomb was detonated outside the Mount Lebanon Hotel in Baghdad, killing seventeen people and wounding forty-five. Al Qaeda and Ansar al-Islam were suspected.

Child suicide bomber arrested in the West Bank, March 24, 2004. A fifteen-year-old Palestinian boy, found to have explosives strapped to his chest, was arrested by Israeli soldiers at the Hawara checkpoint in the West Bank. The al-Aqsa Martyrs' Brigades claimed responsibility for the attempt.

Suicide bombing in Saudi Arabia, April 21, 2004. Four people were killed and one hundred and fifty wounded when a man attempted to drive a car packed with explosives into a government building in Riyadh. When stopped by police, the bomber set off the explosives before reaching his target. Extremists sympathetic to al Qaeda were suspected.

Suicide bombings in Iraq, April 21, 2004. Five suicide car bombs were detonated near police stations in and around Basra, killing sixty-eight people, including many school children, and wounding one hundred. Al Qaeda were suspected.

Boat attacks in Iraq, April 24, 2004. Three boats carrying suicide bombers exploded in and around the Southern Oil Company terminal at Basra, killing three US sailors and wounding several others. The terminal was shut down for a day, costing Iraq 1.9 million barrels in lost exports. Al Qaeda claimed responsibility.

Suicide bombing in Iraq, May 6, 2004. Seven people were killed and twenty-five wounded in a suicide car bomb attack at a checkpoint outside the Coalition-controlled Green Zone in Baghdad.

Saudi Arabian hostage crisis, May 24, 2004. Fifty people were taken hostage at a residential compound for expatriate petroleum industry workers in Khobar. Two earlier attacks took place at the local headquarters of the Arab Petroleum Investments Corporation and of the Petroleum Centre. In all, twenty-two people were killed and twenty-five wounded. A previously unknown group called the Jerusalem Squadron claimed responsibility.

Suicide bombing in Iraq, June 14, 2004. A suicide bomber wearing a vest packed with explosives killed fourteen neighborhood patrol volunteers and wounded ten others in Baquba, north of Baghdad.

Suicide bombing in Iraq, June 17, 2004. Thirty-five people were killed and one hundred and forty-five others wounded when a suicide car bomber attacked the Iraqi Civil Defense Corps centre in Baghdad. Al Qaeda were suspected.

Suicide bombing in Iraq, July 28, 2004. A suicide bomber drove a minibus into a marketplace near a police station in Baquba, north of Baghdad. Sixty-eight people were killed and fifty-six others were wounded.

Church bombings in Iraq, August 1, 2004. Eleven people were killed and dozens wounded in coordinated car bomb attacks outside three churches in Baghdad and one in Mosul.

Airplanes crash over Russia, August 24, 2004. Two planes, carrying ninety people, crashed within twenty minutes of each other after leaving Moscow's Domodedovo Airport. All passengers and crew were killed. Traces of hydrogen were found in the wreckage of both planes and two Chechen women passengers were suspected of being involved. Chechen rebel leader Aslan Maskhadov denied responsibility for the crashes.

Suicide bombing in Russia, August 31, 2004. A female suicide bomber killed nine people and wounded fifty-one others when she attacked the Rizhskaya metro station in Moscow. Chechen separatists were suspected.

School hostage crisis in Russia, September 1, 2004. Thirty-two Chechen separatists stormed School Number 1 in Beslan, holding one thousand children and adults hostage in a gymnasium for three days without food or water. Special Forces stormed the building after explosions were heard and hostages attempted to flee. Three hundred and thirty-one people died in the siege, one hundred and eighty-six of whom were children. Seven hundred people were wounded.

Australian embassy bombing in Indonesia, September 9, 2004. Nine people died and one hundred and eighty others were wounded when a car bomb blast targeted the Australian embassy in Jakarta. Jemaah Islamiah claimed responsibility.

Suicide bombing in Iraq, September 30, 2004. Car bombs exploded at a community celebration in Baghdad, killing thirty-six children and wounding many others. The Martyrs Brigades of the Tawhid and Jihad claimed responsibility.

Hotel bombings in Egypt, October 7, 2004. Thirty-four people were killed and one hundred and five wounded in attacks on the Taba Hilton Hotel and the Ras a-Satan campsite on the Sinai Peninsula. Both locations were known to be frequented by Israelis. Palestinian extremists were suspected.

Murder of Theo Van Gogh, November 2, 2004. Dutch film-maker Theo Van Gogh, director of a controversial film about Islam and women, was stabbed and shot to death in Amsterdam. His killer, Mohammed Bouyeri, was discovered to have links to the extremist Islamic organization, the Hofstad Network.

Suicide bombing in Iraq, December 4, 2004. Two car bombs killed sixteen people and wounded thirty-eight others at a checkpoint outside the Coalition-controlled Green Zone in Baghdad.

Bombing in the Philippines, December 12, 2004. Fourteen people died and sixty others were wounded in an explosion at a market in General Santos City, on the island of Mindanao.

Suicide bombing in Iraq, December 19, 2004. A suicide car bomber drove into a funeral procession in Najaf, killing fifty-one people and wounding ninety-two. Baath Party loyalists were suspected.

Suicide bombing in Iraq, December 19, 2004. Sixteen people were killed and thirty-seven wounded in a suicide car bomb attack at a bus stop in Karbala.

Car bombing in Iraq, December 27, 2004. A car bomb exploded outside the offices of the Supreme Council for the Islamic Revolution in Iraq, killing thirteen people and wounding thirty-nine. Abdel Aziz al-Hakim, Shiite leader of the SCIRI, was believed to be the target, but was unharmed. Sunni extremists and Baath Party loyalists were suspected.

2005

Suicide bombings in Iraq, January 19, 2005. Twenty-six people were killed in a series of four car bombings in Baghdad. The attacks occurred in quick succession at the Australian embassy, a police station, the international airport and a military complex.

Suicide bombing in Iraq, February 8, 2005. A suicide bomber walked into a queue of army recruits standing outside the Iraqi National Guard Headquarters at the Muthanna Airfield in Baghdad, killing twenty-two people and wounding twenty-seven.

Assassination of the former Prime Minister of Lebanon, February 14, 2005. A car bomb blast in front of the St George and Phoenicia Intercontinental Hotel in Beirut killed Rafik Hariri, the former Prime Minister of the country, and nine others, including a former minister, and wounded one hundred. A previously unknown extremist group called Support and Jihad in Syria and Lebanon claimed responsibility.

Car bombing in Thailand, February 17, 2005. Five people were killed and forty others wounded when a car bomb was detonated outside the Marina Hotel in the town of Sungai Kolok.

Ashura attacks in Iraq, February 19, 2005. Sixteen people were killed and one hundred wounded in a series of attacks in and around Baghdad, targeting the Shiite celebrations of Ashura. Sunni extremists were suspected.

Suicide bombing in Iraq, February 28, 2005. One hundred and twenty-five people were killed and one hundred and fifty others wounded in Hilla, when a car bomb exploded outside a government office where army recruits were queuing.

Suicide bombing in Iraq, March 10, 2005. A suicide bomber blew himself up at a funeral being held at a Shiite mosque, killing forty-seven people and wounding more than one hundred.

Car bombing in Qatar, March 19, 2005. A car bomb exploded at a theatre in an expatriate neighborhood of Doha, killing one and wounding twelve others.

Bomb attacks in Thailand, March 27, 2005. Two people were killed and several dozen wounded in three explosions in the southern province of Songkhla, at the region's main airport, a department store and a hotel. Islamic extremists were suspected.

Nail bombing in Egypt, April 7, 2005. In the first attack targeting foreigners in Cairo for seven years, a nail bomb was detonated at the Khan al-Khalili bazaar, killing two people and wounding eighteen others.

Bombings in Myanmar, May 7, 2005. Eleven people died and one hundred and sixty-two others were wounded when three bombs exploded in Yangon, one at the Trade Centre, another at a shopping centre close to military headquarters and the third at another shopping centre close to the airport. A rebel group opposed to the military junta were suspected but denied responsibility.

Suicide bombing in Afghanistan, June 1, 2005. Twenty people were killed and forty-two wounded in a suicide bombing at the funeral of prominent cleric Mullah Abdul Fayaz. Al Qaeda were suspected.

Bombings in Iran, June 12, 2005. Four bombs exploded in the town of Ahvaz on the Iraqi border, followed by three in Tehran. Altogether, ten people were killed and seventy-eight wounded. Iraqi Baath Party loyalists were suspected.

Suicide bombing in Iraq, June 14, 2005. Twenty-two people were killed and eighty others wounded when a suicide bomber blew himself up at the Rafidain Bank in Kirkuk.

Attempted attack in India, July 5, 2005. Five men attacked the Ram Janmabhoomi complex in Ayodhya. All were killed in a gunfight with security forces, and one civilian died. Lashkar-e-Taiba were suspected.

London bombings, July 7, 2005. Four British suicide bombers killed fifty-two people and wounded more than seven hundred and seventy in a series of attacks on the London transport system. Three bombs went off in the underground network and one in a bus, all during the morning rush hour.

Suicide bombing in Iraq, July 16, 2005. A suicide bomber blew himself up near a fuel tanker parked near a petrol station in Musayyib, killing at least sixty people and wounding one hundred.

Attempted London bombings, July 21, 2005. Four bombs, three on the underground network and one on a bus, failed to detonate, causing minor injuries. All four bombers were arrested and charged, eventually to be sentenced to a minimum of forty years each.

Car bombings in Egypt, July 23, 2005. Eighty-eight people were killed and two hundred wounded in a series of car bomb attacks at the Sharm el-Sheikh resort. A group called the Abdullah Azzam Brigades claimed responsibility.

Train bombing in India, July 28, 2005. Thirteen people were killed and fifty wounded in an explosion on a train near Jaunpur in the state of Uttar Pradesh. Islamic extremists were suspected.

Suicide bombing in Iraq, July 29, 2005. Twenty-five people were killed and thirty-five wounded when a suicide bomber blew himself up outside an army recruitment centre in Rabia, near the Syrian border.

Bombings in Bangladesh, August 17, 2005. Three hundred simultaneous explosions took place in fifty cities and towns across the country, killing two people and wounding fifty others. A group called Jamatul Mujahideen Bangladesh claimed responsibility.

Bombings and shootings in Iraq, September 14, 2005. One hundred and fifty people were killed and hundreds of others wounded in a series of bombings and shootings across Iraq. The worst of the incidents occurred in Kadhimiya, a Shiite district of Baghdad, where a car bomb exploded, and in the town of Taji, where gunmen dragged seventeen men from their homes and shot them. Al Qaeda claimed responsibility.

Suicide bombing in Iraq, September 28, 2005. A woman dressed as a man blew herself up outside a new army and police recruitment centre in Tal Afar, killing eight people and wounding fifty-seven. Al Qaeda claimed responsibility.

Attacks in Russia, October 13, 2005. About two hundred militants attacked a number of federal buildings in the town of Nalchik in the southern region of Kabardino-Balkariya. The buildings included police stations, security headquarters, military offices, drugs-control offices and the airport. One hundred and forty-two people were killed and many more wounded. A pro-Chechen rebel group called the Caucasus Front claimed responsibility.

Bombings in Iran, October 15, 2005. Two bombs exploded at a shopping mall in Ahvaz on the Iraqi border, killing four people and wounding seventy-five others.

Car bombings in Iraq, October 24, 2005. A series of car bomb attacks killed one hundred and forty-four people and wounded more than two hundred in Sadr City, Baghdad. Sunni extremists and Baath Party loyalists were suspected.

Suicide bombing in Israel, October 25, 2005. A suicide bomber killed five people and wounded twenty-eight in an attack on a marketplace in the northern town of Hadera. Islamic Jihad claimed responsibility.

Bombings in India, October 25, 2005. Sixty people were killed and one hundred and eighty wounded in bomb blasts that hit two marketplaces and a bus stop in New Delhi. Lashkar-e-Taiba were suspected.

Attack on schoolgirls in Indonesia, October 29, 2005. Three schoolgirls were beheaded and a fourth seriously wounded as they walked to their nearby Christian school in Poso, Central Sulawesi. The extremist Islamic group Tanah Runtuh were found to be responsible.

Bombings in Jordan, November 9, 2005. Simultaneous attacks occurred at three hotels in Amman, killing sixty-seven people and wounding one hundred and fifty others. Al Qaeda were suspected.

Suicide bombings in Iraq, November 18, 2005. Two suicide truck bombs exploded outside the Hamra Hotel in

Baghdad, killing six people and injuring forty. The hotel was well known for housing foreign journalists.

Suicide bombings in Iraq, November 18, 2005. Suicide bombers attacked two Shiite mosques in Khanaqin, near the Iranian border, killing seventy people and wounding one hundred. Al Qaeda and Ansar al-Sunna were suspected.

Suicide bombing in Iraq, December 6, 2005. Thirty-six people were killed and seventy-two others wounded in a suicide attack on a police academy in Baghdad.

2006

Suicide bombing in Iraq, January 4, 2006. Thirty-six people were killed and forty wounded when a suicide bomber blew himself up at a funeral in Muqdadiyah, north of Baghdad.

Suicide bombing in Iraq, January 6, 2006. Sixty people were killed when a suicide bomber blew himself up at the Imam Husayn shrine in Karbala.

Shootings in the Philippines, February 2, 2006. Six people were killed and five others wounded when gunmen attacked a Christian family in the township of Patikul, on the island of Mindanao. Abu Sayyaf were suspected.

Suicide attack at Iraqi funeral kills 36, wounds 40

Bombing in Iraq, February 22, 2006. A bomb attack which destroyed one of the holiest Shiite shrines, the Askariya in Samarra, resulted in immediate reprisals against Sunnis. More than sixty Sunni mosques were burned or occupied and several Sunnis, including a cleric, were shot dead.

Bombings in India, March 7, 2006. Twenty-eight people were killed and more than one hundred wounded in coordinated bomb blasts around Varanasi. Islamic extremists were suspected.

Suicide bombing in Iraq, April 7, 2006. Three suicide bombers, two of whom were disguised as women, attacked the Buratha mosque in Baghdad, killing seventy-four people and wounding one hundred and forty others. Sunni extremists were suspected.

Suicide bombing in Pakistan, April 11, 2006. Fifty-seven people were killed and eighty wounded in a suicide attack on Nishtar Park in Karachi, where tens of thousands of people had gathered to celebrate the birth of the prophet Muhammad.

Suicide bombing in Israel, April 17, 2006. Nine people were killed and dozens more wounded in a suicide bombing at a restaurant in Tel Aviv. Islamic Jihad claimed responsibility.

Bombings in Egypt, April 24, 2006. Twenty-three people were killed and sixty-two others wounded in bomb attacks on two cafeterias and a supermarket in the resort town of Dahab. The group Jama'at al-Tawhid wal-Jihad was suspected.

Suicide bombing in Iraq, May 9, 2006. Seventeen people were killed and sixty-five wounded when a suicide bomber drove a pick-up truck into a marketplace in the northern city of Tal Afar.

Mine attack in Sri Lanka, June 15, 2006. Sixty-four people were killed and eighty wounded in a mine attack on a bus in Kabithigollewa in the Anuradhapura district. It was the worst incident to involve civilians since the ceasefire in 2002. The Liberation Tigers of Tamil Eelam were suspected but denied responsibility.

Shootings in Iraq, July 9, 2006. Gunmen killed forty people at a fake checkpoint in Baghdad, separating out Sunnis and shooting them. The Mehdi Army militia were suspected but denied responsibility.

Train bombings in India, July 11, 2006. Seven explosions on board commuter trains and at stations killed one hundred and seventy-four people and wounded four hundred and sixty-four in Mumbai. Lashkar-e-Taiba and Jaish-e-Muhammad were suspected.

Bombings and shootings in Iraq, July 17, 2006. Gunmen shot into a marketplace in Mahmudiya, south of Baghdad, killing forty-eight people and wounding many more. A group called the Supporters of the Sunni People claimed responsibility.

Car bombing in Iraq, July 18, 2006. Fifty-three people were killed and one hundred and three were wounded in a car bomb attack on a Shiite shrine in the southern city of Kufa.

Suicide bombing in Afghanistan, August 4, 2006. Twenty-one people were killed and thirteen wounded in Panjwayi, in the province of Kandahar, when a suicide car bomber attacked a marketplace.

Bombings in Baghdad, August 13, 2006. A series of explosions killed fifty-seven people and wounded one hundred and fifty in Baghdad.

Temple bombing in India, August 16, 2006. Five people died and fifty others were wounded in an explosion at the temple of the International Society for Krishna Consciousness in Imphal, in the north east of the country. Islamic extremists were suspected.

Shootings in Iraq, August 20, 2006. Gunmen opened fire on a crowd of pilgrims in Baghdad, killing twenty people and wounding three hundred others.

Bombings in India, September 8, 2006. Thirty-one people were killed and one hundred wounded in a series of bomb attacks in Malegaon, in Maharashtra province. Two explosions took place at a Muslim cemetery and a third in the town square.

Bombings in Thailand, September 16, 2006. Five bombs exploded in central Hat Yai, Songkhla Province, killing four people and wounding eighty. The South Thailand Insurgency were suspected.

Assassination attempt on Somali President, September 18, 2006. Eleven people were killed when a car bomb exploded outside the parliament building. Among the dead was the President's brother. The presumed target of the attack, President Abdullahi Yusuf himself, was left unharmed. Islamic extremists were suspected.

Suicide bombing in Sri Lanka, September 18, 2006. Ninety-four people were killed and one hundred and fifty wounded when a suicide bomber drove a truck filled with explosives into a military convoy near the north-eastern town of Habarana. The Liberation Tigers of Tamil Eelam were suspected.

Assassination of Pierre Gemayel, November 21, 2006. The Lebanese Minister of Industry, Pierre Gemayel, was shot by three gunmen who drove into his car in Beirut. He later died in hospital. The Fighters for the Unity and Liberation of Greater Syria claimed responsibility.

Car bombings in Iraq, November 23, 2006. Six car bombs and two mortar rounds killed two hundred and fifteen people and wounded two hundred and fifty-seven others in Sadr City. Sunni extremists and Baath Party loyalists were suspected.

Suicide bombing in Iraq, December 12, 2006. A suicide bomber detonated an explosive-packed truck in Tayaran Square in Baghdad, killing seventy people and wounding two hundred and thirty.

2007

Bombings in Thailand, January 1, 2007. Three people were killed and thirty-eight wounded when eight bombs exploded across Bangkok. Groups loyal to the former Prime Minister Thaksin Shinawatra were suspected.

Suicide bombings in Sri Lanka, January 5, 2007. Five people were killed and thirty wounded when a bomb exploded on a bus near Nittambuwa, north east of Colombo. The Liberation Tigers of Tamil Eelam were suspected, but denied responsibility.

Bombings in the Philippines, January 10, 2007. Six people were killed and thirty-five wounded in explosions in General Santos City, Kidapawan City and Cotabato City. Islamic extremists were suspected.

Car bombing in Iraq, January 22, 2007. Eighty-eight people were killed and one hundred and sixty others wounded in two car bomb blasts in a Baghdad marketplace.

Suicide bombing in Pakistan, January 27, 2007. Sixteen people were killed and thirty-five wounded when a suicide bomber blew himself up at a bazaar in Peshawar's Old City. Among the dead was the Chief of City Police.

Suicide bombing in Baghdad, February 3, 2007. A suicide bomber detonated an explosives-packed truck at a marketplace in Baghdad, killing one hundred and thirty-five people and wounding three hundred and thirty-nine others. Sunni extremists and Baath Party loyalists were suspected.

Suicide bombing in Pakistan, February 17, 2007. Fifteen people were killed and forty-three wounded by a suicide bomb at a lawyer's rally in Islamabad.

Train bombing in India, February 19, 2007. Two bombs exploded on a train traveling from India to Pakistan, killing sixty-eight people and wounding dozens more.

Chlorine bombing in Iraq, February 21, 2007. A truck bomb packed with explosives and chlorine gas exploded in Baghdad, killing two people and wounding thirty-two others.

Suicide bombings in Iraq, March 6, 2007. One hundred and fifteen people were killed when two suicide bombers blew themselves up in Hilla.

Bombings in Iraq, March 27, 2007. One hundred and fifty-two people were killed and three hundred and forty-seven others wounded when a truck bomb exploded in Tal Afar.

Suicide car bombings in Algeria, April 11, 2007. As many as sixty-seven people were killed and one hundred and seventy-seven wounded when two suicide bomb blasts went off in Algiers, near the capital's constitutional court and the UNHCR building. Al Qaeda claimed responsibility, but the Salafist Group for Preaching and Combat were also suspected.

Suicide truck bombing in Iraq, May 13, 2007. Forty-five people were killed and dozens more wounded when a truck bomb exploded at the offices of the Kurdistan Democratic Party in Makhmur, Irbil Province. A senior police officer was among the dead and the town's mayor was wounded.

Assassination attempt on the Prime Minister of Ethiopia, June 3, 2007. A car bomb at the home of Prime Minister Ali Mohamed Gedi in Mogadishu killed six guards, but left him unharmed, in the third attempt on his life. Islamic extremists were suspected.

Car bombing in Lebanon, June 14, 2007. Ten people were killed when a car bomb exploded in Beirut. Among the dead was Walid Eido, an anti-Syrian MP and ally of the assassinated Prime Minister of Lebanon Rafik al-Hariri.

London car bombs, June 29, 2007. Two car bombs planted in inner city London were discovered and disabled before going off. Men linked to al Qaeda operatives were suspected.

Suicide bombing in Pakistan, June 29, 2007. Thirteen people were killed and seventy wounded in a suicide bomb attack at the Red Mosque in Islamabad. It was believed to be a retaliatory strike for the storming of the mosque two weeks earlier, when security forces killed one hundred students and militants.

Glasgow Airport attack, June 30, 2007. A jeep loaded with petrol was driven into the doors of the main terminal and set alight. Only one of the two men in the car was seriously hurt, and he later died in hospital.

Train bombing in Russia, August 14, 2007. A train traveling from Moscow to St. Petersburg was derailed by an explosion, injuring sixty people. While Chechen rebels were considered most likely to be responsible, Russian nationalists were also suspected.

Suicide bombings in Iraq, August 14, 2007. Four suicide bombs exploded in a series of coordinated attacks near Qahataniya, killing three hundred and forty-four people and wounding four hundred. Al Qaeda were suspected.

Bombings in India, August 25, 2007. Two bombs exploded in near simultaneous attacks on an amusement park and a restaurant in Hyderabad, killing forty-two people and wounding fifty-four. Two more bombs were discovered and disabled, while nineteen others that had failed to detonate were later discovered. The group Harkat-ul-Jehadi Islami was suspected.

Suicide bombing in Pakistan, October 18, 2007. A suicide bomber killed one hundred and thirty-four and wounded four hundred and fifty in Karachi when he attacked the procession of former Prime Minister Benazir Bhutto. Bhutto had returned from exile to lead the opposition in the forthcoming elections.

Suicide bombing in Afghanistan, November 6, 2007. Forty people were killed and one hundred and twenty wounded when a suicide bomber blew himself up at a sugar factory in Baglan Province. Among the dead were a delegation of MPs and the children who had gathered to welcome them. The Taliban were suspected but denied responsibility.

Assassination of Benazir Bhutto, December 27, 2007. Former Prime Minister of Pakistan Benazir Bhutto was assassinated in a suicide attack while leaving an election rally in Rawalpindi. Twenty other people were killed and many more wounded.

Glossary

Abu Sayyaf Group Active in the southern Philippines and other parts of Southeast Asia, this group kidnaps Westerners as a means of raising money to wage an armed struggle for the purpose of creating a separate country for Muslims in what is now part of the Philippines.

Afrikaner Resistance Movement (AWB) A right-wing South African organization rooted in that country's Afrikaner population which employed terrorist violence in an unsuccessful effort to prevent the end of apartheid and the start of majority rule.

Al Qaeda "The Base" or "The Center;" the center of a worldwide network of terrorist groups originally created to wage a holy war against the Soviet occupation of Afghanistan.

Armed Islamic Group (GIA) Following the refusal by Algeria's military to accept the results of elections that would have brought about a victory for the Islamic Salvation Front (1991), the GIA waged a near decade-long terrorist campaign aimed at transforming the country into an Islamic republic.

Assassins A band of Shia Muslims active during the Crusades, committed to the purification of Islam through the killing of Sunni Muslim leaders thought to be corrupt.

Basque Homeland and Liberty (ETA) An organization committed to the use of terrorism in order to achieve the establishment of an independent state for the Basque population of northern Spain and southern France.

Bin Laden, Osama (born 1957)   Co-founder of al Qaeda; the son of an exceptionally wealthy Saudi family who went to Afghanistan to help expel the Soviets and then became committed to waging a worldwide holy war to get "Jews and crusaders" to leave the Middle East.

German Red Army Fraction   Also known as the Baader–Meinhoff Gang, a social revolutionary band active during the 1970s and 1980s which developed ties with and received training from Palestinian groups.

Hamas   The Islamic Resistance Movement created in the Gaza Strip during the first Intifada (1987–93) to destroy the state of Israel and create an Islamic state of Palestine in its place.

Heinzen Karl   A mid-nineteenth-century German revolutionary who wrote an essay on "Murder" (1849) calling for and justifying the use of terrorism as a means of ending tyranny.

Hizbollah   This "Party of God" was organized among Lebanese Shiites following the Iranian Revolution. During the 1980s and 1990s it engaged in a series of violent attacks aimed at forcing American and later Israeli forces to withdraw from the country.

Irgun   A Jewish nationalist group headed by Menachem Begin that used terrorist violence in an effort to force the British out of Palestine during the period 1945–48.

Khomeini, Ayatollah Ruhollah   The key religious leader in the 1979–80 Iranian Revolution that deposed the Shah and led to the establishment of an Islamic republic.

Liberation Tigers of Tamil Eelam   An organization of militant Tamils committed to achieving an independent state for their ethnic group in what is presently northeastern Sri Lanka.

McVeigh, Timothy   A disaffected US Army veteran who detonated a truck bomb in front of the Murrah Federal Building in Oklahoma City on April 19, 1995 in retaliation for the government's assault on the Branch Davidian compound near Waco, Texas two years earlier.

Montoneros   An Argentine revolutionary organization active in the 1960s and 1970s which hoped the return of former dictator Juan Peron from exile would lead to the profound changes in society the Montoneros believed essential. When Peron refused to support these changes the organization returned to terrorist violence until it was eliminated by Argentina's military after the latter seized power in 1976.

National Liberation Front (FLN)   An organization that launched an insurgency in 1954 to compel the French to grant Algeria national independence.

National Organization of Cypriot Fighters (EOKA)   An organization led by the Greek Colonel George Grivas that waged a terrorist campaign during the 1950s aimed at getting the British to leave Cyprus.

Palestinian Islamic Jihad (PIJ)   Founded in 1979–80 by Palestinian students in Egypt who had split from the Muslim Brotherhood, the PIJ is committed to the same goal as Hamas.

Palestinian Liberation Organization (PLO)   An organization formed by the Egyptian government in 1964 aimed at destroying Israel and replacing it with a "democratic secular state." Following the June 1967 Arab–Israeli war the PLO became an umbrella organization for most militant Palestinian groups and later still (1974) was designated the sole legitimate spokesman for the Palestinian people by the Arab League.

People's Will (Narodnaya Volya)   A Russian revolutionary group that succeeded in assassinating the Czar in 1881, considered the first modern terrorist organization.

Phoenix Park Murders In 1881 the representative of the British government in Ireland and his secretary were gunned down by Irish nationalists in Dublin's Phoenix Park.

Propaganda by Deed A term adopted by nineteenth-century European anarchists to emphasize the publicity achieved through the use of sensational acts of violence against prominent figures in political and economic life.

Qutb, Sayyid An Egyptian school teacher who visited the United States in 1949 and later became the leader of his country's Muslim Brotherhood. Qutb became the single most powerful advocate of holy war against secular Arab governments and Western influence in the Muslim world.

Red Brigades (BR) An Italian revolutionary organization that kidnapped and killed former prime minister Aldo Moro in 1978.

Reign of Terror The period of Jacobin rule in revolutionary France (1793–94) from which the term "terrorism" derives it name.

Revolutionary Armed Forces of Colombia (FARC) A left-wing revolutionary organization that combines terrorism with rural guerrilla warfare in order to topple the government in Bogotá.

Socialist Revolutionaries (SRs) A party of Marxist revolutionaries active in Russia in the first decade of the twentieth century which carried out a series of assassinations of prominent Czarist officials.

Tupamaros A Uruguayan revolutionary organization that sought to produce a military reaction by carrying out a series of terrorist attacks in the period 1968 – 72. The organization succeeded in this "strategy of provocation." The military intervened, brought an end to Uruguay's democracy, but also eliminated the Tupamaros in the process.

Yousef, Ramzi   A member of al Qaeda and bomb-making specialist who planned and helped carry out the first attack on the World Trade Center in 1993.

Zealots   A band of Jewish fanatics active during the first century A.D. which employed terrorist tactics in order to provoke a war between Judea and Rome in the hope that such a conflict would bring an end to Roman rule and the advent of the "Last Times."

Notes

Chapter one

1. Walter Laqueur, *Terrorism* (Boston: Little, Brown, 1977) p. 5.
2. Martha Crenshaw, "The Psychology of Terrorism," *Political Psychology* 21:2 (2000) p. 406.
3. The sentence was part of a letter to the editor published in the Dutch newspaper *Leidsch Dagblad* (March 17, 1989). The writer objected to a conference on terrorism then underway at the University of Leiden. See also Edward Herman and Gerry O'Sullivan, *The Terrorism Industry* (New York: Pantheon Books, 1989).
4. Bruce Hoffman, *Inside Terrorism* (London: Victor Gollancz, 1999) p. 43.
5. Alex Schmid, Peter Jongman et al., *Political Terrorism* (New Brunswick, NJ: Transaction, 1988) p. 28.
6. The German and British definitions were taken from Alex Schmid, "The Response Problem as a Definition Problem," *Terrorism and Political Violence* 4:4 (1992) pp. 8–9; The American comes from Hoffman, *Inside Terrorism* p. 38.
7. Jessica Stern, *The Ultimate Terrorists* (Cambridge, MA: Harvard University Press, 1999) p. 31.
8. See, for example, the experience of Italy's Red Brigades, David Moss, *The Politics of Left-Wing Violence in Italy 1969–1985* (New York: St. Martin's, 1989) pp. 77–79.
9. Thomas Friedman, *From Beirut to Jerusalem* (New York: Farrar, Strauss, Giroux, 1989) pp. 76–105.
10. See, for example, David Veness, "Low Intensity and High Impact Conflict," in Max Taylor and John Horgan (eds.), *The Future of Terrorism* (London: Frank Cass, 2000) pp. 8–14.

11. Quoted in Walter Laqueur, *Guerrilla: A Historical and Critical Study* (Boston: Little, Brown, 1976) pp. 244–245.

12. See, for example, Brian Crozier, *The Rebels* (Boston: Beacon Press, 1960) pp. 159–161; Thomas Thornton, "Terror as a Weapon of Political Agitation," in Harry Eckstein (ed.), *Internal War* (New York: Free Press, 1964) pp. 92–95.

13. See, for example, David Scott Palmer, "The Revolutionary Terrorism of Peru's Shining Path," in Martha Crenshaw (ed.), *Terrorism in Context* (University Park: Pennsylvania State University Press, 1995) pp. 249–308.

14. Paul Pillar, *Terrorism and U.S. Foreign Policy* (Washington: Brookings Institution Press, 2001) pp. 217–218.

15. See, for example, Rohan Gunaratna, *Inside al Qaeda* (New York: Berkley Books, 2002) pp. 72–110.

Chapter two

1. For a summary see David Rapoport, "Fear and Trembling: Terrorism in Three Religious Traditions," *American Political Science Review* 78:3 (1984) pp. 658–677. Rapoport reports they were actually two groups with virtually identical objectives.

2. Bernard Lewis, *The Assassins: A Radical Sect in Islam* (London: Weidenfeld & Nicholson, 1967).

3. See, for example, Norman Cohn, *The Pursuit of the Millennium* (New York: Oxford University Press, 1961) pp. 37–74.

4. Quoted in Simon Reeve, *The New Jackals* (Boston: Northeastern University Press, 1999) p. 268.

5. Karl Heinzen, "Murder," in Walter Laqueur (ed.), *The Terrorism Reader* (New York: New American Library, 1978) pp. 53–54.

6. David Rapoport, "The Fourth Wave: September 11 in the History of Terrorism," *Current History* (December 2001) pp. 419–424.

7. Anna Geifman, *Thou Shalt Kill* (Princeton: Princeton University Press, 1993) pp. 45–83.

8. Albert Parry, *Terrorism from Robespierre to Arafat* (New York: Vanguard Press, 1976) pp. 78–91.

9. Tim Pat Coogan, *The IRA* (New York: Palgrave, 2002) pp. 15–20.
10. See J. Bowyer Bell, *A Time of Terror* (New York: Basic Books, 1978) p. 154.
11. See, for example, *Guerrilla* (Boston: Little, Brown, 1976) pp. 239–277.
12. Hoffman, *Inside Terrorism*, pp. 57–60.
13. See, for example, Martha Crenshaw, "The Effectiveness of Terrorism in the Algerian War," in Crenshaw (ed.), *Terrorism in Context* (University Park: Pennsylvania State University Press, 1995) pp. 473–513.
14. William Quandt, Fuad Jabber, and Anna Mosely Lesch, *The Politics of Palestinian Nationalism* (Berkeley and London: University of California Press, 1973) pp. 52–93.
15. For a general discussion see, for example, Juliet Lodge (ed.), *Terrorism: A Challenge to the State* (New York and London: St. Martin's Press, 1981).

Chapter three

1. Gary Sick, *All Fall Down* (New York and London: Penguin Books, 1985) pp. 3–24.
2. Robin Wright, *In the Name of God* (New York and London: Simon & Schuster, 1989) pp. 35–81.
3. Robin Wright, *Sacred Rage* (New York and London: Simon & Schuster, 1986) pp. 69–110.
4. See, for example, Peter Bergen, *Holy War, Inc.: Inside the Secret World of Osama bin Laden* (New York: Simon & Schuster, 2001) pp. 92–166.
5. Gabriel Almond, R. Scott Appleby, and Emmanuel Sivan, *Strong Religion: The Rise of Fundamentalisms around the World* (Chicago and London: University of Chicago Press, 2003).
6. Yonah Alexander (ed.), *Palestinian Religious Terrorism: Hamas and Islamic Jihad* (Ardsley, NY: Transnational, 2002) pp. 1–44.
7. See, for example, John Esposito, *Unholy War* (Oxford and New York: Oxford University Press, 2002) pp. 102–105.
8. See, Yossef Bodansky, *Bin Laden: The Man who Declared War on America* (Rocklin, CA: Forum, 1999) pp. 56–90.

9. Quoted in Rohan Gunaratna, *Inside al Qaeda* (New York: Berkeley Books, 2002) p. 61.
10. Gunaratna, ibid., pp. 72–126.

Chapter four

1. See, for example, Leonard Weinberg and William Eubank, *The Rise and Fall of Italian Terrorism* (Boulder: Westview Press, 1987) pp. 53–76; Robert Clark, *The Basques: The Franco Years and Beyond* (Reno: University of Nevada Press, 1979) pp. 189–225.
2. Alan Krueger and Jitka Maleckova, "Education, Poverty, Political Violence and Terrorism: Is There a Causal Connection?" NBER Working Paper 9074, July 2002.
3. See, for example, Ehud Sprinzak, "The Psychopolitical Formation of Extreme Left Terrorism in a Democracy," in Walter Reich (ed.), *Origins of Terrorism* (Cambridge and New York: Cambridge University Press, 1990) pp. 65–85.
4. Tore Bjorgo (ed.), *Terror from the Extreme Right* (London: Frank Cass, 1995).
5. See Bernard Lewis, *The Crisis of Islam* (New York: Modern Library, 2003) pp. 64–81.
6. Leonard Weinberg and Ami Pedahzur, *Political Parties and Terrorist Groups* (London: Routledge, 2003) pp. 1–16.
7. Martha Crenshaw, "The Psychology of Terrorism," *Political Psychology* 21:2 (2000) pp. 405–419; Leonard Weinberg and Paul David, *An Introduction to Political Terrorism* (New York: McGraw Hill, 1989) pp. 83–117.
8. Michele Zanini and Sean Edwards, "The Networking of Terror in the Information Age," in John Arquilla and David Ronfeldt (eds.), *Networks and Netwars* (Santa Monica: Rand, 2001) pp. 29–60.

Chapter five

1. Alex Schmid, "Magnitudes of Terrorist Victimization," in Dilip Das and Peter Kratcoski (eds.), *Meeting the Challenges of Global*

Terrorism (Oxford and New York: Lexington Books, 2003) pp. 33–68.

2. See, for example, United States Department of State, *Patterns of Global Terrorism, 2003* (Washington, 2004).

3. Source: MIPT Oklahoma City National Memorial Institute for the Prevention of Terrorism, 2003.

4. Source: Alex Schmid, "Magnitudes of Terrorist Victimization," p. 43.

5. See especially, Alex Schmid and Jenny de Graaf, *Violence as Communication: Insurgent Terrorism and the Western News Media* (Beverly Hills: Sage, 1982).

6. Brigitte Nacos, *Mass-Mediated Terrorism* (Lanham, MD and Oxford: Rowman & Littlefield, 2002) pp. 83–91.

7. Gabriel Weimann and Conrad Winn, *The Theater of Terror* (New York and London: Longman, 1994) pp. 51–89.

8. Thomas Friedman, *From Beirut to Jerusalem* (New York: Farrar, Strauss, Giroux, 1989) pp. 76–105.

9. Paul Wilkinson, *Terrorism versus Democracy: The Liberal State Response* (London: Frank Cass, 2001) pp. 94–123.

10. Michael Addison, *Violent Politics: Strategies of Internal Conflict* (Oxford: Palgrave, 2002) pp. 132–180.

11. Jane Boulden and Thomas Weiss (eds.), *Terrorism and the UN Before and After September 11* (Bloomington: Indiana University Press, 2004) pp. 3–26.

Chapter six

1. See, for example, William Cleveland, *A History of the Modern Middle East* (Boulder and Oxford: Westview Press, 2000).

2. For general discussions see Martha Crenshaw, "Theories of Terrorism: Instrumental and Organizational Approaches," in David Rapoport (ed.), *Inside Terrorist Organizations* (New York: Columbia University Press, 1988) pp. 13–31; and Martha Crenshaw, "The Logic of Terrorism: Terrorist Behavior as a Product of Strategic Choice," in Walter Reich (ed.), *Origins of Terrorism* (Cambridge and New York: Cambridge University Press, 1990) pp. 7–24.

3. See, for example, Roger Fontaine, "Argentina," and Gunduz Aktan and Ali Kokner, "Turkey," in Yonah Alexander (ed.), *Combating Terrorism* (Ann Arbor: University of Michigan Press, 2002) pp. 62–83, 260–298.

4. For an account see Thomas Friedman, *From Beirut to Jerusalem* (New York: Farrar, Strauss, Giroux, 1989) pp. 76–105.

5. For a discussion of the problems posed for democracies in using these techniques see Paul Wilkinson, *Terrorism and the Liberal State* (New York: New York University Press, 1979).

6. Brian Crozier, *The Rebels* (Boston: Beacon Press, 1960) pp. 159–191; Thomas Thornton, "Terror as a Weapon of Political Agitation," in Harry Eckstein (ed.), *Internal War* (New York: Free Press, 1964) pp. 92–95.

7. Walter Laqueur, *Guerrilla* (Boston: Little, Brown, 1976) p. 271.

8. Roy Licklider, "The Consequences of Negotiated Settlements in Civil Wars, 1945–1993," *American Political Science Review* 89 (September 1995), pp. 681–690; Louis Kriesberg, *Constructive Conflicts* (Lanham, MD: Rowman & Littlefield, 1998) pp. 263–297.

9. The literature is voluminous. See, for example, Martin Gilbert, *Israel: A History* (New York: William Morrow, 1998) pp. 250–251.

10. David Welsh, "Right-Wing Terrorism in South Africa," in Tore Bjorgo (ed.), *Terror from the Extreme Right* (London: Frank Cass, 1995) p. 254.

11. See, for example, Ed Moloney, *A Secret History of the IRA* (New York: W. W. Norton, 2002) pp. 196–245.

12. See, George Mitchell, *Making Peace* (New York: Alfred Knopf, 1999) pp. 3–45.

13. See, for example, Alessandro Silj, *Never Again without a Rifle* (New York: Karz, 1979) pp. 140–157.

14. Walter Laqueur, *Terrorism* (Boston: Little, Brown, 1977) p. 73.

15. Quoted in Leonard Weinberg and Paul Davis, *Introduction to Political Terrorism* (New York: McGraw-Hill, 1989) p. 101.

16. David Rapoport, "The Fourth Wave: September 11 and the

History of Terrorism," *Current History* (December 2001) pp. 419–424.

17. Ibid., p. 420.

18. Ibid., p. 424.

19. Ehud Sprinzak, "Right-Wing Terrorism in Comparative Perspective: The Case of Split Delegitimization," in Tore Bjorgo (ed.), *Terror from the Extreme Right* (London: Frank Cass, 1995) pp. 17–43.

20. Ibid., p. 21.

21. Christopher Hewitt, "The Political Context of Terrorism in America," in David Rapoport and Leonard Weinberg (eds.), *The Democratic Experience and Political Violence* (London: Frank Cass, 2001) pp. 325–344.

22. See, for example, Sidney Tarrow, *Power in Movement* (New York: Cambridge University Press, 1994) pp. 17–18.

23. Cynthia Irvin, *Militant Nationalism* (Minneapolis: University of Minnesota Press, 1999) p. 25.

24. Ibid., p. 28.

Index